3⁹⁵

DISTANT VOICES

Selected books by Denys Thompson

What to Read in English Literature
Uses of Poetry (*C.U.P.*)
(*ed.*) Matthew Arnold: Selected Poems and Prose
(*ed.*) Children as Poets
(*ed.*) Discrimination and Popular Culture

Distant Voices

POETRY OF THE PRELITERATE

Edited by

DENYS THOMPSON

HEINEMANN
LONDON
ROWMAN AND LITTLEFIELD
TOTOWA, NEW JERSEY

Heinemann Educational Books
LONDON EDINBURGH MELBOURNE AUCKLAND
TORONTO HONG KONG SINGAPORE KUALA LUMPUR
IBADAN NAIROBI JOHANNESBURG
NEW DELHI LUSAKA KINGSTON

ISBN (U.K.) 0 435 14894 X
ISBN (U.S.) 0–8476–6102–4

First published in Great Britain 1978
by Heinemann Educational Books

First published in the United States 1978
by Rowman and Littlefield, Totowa, N.J.

Published by
Heinemann Educational Books Ltd
48 Charles Street, London W1X 8AH
Filmset by Keyspools Ltd, Golborne, Lancs
Printed and bound in Great Britain by
Cox & Wyman Ltd,
London, Fakenham and Reading

CONTENTS

LIST OF ILLUSTRATIONS

INTRODUCTION

This is a collection of poems by people who did not use writing, or only a very little for such needs as keeping accounts and records. They form the great majority of all the human beings who have ever lived. They could neither read nor write, but to call them 'illiterate' is to introduce irrelevant notions of inadequacy; 'preliterate' is the more appropriate word. 'Primitive' too may have the wrong connotations, for the peoples whose poetry is drawn on had highly developed languages, and language does not flourish in a vacuum. In fact their cultures were often far advanced all round, in religion, philosophy and the arts, from that of living together to the making of pottery, fabrics and other objects that are now museum treasures. They produced a variety of poetry that includes great myths and epics such as Homer's, as well as much else that differs in kind and aim from the written poetry we are accustomed to. One certain thing is that this preliterate poetry played a more vital part in the life of its time than any printed verse has ever done, and one larger than we can readily imagine.

It was the vehicle for law and history, religion and technology, mores and ethics. It supplied the means of the education on which society depended for its continuity and coherence. Thus for example at Athens, well into the fifth century B.C., Homer was still the encyclopaedist of the city state, and poetry enjoyed what E. A. Havelock has termed 'preserved communication'. Public business depended on verse, and it was necessary for political and even military leaders to be skilled in it; Agamemnon mobilizing his fleet at Aulis may have had to get his orders expressed in rhythmic verse. Elsewhere, as in Greece, 'Poetry was not literature but a political and social necessity. It was not an art form, nor a creation of the private imagination, but an encyclopaedia maintained by co-operative effort.' Accordingly poets were powerful people, and provided their community with a supply of natural leaders.

I

The poets represented here mostly come from cultures less esteemed than that of Athens, but they were in no sense 'disadvantaged' or deprived. Though oral, their compositions have to be called 'literature' because there is no other word. Oral poems are positively not a rudimentary form of written poetry, but an independent mode; for – as the Chadwicks remind us in their great work – 'the connection between literature and writing is accidental'. The Chadwicks were academics, working entirely on research into printed records, but there is a similar implication in the conclusions of two anthropologists in the field, C. H. and R. M. Berndt, with immediate knowledge of as 'primitive' a people as one can conceive, the aborigines of Australia. They point out that their subjects are not survivals with a stone-age culture:

They are our contemporaries, motivated by the same basic urges as ourselves, but with a different way of living, a different outlook, different values ... Part of the trouble has been the assumption that an emphasis on material objects, and on technical achievements, must always go hand-in-hand with highly developed mental ability or an advanced civilisation. The measuring-rod here was usually our own Western European-type culture, for a long time depicted as far superior in every way to all others. This view has been profoundly shaken in recent years.

The World of the First Australians

So profoundly shaken, one might add, that it has been advanced (e.g. by Stanley Diamond) as the main function of anthropology that it should tell civilized societies what they need to learn from primitive people.

How is it that poems by unlettered authors are available to us? So far as English is concerned the first communicators were the monks who in Saxon times and the early middle ages transcribed the whole of Anglo-Saxon literature and other pagan material. Of course a great deal must have been lost, because the church disapproved of popular song, and put it down whenever it could. In the sixteenth century, ballads and folk songs began to be printed as broadsheets, and then travellers and, further afield, explorers recorded what impressed them. For instance in 1795 Mungo Park, weary with searching for the source of the Nile, was most hospitably entertained by African villagers. After giving him a meal, the women went on with their spinning, a labour which they lightened by extempore songs, one of them about him: 'It was sung by one of the young women, the rest joining in a sort of chorus. The air was sweet and plaintive, and the words, literally translated, were these:

> The winds roared, and the rains fell,
> The poor white man, faint and weary,
> Came and sat under our tree.
> He has no mother to bring him milk,
> No wife to grind his corn.
>> *Let us pity the white man;*
>> *No mother has he,* etc.'

After the explorers came the nineteenth-century administrators, officials, missionaries, traders and settlers, and many of them noted the poetry that impressed them. In the nineties for example a tough gold prospector recorded this from an Athabascan Indian:

Song to a Dead Bear

We apologise for depriving you of your life,
You who are the real owner of the forests and woods and rivers,
Which God gave you
To be your own place to live in.

We are compelled to take your spirit from you
In order that we may live,
For our own immediate food;
And also to take your skin to sell
So that we may support our wives and children.

ANGUS GRAHAM, *The Golden Grindstone*

Then the anthropologists, Seligmann, Malinowski, the Berndts, to name only a few of the many hundreds, recorded a variety of ritual and spontaneous songs; and from Walter Scott onwards collectors like Cecil Sharp, Verrier Elwin in India and Hugh Tracey in South Africa have written down whole volumes of songs. The vast field was explored by the Chadwicks for their pioneer research, drawn on by C. M. Bowra for his *Primitive Song* (a strongly recommended introduction), and well traversed by Willard Trask for his standard anthology *The Unwritten Song*.

Except for a few English ones, all the poems here are translations, some of them from the languages of the original French, German or Italian collectors. Inevitably there is loss in translation and still more through lack of context; rapport with the audience is an element of the original performance that cannot be transferred, nor can the music and dance and movement. The oral poet, the only kind for thousands of years, composed every type of poetry known to us, and he employed all the resources of his craft: rhyme, rhythm, metre; assonance, onomatopoeia; pattern, antithesis, repetition, refrain and parallelism; simile, metaphor, imagery. Sometimes a special poetic diction was developed, and thus part of the vocabulary might acquire reverberation through its connection with religious and other occasions, exerting a powerful pull on the emotions; though, without writing, words could never take on the charge of associations that so greatly enrich the English language and enable the poet to draw on emotional capital stored up over hundreds of years. The move from the original to a modern European tongue must shed some of the effects just mentioned, but so far as one can tell rather less than might be expected.

To start with an item that needs no translation, a little aboriginal poem from Australia, of which the last line is an imitation of the call of the plover as it is heard before rain:

Rain Chant

Dad a da da
Dad a da da
Dad a da da
Da kata kai

4

Ded o ded o
Ded o ded o
Ded o ded o
Da kata kai

Such imitative poems often come across quite well in translation.
Here is another example, a Navajo Indian poem, that also enacts
the sound and rhythm of rain:

Corn Song

The corn grows up.
The waters of the dark clouds drop, drop.
The rain descends.
The waters from the corn leaves drop, drop.
The rain descends.
The waters from the plants drop, drop.
The corn grows up.
The waters of the dark mists drop, drop.

The beating of rain, the fall of waves, the pulse of the blood, the
movement of a march or a lullaby, the tempo of paddling a boat,
shouts of exultation and cries of mourning can be sensed in the
poetry of most languages; the archetypal themes of literature have
both physical and psychological roots. The next example shows
how a literal prose translation can reproduce the pattern and
something of the movement of the original. The last two lines of
the poem, No. 58 in this book, collected from the Veddas of
Ceylon in 1910, run thus in their language, with lines repeated:

Waeccen pinnen pana noyeyi,
Waeccen pinnen pana noyeyi,
Kudi peta naettan pana yanneyi,
Kudi peta naettan pana yanneyi.

The translation, without repetition:

Owing to rain or dew, life will not depart,
If there be no wife, life will depart.

5

If we read some of the translations of Hebrew poetry in the Authorised Version without recourse to the text it is clear that some of the original power is transmitted. The antitheses in Ch. 3 of *Ecclesiastes* supply a simple example:

> To everything there is a season,
> And a time to every purpose under the heaven:
> A time to be born, and a time to die;
> A time to plant, and a time to pluck up that which is planted . . .
> A time to rend, and a time to sew;
> A time to keep silence, and a time to speak;
> A time to love, and a time to hate;
> A time for war, and a time for peace.

Still more in the powerful lament of David for Saul and Jonathan (No. 114) we feel the impact of what was not inserted by the translators: the rhythm, the emphases, the imagery and the tolling bell sound of the near-refrain 'How are the mighty fallen', with the variation on the final repeat stressing the message, 'And the weapons of war perished!' Usually the best translations are literal, and are effective when set out as verse; arrangement brings out parallelism, contrast, emphasis and some of the rhythm. Cut-up prose, yes – but so at first sight is some of the best work of Pound and Eliot, in which the reader must be sensitive to the rhythms which are very much there and need only a slightly co-operative ear to come into full being. The worst translations are those which aimed at being poetic at a time when the conventions of poetry were bad, as in the second half of the nineteenth century. There are one or two examples in the pages that follow, in which it is fairly clear that the translator's additions form a barrier between the oral poet and the modern reader. As well as imagining the music, the audience and the occasion, the reader of today should supply all he can by reading aloud or at least forming the words with the mouth – a form of co-operation that is required anyway to bring all printed poetry to life.

The societies that produced poetry as surely as the earth throws up wild plants were characteristically small, homogeneous, and living off the land by hunting, cattle-raising or tilling the soil. Often their outlook was animist. In the words of Yeats:

They saw in the rainbow the still bent bow of a god, thrown down in his negligence; they heard in the thunder the sound of his beaten water-jar, or the tumult of his chariot-wheels; and when a sudden flight of wild ducks, or of crows, passed over their heads, they thought they were gazing at the dead hastening to their rest.

The poems were always sung or chanted, sometimes danced and accompanied by musical instruments. They were an integral part of every activity and phase of life from birth to death, to a degree difficult to conceive now. They were regarded in some cases as strictly functional – to celebrate a birth, to help the new-born child to a place in the scheme of things, to obtain a husband or a wife, to solemnize a wedding or a funeral, to secure good hunting or a rich yield from crops or animals, to defuse a quarrel, to ease illness, to accompany rites of passage, to placate the powers or seek their help. A large class of songs was interwoven with the daily round of getting food or making shelter; they made the power of muscle more effective and rendered easier all tasks that needed united action or went with a swing. Three thousand years ago for example the Greeks had songs for weaving, treading grapes, stamping barley, making ropes, carrying water and baking bread; watchmen, shepherds and others also had their own songs. From all over the world comes the same story: songs for rowing, paddling, hauling timber, marching, launching boats. Africa has always been strong in work songs for anything that goes to a rhythm – hoeing, weeding, mowing, sawing, throwing up water from a deep well on a human chain, while there are domestic and solitary songs for women grinding corn or pounding rice. With two main exceptions not many work songs have survived in the British Isles. Sea shanties were employed to promote rhythmical action and make more efficient use of man-power; and in Gaelic there were numerous songs, now translated, to go with reaping, milling, spinning, waulking cloth and so on.

7

All these tended to be closely geared in with the job in hand, even as late as the time of Cecil Sharp; he records that when he was collecting:

I have many times sat by the side of a stonebreaker on the wayside and taken down songs – at the risk too of my eyesight, for the occupation and the song are very often inseparable.

And a friend of R. R. Terry's seeking to obtain a song from an old Irish woman, reputed to be the best keener in the district, found that she was distressed and could not sing, till he lay down and pretended to be a corpse.

It was common too for everyone to improvise verse on occasion, as Bede tells us in his *History* (IV, 24). Usually this would not be difficult, since the language of oral societies tended to be poetic; the earliest speech was probably expressive and poetic rather than prosaic and indicative. The language was concrete, it reflected first-hand experience, it spoke of what people knew immediately. Imagery came from the weather, the seasons, the environment and the life within it. Examples may be found in the diction, imagery and rhythm of much rustic speech; in pre-industrial England the names given to plants, places and animals were often remarkably beautiful. At first a general possession, poetry separated out for various functions: cosmology, ritual, history and law; it was a generally useful aid to memory. Charms and spells had to be accurate, or they would lose their force; weather lore, information about farming and house-keeping, rules for navigation are other examples. Whole books of biography, science and medicine were composed in verse, and priests and teachers relied heavily on metrical mnemonics. The poets whose compositions have survived were only a little more skilled at their craft than the rest of the community.

The audience was very important. In the age of print the poet sits down and commits to writing the poem that has been growing in his head; he can do so when he feels like it, when there is a stimulus, when the matter is ripe. He can take as long as he likes; the process of writing clears the mind; he can revise and rewrite. He composes with an eventual audience in mind, but without the immediate reaction – from enthusiasm to sleep – of listeners, he must be his own first audience and get the poem right before launching it. This mode of composition has produced incomparably fine poetry, of a range and quality beyond the compass of the oral poet. Except for the woman at her grinding or spinning, the oral poet needed an audience and an opportunity; the poem did not exist till it was realized in performance. Even the traditional folk song took as many shapes as it had performers, while the epic or ballad could be even more fluid, consisting of an outline story which the individual singer clothed from his stock-in-trade of spare parts. Talented performers tried out variations and innovations, which went into the repertoire if socially approved. Only in the case of poems for ritual or magic or handing down laws and religious doctrine was accuracy required, and obtained; the sacred books of India, the Vedas, were transmitted for hundreds of years with complete fidelity.

Two factors militated against the composition of what to us is now the most familiar type of verse, the personal lyric. Some cultures turned out nothing but functional poetry, sung as it was required for particular events, to further the aims of the group, or to ease and grace the job in hand. Such verse does not become obsolete because its aims are forgotten; sea shanties, used to compensate inadequate techniques of manipulating a ship's gear, are many of them of lasting beauty. Moreover the need of small societies to hold together as a group for mere survival, sometimes under a leader with whom his people came to identify, meant that the concerns of the individual had not the importance they have acquired since. The individual consciousness was in some directions not fully developed; a poem like Wordsworth's 'Strange fits of passion have I known' would not have been understood. Despite the obstacles, there is a surprising amount of personal poetry in the oral literature of all ages; the voice of a suffering human being is recognizable across tens of centuries, as in

9

this Chinese poem of the third century B.C.:

> With flowers blooming and birds singing,
> Spring is here calling us to visit friends far and near.
> Other women are accompanied by their husbands and sons,
> Poor me, I shall go to the wall where my husband's bones are.
> Great Wall! Great Wall! If you can save us from enemies,
> Why not save first our dear ones?

(The Great Wall was built by forced labour under harsh conditions.)

What did their poetry do for the people whose lives it pervaded? First, it helped them to adjust themselves to their environment and to be at home in it; it also allowed them to believe that they had a measure of control over it, and thus to rid themselves of their worst fears about the gods and the powers of nature. Their poetic myths provided accounts of the creation and running of the universe that may not accord with whatever theory is current in 1978, but they were at least as effective in dispelling their terrors as modern science is in allaying our own fears about atomic or ecological catastrophe. Next, poetry enabled them to cope with the changes and chances of life; it made sense of the weather and the seasons and offered support in times of crisis. For example, the elegies recited at a death sustained the bereaved person in his or her grief, provided a ritual form of expression and allowed the community to share the sorrow. Collective mourning of this kind affords a glimpse of the original nature and purpose of poetry. Another function of poetry was to act as a vehicle for the traditions of a community, and as an agent in favour of conformity. In some cases it institutionalized and provided a safety valve for dissent and complaint. Poetry made available a knowledge of life, and offered patterns of conduct. The understanding and digestion of experience were furthered by symbolizing, in which primitive poetry is characteristically rich, with the natural environment providing imagery in abundance. The people of Chattisgarh in India for instance – where life is hard and dusty and made tolerable only by poetry – converse all day long in symbols. When a man has daughters to marry he tells his friends he has millet in the house, and when he asks for a girl in marriage he says he has come for a flower to put in his hair. As Carlyle wrote in 1834, 'It is in and through Symbols that man, consciously or unconsciously, lives, works, and has his being: those ages, moreover, are accounted the noblest which can the best recognize symbolical worth, and prize it the highest.'

One of the fullest claims for the part played by oral poetry is that stated by C. M. Bowra in discussing the songs of primitive peoples. Poetry, he writes, is indispensable to those who practise it. It formulates and answers their nagging questions, enables them to pursue action with zest and confidence, puts them in contact with gods and spirits, and makes them feel less strange in the natural world. It gives a solid centre to what would otherwise be chaos, supplies a continuity, and keeps their minds and energies awake. It enables them to absorb experience with their whole natures, and enhances the desire and strengthens the capacity to live. Through their poetry, Bowra concludes, life is sustained, renewed and fulfilled.

The present selection is only a very small sample of what is available, and does not represent the whole range of oral poetry, which of course includes myth, epic, ballad and narrative. Though it does not draw much on European sources, partly because print brought to an end all oral traditions and partly because the surviving oral poetry is well known, a few poems from England, Wales, Scotland, and Ireland are included to show the kinship, in feeling and imagery, between poets far apart in space and time. How close is an early Chinese song:

> The cloth-plant grew till it covered with thorn-bush
> The bindweed spread far over the wilds.
> My lovely one is here no more.
> With whom? – no, I sit alone . . .

to the English folk song:

I leaned my back against an oak,
I thought it was a trusty tree.
But first it bent and then it broke;
My true love has forsaken me.

It is hoped that it will be enjoyed widely enough to encourage the making of more collections – in the case of Gaelic poetry for example there must be well over a thousand poems already translated from which there is no selection in print – and that it will demonstrate the value of what the preliterates can offer us. That is, poetry which excels at conveying impressions, sensations and emotions that are basic in human nature.

That centrality is what matters today. The poems come from people at an earlier but not inferior stage in the development of man; as we have noted, he was less conscious of himself as an individual, his life was less private, and his consciousness of the world about him was unified, the result of a life led and aims shared by all. The strength of the poems rests in their closeness to common experience, the fulness of their response to the demands and contingencies of life, and the way in which they are often expressed symbolically. They are not alien and remote from us, or unintelligible, but are near the core of humanity which we share with their authors. This aspect of the poetry makes it much more sympathetic than most modern verse, which is so markedly not central, not engaging, not intelligible, stuck in backwaters away from the main stream of human experience, offering the reader what may be unique but lacks appeal. Perhaps it is not so much that poets are writing the 'wrong' kind of verse, as that the wrong people feel impelled to offer us their peripheral experiences.

This central core needs to be kept in sight and maintained at a time when the human norms are slighted or obscured. In the eyes of those who run the economy (whatever their political labels) we are consumers to be controlled by the media; to various reductionist writers and biologists, mere animals; to the pornographers of perversion and cruelty a sub-species with great potentialities for exploitation. There is no need to idealize preliterate people; warfare and cannibalism were institutions among some of them (cf. Stanley Diamond in *Tract* No. 18, *The Primitive and the Civilized*). They rarely lived much above subsistence level, they endured toil and poverty and starvation, but they produced poetry that deals directly with the main concerns of mankind, addressed to the whole of the group that the poets knew, and within the scope of all to enjoy. This much cannot be claimed for the 'art' poetry of the past three or four hundred years. This at its best is wonderful – it has widened human consciousness, opened up new paths and potentialities – but at present it is accessible only to a few. By contrast the ready availability of preliterate verse should win it readers who are discouraged at the threshold of modern poetry.

★   ★   ★   ★   ★

The stimulus and help of the following books are acknowledged with gratitude:

C. M. Bowra, *Primitive Song*
    An exploratory and attractive work on the songs of technically primitive people, such as bushmen, aborigines and pygmies.

David Buchan, *The Ballad and the Folk*
    Excellent on the background and composition of oral poetry; of wider relevance than the title suggests.

H. M. and N. K. Chadwick, *The Growth of Literature*
    A comprehensive survey of the world's oral poetry in three massive and illuminating volumes.

E. A. Havelock, *Preface to Plato*
    Includes a vigorous explanation of the reasons for the power of poetry in classical Greece.

Cecil Sharp, *English Folk Song*
    Penetrating insights of the man who recorded English folk song, just in time.

Willard R. Trask, *The Unwritten Song*, 1 and 2
    A very fine collection of oral poetry, strong on America and the Pacific, and the first of its kind.

I

Love and Courtship

I

Grass Song

Sung in the evening by women, beating time with handfuls of dry grass.

This grass in my hand before it was cut
Cried in the wind for the rain to come:
All day my heart cries in the sun
For my hunter to come.

BUSHMAN, KALAHARI DESERT

2

Dance Song

She burst into the dance.
None of us knows her name.
A silver amulet
Swings between her breasts.

She sprang into the dance,
Rings tinkling at her ankles,
Silver bracelets.

For her I sold
An apple orchard.

She burst into the dance,
Her hair streamed loose.

For her I sold
A field of olive-trees.

She sprang into the dance,
Her necklace of pearls glittered.

For her I sold
My grove of fig-trees.

She sprang into the dance,
With a flower of a smile.

For her I sold
All my orange-trees.

BERBER, ALGERIA

3

Love Song

First, I admire you for your hair dressed like a rooster's tail.
Second, I love you because you speak so charmingly.
Third, I love you for your features, which are sweet to look at.
Fourth, I love you for your clothes, which are all the same colour.
Fifth, I love you because you have pins in your hair and a Chinese
    fan in your hand.
Sixth, I love you because your hair is green.
Seventh, I love you because your parents brought you into the
    world.

Eighth, I love you because your phoenix eyes look at me most
    lovingly.
Ninth, I love you because we are going to be married and live
    together.
Tenth, I love you because you will not marry anyone but me.

VIETNAM

4

Courting Song and Reply

The girl:
Oh, my handsome boy!
You think I ought to say something nice to you?
Just you listen, and I'll tell you something!
You act like Kokon Morok himself,
My handsome boy!
You want me to tell you something more!
Now just you listen!
The way the snail twines, put your arms around me that way,
My handsome boy!
Haven't you had enough yet?
As men throw themselves into the rushing stream, so you may
    handle me,
My handsome boy!
Say more to you than that? – what makes you think so?

The boy:
Oh, you beautiful girl!
You think I ought to say something to you, too.
Just you listen!
What do you mean by jeering at me like that?

Oh, you beautiful girl!
Do you want to hear something else nice?
Just you listen!
As the flood carries stones away with it, so you carry me away,
You beautiful girl!
I had something to say to you – it was you who wanted it!

NEW GUINEA, ABOUT 1850

5

The Lightning Snakes

The tongues of the Lightning Snakes flicker and twist, one to
    the other . . .
Flashing among the cabbage palm foliage . . .
Lightning flashing through clouds, flickering tongue of the
    Snake . . .
Always there, at the wide expanse of water, at the place of the
    sacred tree . . .
Flashing above the people of the western clans,
All over the sky their tongues flicker, above the Place of the
    Rising Clouds, the Place of the Standing Clouds,
All over the sky, tongues flickering, twisting . . .
Always there, at the camp by the wide expanse of water . . .
All over the sky their tongues flicker; at the Place of the Two
    Sisters, the place of the Wawalag.
Lightning flashing through clouds, flickering tongue of the
    Lightning Snake . . .
The blinding flash lights up the cabbage palm foliage . . .
Gleams on the cabbage palms, and their shining leaves . . .

ABORIGINAL, AUSTRALIA, FROM A LOVE SONG CYCLE

6

Song

Youth looks on youth and starts pursuing.
If my veil lifts it is the wind's doing.

Looking into your eyes – O, all-my-good!
My being is dissolved in a burning flood.

Youth looks on youth, and starts pursuing.
If my veil lifts, it is the wind's doing.

HINDI, INDIA

7

A Woman Sings of Her Love

Oh, you are a kilt which a young dandy set out to choose,
Oh, you are like a costly ring for which thousands were paid,
Will I ever find your like – you who have been shown to me only
    once?
An umbrella comes apart; you are (as strong) as looped iron;
Oh, you who are as the gold of Nairobi, finely moulded,
You are the risen sun, and the early rays of dawn.
Will I ever find your like, you who have been shown to me only
    once?

SOMALI, AFRICA

8

When I see the beauty on my beloved's face,
I throw away the food in my hand;
Oh, sister of the young man, listen;
The beauty on my beloved's face.

Her neck is long, when I see it
I cannot sleep one wink;
Oh, the daughter of my mother-in-law,
Her neck is like the shaft of the spear.

When I touch the tattoos on her back,
I die;
Oh, sister of the young man, listen;
The tattoos on my beloved's back.

When I see the gap in my beloved's teeth,
Her teeth are white like dry season simsim;
Oh, daughter of my father-in-law, listen;
The gap in my beloved's teeth.

The daughter of the bull confuses my head,
I have to marry her;
True, sister of the young man, listen;
The suppleness of my beloved's waist.

ACOLI PEOPLE, NORTHERN UGANDA

9

Woman, lovely as lightning at dawn,
Speak to me even once.

I long for you, as one
Whose dhow in summer winds
Is blown adrift and lost,
Longs for land, and finds –
Again the compass tells –
A grey and empty sea.

SOMALI, AFRICA

10

How am I to cross the hills?
Without you the level plain
Is like a mountain
Without you the flooded river
Is a parched plain in time of drought
Without you the sarai tree in bud
Is dry and blackened in a forest fire.

CHATTISGARH, INDIA

11

Serenade

O lady, be calm and cry not but sing to your suitors
Sing to those who guide you and to the discerning passers-by.

Sing to the son of Shaka's people, cast aside your grief and sorrow
and distress.
O lady, be calm, let me give you gifts, fine clothes from our
homeland the Hejaz
Let me adorn you with a chain and beads of gold devised in
Shiraz
Let me build for you a great white house of lime and stone.
Let me furnish it for you with furnishings of crystal that those
who see it shall sing its praise
Spread beneath with rushes soft from the lake-sides of Shaka and
Ozi
Let me satisfy your good parents and let them rest at ease with
minstrels' songs
Let them lie at ease with food of young camels and of oxen, sheep
and goats
Because, my lady, O lady mine let me tell you, you are my
beloved.

SWAHILI, AFRICA

12

Shall I compare thee to a white *mehari*, to a camel of Termai?
To a herd of Kita antelopes? To the fringe of Jerba's red scarf?
To grapes which have just ripened?
In a valley where alongside of them ripens the date?
Amûmen is the thread on which have been strung the pearls of
my necklace.
He is the cord on which are hung the talismans on my breast.
He is my life.

TUAREG WOMAN, AT AN AHAL

22

13

The parrot weeps without its cage
My life weeps without support
How empty the house is
Without a girl
Day by day my body decays
There is no one to help me
No one ahead and no one behind
No one to give me wisdom
How empty the house is
Without a girl.

GOND ABORIGINAL, INDIA

14

Love Song

I know not whether thou hast been absent:
I lie down with thee, I rise up with thee,
In my dreams thou art with me.
If my eardrops tremble in my ears,
I know it is thou moving within my heart.

AZTEC

The wind and the rain are beating down.
Take shelter or your clothes will be drenched.
The rain is falling, falling.
   In all my dreams I searched for you,
   But I did not find even the echo of your steps.

I have built a fence by the roadside.
I have made a fence for my garden.
Where have you hidden, thief of my heart?
   In all my dreams I searched for you,
   But I did not find even the echo of your steps.

I have cut tall bamboos; I have cut short bamboos.
Large are the hollows of the dwarf bamboos.
The thief who crouched behind my fence has hidden in those
     hollows.
   In all my dreams I searched for you,
   But I did not find even the echo of your steps.

GOND ABORIGINAL, INDIA

16

The nightingale,
From singing
Grown thin:
I, from awaiting
Him I love,
Grown thin.

JAPANESE, 15TH–16TH CENTURY

24

Lovers Disturbed by the Dawn

It is growing lighter: we can see the fields
The hour of parting has come
My heart is full of anger against the dawn
For in this field we must part from one another
Now home will be no longer home to me
The forest is no more a forest
I will be restless in the village where I found rest till now
But part we must, for our enemy the dawn has come.

GOND ABORIGINAL, INDIA

Lujhki Karam

Song for a dance at the Karam festival

In an upper field, I said, 'Girl, please let me.'
No, elder brother, the place is muddy
The place is muddy
My heart is like gold
My clothes are like flowers
No, elder brother, they will get muddy
Near us are people
Over us is God
Elder brother, how can I let you?

URAON SONG, INDIA

Passion-Song of the Maidens

First voice:
The difficult entrance, the veiled gateway

Second voice:
Now is stormed, is carried by assault.

Chorus:
The intruder thrusts against the nub of desire.
Here is a maid; there below is the cleft portal.
Perhaps it is Tu-of-the-long-blade who has flung her upon the
    ground.
Extended by the finger nails,
A net lies open; it has found a handle.
Drawn tightly, the net is drawn tightly,
O rapturous little evoker of delight!
O lusty fellow probing the slippery wound!
The fount of passion gushes forth,
The blade plies in and out,
Anon brought up sharply against the inner gate.
Elsewhere a sudden flow escapes;
The lovers are united in vigorous interplay, made audible in
    mutual embraces.

TUAMOTUS, POLYNESIA

Berber dance
  Jon Gardey, Robert Harding Associates

The Worthless Lover

Trousers of wind and buttons of hail;
A lump of Shoa earth, at Gondar nothing left;
A hyena bearing meat, led on a leather thong;
Some water in a glass left standing by the fire;
A measure of water thrown on the hearth;
A horse of mist and a swollen ford;
Useless for anything, useful to no one;
Why am I in love with such a man as he?

AMHARA, AFRICA

Brief Moment

By Him who brings weeping and laughter,
    who deals death and life as He wills –
She left me to envy the wild deer
    that graze twain and twain without fear.
O love of her, heighten my heart's pain,
    and strengthen the pang every night.
O comfort that days bring, forgetting–
    the last of all days be thy tryst.
I marvelled how swiftly the time sped
    between us the moment we met:
But when that brief moment was ended,
    how wearily dragged he his feet!

ANCIENT ARABIC

Kalahari women
  BBC copyright

Old Thyme

Come all young women and maids
  That are all in your prime,
Mind how you weed your gardens gay,
  Let no one steal your thyme.

Once I had thyme enough,
  To last me night and day,
There came to me a false young man
  Stole all my thyme away.

And now my thyme is done,
  I cannot plant no new,
There lays the bed where my old thyme grew,
  'Tis all over-run with rue.

Rue is a running root,
  Runs all across amain,
If I could pluck that running root
  I'd plant my old thyme again.

NORFOLK

At the River

A blond girl was singing on the Trikhas bridge
piercing songs, full of grief.

And from her mournful sound, her grievous song,
the bridge cracked, the river stopped,
and the spirit of the river jumped out onto the bank.
A traveller called out from the far ridge:
'Change the tune, *kori*, sing a different song
so the river can run again and the bridge be put together again,
so the spirit of the river can return to his place.'
'How can I change the tune, how can I hush my song?
This song I'm singing is a lament
because there's no cure for the pain in my heart.
I lost my mother and my father and nine soldier brothers,
and my beloved was sick in bed
and he sent me searching for a cure that was nowhere in this
        world:
rabbit's cheese and wild goat's milk.
And, by the time I had gone up into the wild mountains and
        down to the plains
to hunt the rabbit, to catch the wild goat,
to build a marble *mandra* to make the cheese,
my beloved got married to another woman:
he took a rock for his mother-in-law and the black earth for his
        wife.'

GREEK

24

O Waly, Waly

The water is wide, I cannot get o'er,
And neither have I wings to fly.
Give me a boat that will carry two,
And both shall row, my love and I.

O, down in the meadows the other day,
A-gath'ring flowers, both fine and gay.
A-gath'ring flowers, both red and blue,
I little thought what love can do.

I put my hand into one soft bush
Thinking the sweetest flower to find.
I pricked my finger right to the bone,
And left the sweetest flower alone.

I leaned my back up against some oak
Thinking that he was a trusty tree;
But first he bended and then he broke;
And so did my false love to me.

A ship there is and she sails the sea,
She's loaded deep as deep can be,
But not so deep as the love I'm in:
I know not if I sink or swim.

O, love is handsome and love is fine,
And love's a jewel while it is new,
But when it is old, it groweth cold,
And fades away like morning dew.

ENGLISH

25

May the man who gained my trust yet did not come
Turn to a devil, sprouting triple horns.
Then he would find himself shunned by mankind.

May he become a bird of the water-paddy
With frost and snow and hailstones raining down.
Then he would find his feet were frozen fast.

May he become the duckweed on the pond.
Then he would sway and shiver as he walked.

JAPANESE, 12TH CENTURY

26

The Seeds of Love

I sowed the seeds of love,
I sowed them in the spring –
I gathered them up in the morning so soon,
While the small birds did sweetly sing.

My garden was planted well
With flowers everywhere,
But I had not the liberty to choose for myself
Of the flowers that I loved so dear.

My gardener he stood by,
I asked him to choose for me;
He chose me the violet, the lily and the pink,
But these I refused all three.

The violet I did not like
Because it fades so soon.
The lily and the pink I did overthink,
And I vowed I would wait till June.

For in June there's a red rosebud,
And that's the flower for me,
So I pulled and I plucked at the red rosebud
Till I gained the willow tree.

For the willow tree will twist
And the willow tree will twine,
I wish I was in the young man's arms
That once had this heart of mine.

Come all you false young men
That leave me here to complain.
For the grass that now is trodden under foot
In time it will rise again.

ENGLISH

27

The Lazy Wave

The lazy wave slides over the sand,
My love and I were hand in hand.
It ran till it came where we did stand,
And faded away in the Severn sand.

Oh love that be new runs in on the tide,
But love that be ebbing will never abide.
Like the lazy wave it do fade away,
And leave you alone for ever a day.

The ships they go sail in the Severn Sea
But never a lad looks out for me.
My heart is a-broked, the heart that I gave
Wasted and gone like the lazy wave.

So lonely I wander by Severn Side
Watching and waiting the turn of the tide.
But no one returns for to claim his bride
And the lazy wave it do fade and hide.

SOMERSET

28

The man who was my lover
He is dead.
I am lonely.
If I could go to him
I would go
No matter how far away.

NAVAJO INDIAN

29

Wulf

Wulf is the woman's outlawed lover, and Eadwacer her tyrannous husband.

It is as if they gave a prey to my people.
Will they feed him, if he should feel want?
It is not so with us.

Wulf is on one island, I on another;
Marshes surround that island;
Cruel men dwell there.
Will they feed him, if he should feel want?
    It is not so with us.

I waited for my Wulf with far-ranging longing,
When the rain poured down and I sat weeping.
When a warrior there put his arms around me,
It pleased me then, but it was also pain.
Wulf, my Wulf, my longings for you
And your rare visits have made me sick,
With a stricken heart, and not a want of food.
Do you hear, Eadwacer? Wulf will carry
Our wretched whelp off to the wood.
Men can easily sunder that which was never
Joined together, the song of us two together.

ANGLO-SAXON

30

A Tristful Girl

Rain fell in the evening
And a frosty night came,
I rose to look for my sweetheart
And I found the green meadow,
And on the meadow my sweetheart's cloak,
And on the cloak his silk handkerchief,
And on the handkerchief his guitar,
By the guitar an apple.

I thought all thoughts.
If I should take his cloak,
He is young, inexperienced, and I am afraid
He might catch cold –
If I should take his handkerchief.
I gave it to him as a sign of my love.
If I took his guitar,
His guitar was given him by my brothers.
I thought of everything and I decided
To bite his apple.
So that he may know I had come
To see my sweetheart.

YUGOSLAV TRADITIONAL BALLAD

31

If I might be an ox,
An ox, a beautiful ox,
Beautiful but stubborn;
The merchant would buy me,
Would buy and slaughter me,
Would spread my skin,
Would bring me to the market.
The coarse woman would bargain for me;
The beautiful girl would buy me.
She would crush perfumes for me;
I would spend the night rolled up around her;
I would spend the afternoon rolled up around her.
Her husband would say: 'It is a dead skin.'
But I would have her love.

GALLA PEOPLE, ABYSSINIA

35

Breaking a Willow-branch

Mounting your horse, you did not take your whip,
Instead you broke a branch from the willow-tree.
Walking and sitting I played on my flute,
Its sadness would break any traveller's heart.

Deep down within me I was miserable,
Oh! How I wished that I could be your whip!
Coming and going, I'd be worn at your wrist,
Journeying and halting to rest upon your knee.

Far off you can descry the Meng-chin ford,
And all its clumps of dancing willow-trees.
But I am only a girl of a nomad tribe,
And cannot understand your Chinese songs.

CHINESE, PERHAPS ORIGINALLY
TRANSLATED INTO CHINESE FROM ONE
OF THE NOMAD LANGUAGES

2

Marriage and Children

A Song before Marriage

How shall I buy
A red and yellow cloth?
How shall I buy, mother
A beautiful girl?
With money I shall buy
The red and yellow cloth
With words I shall buy
The beautiful girl
Where shall I put
The red and yellow cloth?
Where shall I put
The lovely girl?
In a chest I shall put
The red and yellow cloth
In a room I shall put
The beautiful girl.

URAON, INDIA

34

Song for a Marriage Ceremony

Out of the house she comes
To the green, green marriage-booth
But why is her body drooping?
Why is your mind so sad, my bride
Why droops your body like a flower?

Without my mother, my mind is sad
Without my father, my body droops
If today your mother were living
She would have shaded your head with her cloth
If today your father were living
He would have guarded you with his sword
I have plucked a flower
And sent it to call them
Go, go, little flower
To the land of my father and mother
Now mother is coming in a litter
And father is coming on a horse
Mother, here is your loving child
Mother, take her for a moment in your lap
Henceforth she will be a stranger to you.

GOND ABORIGINAL, INDIA

35

Song to a Bride

Slowly, slowly,
Child, counting your steps,
Go away, go away with tears,
With a large heart, with a weary heart,
Without turning your face,
From the house, from the village,
Where your eyes so gaily
Laughed at every comer.

Counting, counting your steps,
Today you go away.
With a large heart, with a weary heart,
Go away, go away below!
Counting, counting your steps,
With a large heart, with a weary heart,
Today you go away.

Keep on your heart
And guard well the flower
Of your mother's garden,
The flower which will say to you:
'I am still loved below!'
Keep on your heart
And guard well the flower
In memory for ever.

Counting, counting your steps,
Today you go away,
With a large heart, with a weary heart,
Go away, go away below!
With a large heart, with a weary heart,
Today you go away.

GABON PYGMY, AFRICA

36

Song for the Departure of the Bride and Bridegroom

The mother
Who gave the lota of water with her own hands

Is weeping
The father
Who counted the dowry with his own hands
Is weeping
The elder sister
Who pinned the flowers in the hair with her own hands
Is weeping
The elder brother
Is catching his sister
And giving her away
The sister's beauty
Is filling the whole village.

URAON, INDIA

37

Less Gaiety now Another Boy has got Married

The nest of the white ant is graced by the cobra
The cobra is taken by the charmer
The nest is vacant
The river's pool glistens with the fishes
The big net is thrown by the boy who fishes
The pool is stagnant
The jungle sprang with the deer
The deer died in the trap
The jungle withers
The village lives in its boys
The bridegroom is taken to the spring
The village dies.

URAON, INDIA

38

Birth

Slowly the unborn babe distends life's pathway,
    torn by the child's head;
Now the living child,
    long cherished by the mother beneath her heart,
Fills the gateway of life.

There is room to pass safely through –
    The child slips downward,
    It becomes visible,
    It bursts forth into the light of day,
The waters of childbirth flow away.

POLYNESIAN

39

Song at Birth

My heart is joyful,
My heart takes wing in singing,
Under the trees of the forest,
Forest our home and our mother.
In my net I have taken
A little, a very little bird.
My heart is caught in the net,
In the net with the bird.

PYGMY, AFRICA

Lullaby

Someone would like to have you for her child
But you are my own.
Someone wished she had you to nurse you on a good mat;
Someone wished you were hers: she would put you on a camel
     blanket;
But I have you to rear you on a torn mat.
Someone wished she had you, but I have you.

AKAN, WEST AFRICA

41

Kahuto, the Owl
A bedtime lullaby

Hoot! wife of mine, owl wife
Hoot! roast for you and me
Hoot! let's go and see the dance
Hoot! at King Eagle's
Hoot! at Torowala on the hill
   A pig yam for me
Hoot! how are we to go?
Hoot! let's go by sea
Hoot! my feet will get wet
Hoot! or how are we to go?
Hoot! let's go by the path
Hoot! my feet will get dirty
Hoot! let's fly like birds
   Come on! Come on!

SOLOMON ISLANDS

42

Lullaby

Sleep, baby, sleep:
Sweet baby, go to sleep.
Too sweet for words, how could you tell
How sweet my baby is –
More than the trees on every hill,
More than every blade of grass,
More than all the stars in the sky,
More than the rice stalks in the field?
This babe asleep
Is more, more sweet
Than all of these.

JAPANESE, 17TH CENTURY

43

Lullaby: Complaint of the Wild Goose

We were nine to leave the lake in the north;
Of the nine travellers, I am the last.
Noble hunting falcon, have pity on me.

My country is far; the winds are contrary;
My wings grown heavy, I followed behind, alone.
Noble hunting falcon, have pity on me.

44

The leaders are at the nest, the stragglers are passing the halting-
    place;
Winter is coming, the sky is clouded.
Noble hunting falcon, have pity on me.

The sky is gray, the winds rise;
I hear my brothers flying on through the fog.
Noble hunting falcon, have pity on me.

WESTERN MONGOLIA

44

Good Fortune for a Daughter

By this crowning with a fillet, by this anointing with oil,
Thou art beautiful, thou art the first of thy generation.
Thou shalt overturn the hearts of the old men,
Thou shalt overturn the hearts of the warriors;
They shall gaze upon thee and eagerly speak thy name.
Thou art become the child of the Sun;
Thy feet shall tread high places;
Thy heart shall burn, thy body shall shine;
Thy face shall be beautiful and terrible;
Thy word shall be a judgment that is judged,
And thy name only, Joan Ruth, shall be in the mouth of all
    people,
Thine, thine, thine!
The Sun is risen.

GILBERTESE SPELL, TO BE SAID AT DAWN

Song for a Girl on Growing up

The black turkey gobbler, under the east, the middle of his trail;
    towards us it is about to dawn.
The black turkey gobbler, the tips of his beautiful tail; above us
    the dawn whitens.
The black turkey gobbler, the tips of his beautiful tail; above us
    the dawn becomes yellow.
The sunbeams stream forward, dawn boys, with shimmering
    shoes of yellow.
On top of the sunbeams that stream toward us they are dancing.
At the east the rainbow moves forward, dawn maidens, with
    shimmering shoes and shirts of yellow dance over us.
Beautifully over us it is dawning.

Above us among the mountains the herbs are becoming green.
Above us on the top of the mountains the herbs are becoming
    yellow.

Above us among the mountains, with shoes of yellow I go
    around the fruits and the herbs that shimmer.
Above us among the mountains, the shimmering fruits with
    shoes and shirts of yellow are bent toward him.
On the beautiful mountains above it is daylight.

MESCALERO APACHE

The Father's Song

Great snowslide,
Stay away from my igloo,
I have my four children and my wife;
They can never enrich you.

Strong snowslide
Roll past my weak house.
There sleep my dear ones in the world.
Snowslide, let their night be calm.

Sinister snowslide,
I just built an igloo here, sheltered from the wind.
It is my fault if it is put wrong.
Snowslide, hear me from your mountain.

Greedy snowslide,
There is enough to smash and smother.
Fall down over the ice,
Bury stones and cliffs and rocks.

Snowslide, I own so little in the world.
Keep away from my igloo, stop not our travels.
Nothing will you gain by our horror and death,
Mighty snowslide, mighty snowslide.

Little snowslide,
Four children and my wife are my whole world, all I own,
All I can lose, nothing can you gain.
Snowslide, save my house, stay on your summit.

ESKIMO

The Mother's Song

It is so still in the house.
There is a calm in the house;
The snowstorm wails out there,
And the dogs are rolled up with snouts under the tail.
My little boy is sleeping on the ledge,
On his back he lies, breathing through his open mouth.
His little stomach is bulging round –
Is it strange if I start to cry with joy?

ESKIMO

Power of Raven

Power of raven black be thine,
Power of eagle's back be thine,
   Hound-chase power.
Power of stormy wrack be thine,
Power of moonbeam track be thine,
   Sun's face power.
Power of ocean tack be thine,
Power of land attack be thine,
   Heav'n grace power.

Good of ocean space be thine,
Good of land and place be thine,
   Of heav'n's city.
Every day joy's trace be thine,
No day sorrow's case be thine,
   Honour, pity.
Love of every face be thine,
Pillow-dying grace be thine,
   Saviour, with thee.

GAELIC, SOUTH UIST

49

A Maori Mother Begs her Son
not to Avenge his Father

Let there not be war; for a man of war can ne'er be satiated;
But let my son be instead a man of wisdom and learning –
A keeper of the traditions of his house.
Let there be no war.
Plant deeply the spirit of peace,
That your rule may be known – the land of enforced peace.

RAROTONGA, POLYNESIA

50

The fire is burning at Birginbirgin and Gamwardla and Nuga,
Burning out the wallaby and the kangaroo.

Ah, my daughter, my brother, my nephew, my grandchild, my
    cousins,
We came here from our home, my daughter, my grandchild.
We travelled and hither we came,
We came to this unfriendly place, my daughter, my grandchild.
My baby died here!
Both of us came here with our child, here we found sickness.
My country is far away, hither we came,
Travelling from place to place, my brother, my brother's child.
Crying I carried him sick.
Who is watching and staring while father cries?
Ah, my daughter, my daughter, my grandchild!

ARNHEM LAND, AUSTRALIA

51

Kodai, how the world desires you
I took a pot to beg; as I went my shoes grew heavy
Weaker I got and weaker until my wife abused me
One would give a handful, another a pinch, yet a third gave only
    curses.
On the road the dogs barked and the housewives cursed me
I took a pot to beg: when I came home I put it down
With chatni and chilly I ate the rice; there was no vegetable or
    curry
The earth has lost its honour, the rain stays in the sky
Everywhere sin has increased and heavy is the world.

CHATTISGARH, INDIA

kodai, millet grain

52

Pleasant is November. The fair lady
Sees the paddy all round
And writes to her lord
My husband left me
And went to another land
And he does not care for me any more
I was only twelve years old
When he had my marriage finished
And brought me here
Now in my full bloom
When I am like a pomegranate
My husband is a cloud in another land
Now when the lemons and oranges are ready
My husband forgets me
The garden is blossoming, O my heartless darling
And in it the bee hovers
Cannot your heart see
That the garden withers for want of you?

PATNA DISTRICT, INDIA

53

My Little Son

My little son
Where have they hidden you?
My little son
Have they put you behind the grain-bin?

Have they hidden you down in the wheatfield?
Have they taken you to the forest
And covered you with leaves?
O where have they hidden you
My little son?

GOND ABORIGINAL, INDIA

54

Lament

I silent sit as throbs my heart
   For my children;
And those who look on me
As now I bow my head
May deem me but a forest tree
   From a distant land.
I bow my head
As droops the tree-fern.
And weep for my children.
O my child! so often called,
'Come O my child!'
Gone! Yes with the mighty flood,
I lonely sit midst noise and crowd,
My life ebbs fast.

MAORI, NEW ZEALAND

55

Apukura's Wail

O son, O son of mine, O son!
Hear me, bird, that flies up there!
Have you seen dead my precious one,
Who went among the thousands of Monono?
    Feathers on your legs,
    Feathers on your wing –
    Your beak bends low.
    Alas, my son!

The canoe which I provided,
The canoe on which the son embarked,
The son so loved by me,
Cast up upon some other land!
    O son, alas, my son!

You are a moon that will not rise again,
O son, O son of mine, O son!
The cold dawn breaks without you,
O my son, O son of mine, O son!

MANGAREVA, POLYNESIA

56

Children's Begging Song

The swallow has come, has come,
Bringing fine days and fine weather.
She is white in her belly, and black in her back.

Roll out the pudding from your rich house,
And a beaker of wine, and a basket of cheese.
Buns too and pulse-cake the swallow will not reject.

Are we to get it or to go away?
If you will give us something, well and good.

But if not, we will not put with it.
Let us take the door or the lintel,
Or the lady who is sitting inside.
She is small and we shall easily carry her.

But if you will give us something,
You may get something big in return!
Open, open the door to the swallow.
For we are not elders – we are children.

RHODES, 7TH CENTURY B.C.

57

Keep it Dark!

Keep it dark!
  Don't tell your wife,
  For your wife is a log
  That is smouldering surely!
Keep it dark!

Keep it dark!
   Don't tell your wife,
   For your wife is a pot
   That resounds to the breeze.
   And then 'Bang'!
   It's all out and about!
Keep it dark!

TRADITIONAL DRINKING SONG FROM SOUTHERN RHODESIA

58

For want of gruel or food, life will not depart;
Owing to cold or wind, life will not depart;
Owing to rain or dew, life will not depart.
If there be no wife, life will depart.

VEDDA SONG, CEYLON

59

Song of a Wife

   Just as eventide draws near,
   My old affection comes
   For him I loved.
   Though severed far from me,
   And now at Hawaiki,
   I hear his voice, far distant;
   And though far beyond
   The distant mountain-peak,
   Its echoes speak
   From vale to vale.

NEW ZEALAND

3

The Daily Round

Song to the Sun

The day breaks – the first rays of the rising Sun, stretching her
    arms.
Daylight breaking, as the Sun rises to her feet,
Sun rising, scattering the darkness, lighting up the land ...
With disk shining, bringing daylight, as the birds whistle and call,
People are moving about, talking, feeling the warmth,
Burning through the gorge she rises, walking westwards,
Wearing her waistband of human hair.
She shines on the blossoming coolibah tree, with its sprawling
    roots,
Its shady branches spreading.

SONG OF THE MUDBARA TRIBE
IN THE NORTHERN TERRITORY OF AUSTRALIA

61

On the weeping forest, under the wing of the evening,
The night, all black, has gone to rest happy;
In the sky the stars have fled trembling,
Fireflies which shine vaguely and put out their lights;
On high the moon is dark, its white light is put out.
The spirits are wandering.
Elephant-hunter, take your bow!
Elephant-hunter, take your bow!

In the frightened forest the tree sleeps, the leaves are dead,
The monkeys have closed their eyes, hanging from branches on
     high.
The antelopes slip past with silent steps,
Eat the fresh grass, prick their ears attentively,
Lift their heads and listen frightened.
The cicada is silent and stops his grinding song.
Elephant-hunter, take your bow!
Elephant-hunter, take your bow!

In the forest lashed by the great rain,
Father elephant walks heavily, *baou, baou,*
Careless, without fear, sure of his strength,
Father elephant, whom no one can vanquish;
Among the trees which he breaks he stops and starts again.
He eats, roars, overturns trees and seeks his mate.
Father elephant, you have been heard from afar.
Elephant-hunter, take your bow!
Elephant-hunter, take your bow!

In the forest where no one passes but you,
Hunter, lift up your heart, leap, and walk.
Meat is in front of you, the huge piece of meat,
The meat which walks like a hill,
The meat which makes glad the heart,
The meat that will roast on the hearth,
The meat into which the teeth sink,
The fine red meat and the blood that is drunk smoking.
Elephant-hunter, take your bow!
Elephant-hunter, take your bow!

GABON PYGMY, AFRICA

Eskimo family
National Film Board, Canada

Those game animals, those long-haired caribou,
Though they roam everywhere, I am quite unable to get any.
I carried this bow of mine in my hand always.
At last I pondered deeply:
It is all right, even if
I am quite unable to get them in the present winter.

Those game animals, those seals,
Though they keep visiting their holes, I am quite unable to get
      any.
I carried this harpoon of mine in my hand always.
At last I pondered deeply:
It is all right, even if
I begin at last to be greatly afraid in this present summer.

Those game animals, those fish.
Though I go out in the middle of the lake, I am quite unable
      to get any.
At last I pondered deeply:
It is all right, even if
I begin at last to be afraid to the hummocky ice within.

Those seals, those fearful brown bears,
Constantly walking about here, I begin to be terrified.
This arrow of mine is fearless, this arrow.
Am I to allow myself to be terrified at last?

ESKIMO

Hebridean women dyeing wool
The Mansell Collection

63

The Shot Deer

Tear on tear
Weeps the dew,
As the grey deer
Slips to view.
And her spouse
Cries to her:
From shadows
Of deep boughs.
Do not stir!
Questing food,
The swift moving –
Through wide wood,
The light-loving –
Fears no check.
Till a hum –
In her meek
Slender neck
Shivers, dumb!
Fleetness, vain!
And love, too!
Red flowers stain
Deer and dew.

HINDI, INDIA

64

Hunting Song

The deer speaks

Here I come forth.
On the earth I fell over;
The snapping bow made me dizzy.

Here I come forth!
On the mountain I slipped;
The humming arrow made me dizzy.

The fence of bows!
Within it I run about
In every direction, looking.

The fence of arrows!
Within it I run about
In every direction, looking.

Already they have killed me.
This is my flesh they cut,
And here they threw it down.

FROM A DEER–HUNTING CEREMONY
OF THE PAPAGO INDIANS

65

A spell confided to Kaj Birket-Smith by a West Greenlander as an aid to catching game.

Why am I no longer able?
Why cannot I now make a kill?
What prevents me – what prevents me?
Hither, thou my quarry!
Hither, thou my quarry!
    Aja, aja.

ESKIMO

66

Charm for Striking Fear into a Tiger
and Hardening one's own Heart

O Earth-Shaker, rumble and quake!
Let iron needles be my body-hairs,
Let copper needles be my body-hairs!
Let poisonous snakes be my beard,
A crocodile my tongue,
And a roaring lion in the dimple of my chin.
Be my voice the trumpet of an elephant,
Yes, like the roar of the thunderbolt.
May your lips be fast closed and your teeth clenched;
And not till the heavens and the earth are moved
May your heart be moved
To be angry with me or to seek to destroy me . . .

Let splendour reside in my person.
Whoever talks of encountering me,
A cunning lion shall be his opponent.
O all things that have life,
Endure not to confront my gaze!
It is I who shall confront the gaze of you,
By the virtue of 'There is no god but God.'

MALAY

67

Rain Song

Hi-iya naiho-o! The earth is rumbling
From the beating of our basket drums.
The earth is rumbling from the beating
Of our basket drums, everywhere humming.
Earth is rumbling, everywhere raining.

Hi-iya naiho-o! Pluck out the feathers
   From the wing of the eagle and turn them
Toward the east where lie the large clouds.
   Hi-iya naiho-o! Pluck out the soft down
From the breast of the eagle and turn it
   Toward the west where sail the small clouds.
Hi-iya naiho-o! Beneath the abode
   Of the rain gods it is thundering;
Large corn is there. *Hi-iya naiho-o!*
   Beneath the abode of the rain gods
It is raining; small corn is there.

PIMA INDIAN

68

Rain Storm

'Twas in Koolau I met with the rain:
It comes with lifting and tossing of dust,
Advancing in columns, dashing along.
The rain, it sighs in the forest;
The rain, it beats and whelms, like surf;
It smites, it smites now the land.
Pasty the earth from the stamping rain;
Full run the streams, a rushing flood;
The mountain walls leap with the rain.
See the water chafing its bounds like a dog,
A raging dog, gnawing its way to pass out.

HULA SONG, HAWAII

69

Fresh water running, splashing, swirling,
Running over slippery stones ... clear water ...
Carrying leaves and bushes before it ...
Swirling around ...

Water running, running from pool to pool ...
Water running in streams,
Foaming, carrying leaves and bushes before it ... churning,
Bubbling up among the Miljarwi clansfolk.
Water flowing over the rocks ... flowing each side of the termite
    mounds,
Running fast towards Nalibinunggu clansfolk ... Ridarngu
    ... Gaiilindjil ... Ridarngu,
Toward the Bunangaidjini Wonguri ...
Fast-running water.

Water dammed up by barriers of stone . . .
Breaking out, foaming, like sacred feathered armbands . . .
Carrying away the debris . . .
Sound of rushing water . . . running,
Smaller streams joining together, roaring down . . .
Washing out tree roots at Buruwandji . . . running past the Rocks.

ABORIGINAL, AUSTRALIA

70

Corn Song

The corn grows up.
The waters of the dark clouds drop, drop.
The rain descends.
The waters from the corn leaves drop, drop.
The rain descends.
The waters from the plants drop, drop.
The corn grows up.
The waters of the dark mists drop, drop.

NAVAJO INDIAN

71

Famine

Clouds covered the world's four corners
Covered them darkly
But not a cloud thundered

There was not a whisper from a cloud
Not a cloud shed a drop of rain
Clouds covered the world's four corners
Covered them darkly
Clouds thundered, they covered the world
But not a cloud shed a drop of rain
Clouds covered the world
Covered it darkly.

GOND ABORIGINAL, INDIA

72

Rain Magic

Gentle breeze is the father of rain.
Soft wind is the father of cloudburst.
Rain will not drench me today;
Rain will pack its belongings and go away.
　　The antelope is humming,
　　the buffalo is grumbling,
　　the pig grunts in its belly.
Words have angered the red monkey,
but today he was given the right words
and his anger will disappear.

YORUBA INCANTATION TO STOP RAIN, NIGERIA

At Reaping

God, bless Thou Thyself my reaping,
Each ridge, and plain, and field,
Each sickle, curved, shapely, hard,
Each ear and handful in the sheaf,
  Each ear and handful in the sheaf.

Bless each maiden and youth,
Each woman and tender youngling,
Safeguard them beneath the shield of strength,
And guard them in the house of the saints,
  Guard them in the house of the saints.

Encompass each goat, sheep and lamb,
Each cow and horse, and store,
Surround Thou the flocks and herds,
And tend them to a kindly fold,
  Tend them to a kindly fold.

For the sake of Michael head of hosts,
Of Mary fair-skinned branch of grace,
Of Bride smooth-white of ringletted locks,
Of Columba of the graves and tombs.

GAELIC

74

The Magnificent Bull

My bull is white like the silver fish in the river
white like the shimmering crane bird on the river bank
white like fresh milk!
His roar is like the thunder to the Turkish cannon on the steep
    shore.
My bull is dark like the raincloud in the storm.
He is like summer and winter.
Half of him is dark like the storm cloud,
half of him is light like sunshine.
His back shines like the morning star.
His brow is red like the beak of the hornbill.
His forehead is like a flag, calling the people from a distance,
He resembles the rainbow.

I will water him at the river,
With my spear I shall drive my enemies.
Let them water their herds at the well;
the river belongs to me and my bull.
Drink, my bull, from the river; I am here
to guard you with my spear.

DINKA TRIBE, AFRICA

75

O Lamb Give me my Salt

O Lamb give me my salt,
Salt the market folks gave me;

The market folk ate my fruits,
Fruits the fruit picker gave me;
The farmer broke my hoe,
Hoe the smith gave me;
The smith ate my yam,
Yam an old woman gave me;
The old woman ate my bird,
The bird my trap gave me,
My faithful, useful trap.

OLD IBO POEM, NIGERIA

76

The War Song of Deborah

The kings came and fought,
Then fought the kings of Canaan
In Taanach by the waters of Megiddo;
They took no gain of money.
They fought from heaven;
The stars in their courses fought against Sisera.
The river of Kishon swept them away,
That ancient river, the river Kishon.
O my soul, thou hast trodden down strength.
Then were the horsehoofs broken
By the means of the prancings, the prancings of their mighty
        ones.

THE BOOK OF JUDGES, AUTHORISED VERSION OF THE BIBLE

77

Caravaners' Song

In summer they even make the dust rise;
In winter they even trample the mud!
If they talk with the dark maiden,
And smile upon the red maiden,
Poverty will never leave them.
Poverty is a terrible disease;
It penetrates the sides,
It bends the vertebrae,
It dresses one in rags,
It makes people stupid;
It makes every desire remain in the breast;
Those who are long, it shortens;
Those who are short it destroys wholly.
Not even the mother that has borne the poor man loves him any
     longer!
Not even the father who has begotten him any longer esteems
     him!

SOUTHERN ETHIOPIA

78

The Poor Man

The poor man knows not how to eat with the rich man.
When they eat fish, he eats the head.

Invite a poor man and he rushes in
licking his lips and upsetting the plates.

The poor man has no manners, he comes along
with the blood of lice under his nails.

The face of the poor man is lined
from the hunger and thirst in his belly.

Poverty is no state for any mortal man.
It makes him a beast to be fed on grass.

Poverty is unjust. If it befalls a man,
though he is nobly born, he has no power with God.

SWAHILI, AFRICA

79

When we went away
The millets were in flower.
Now that we are returning
The snow falls and the roads are all mire.
The king's business was very difficult
And we had not leisure to rest.
Did we not long to return?
But we were in awe of the orders in the tablets.

CHINESE, PERHAPS 1000 B.C.

What Plant is not Yellow?

What plant is not yellow?
What day is without a march?
What man is not on the move
Serving in the four quarters?

What plant is not black?
What man is not wifeless?
Heigho, for us soldiers!
We alone are not treated as men.

Not rhinoceroses, not tigers,
Yet we are loosed in this mighty waste.
Heigho, for us soldiers!
Day and night we never rest.

The fox with his broad brush
Lurks among the gloomy grass;
But our wagon with its bamboo body,
Rumbles along the road of Chou.

FROM 'THE BOOK OF SONGS', CHINESE, ABOUT 600 B.C.

81

The Sweetest Thing

There is in this world something
that surpasses all other things
in sweetness.

It is sweeter than honey
it is sweeter than salt
it is sweeter than sugar
it is sweeter than all
existing things.
This thing is sleep.
When you are conquered by sleep
nothing can ever prevent you
nothing can stop you from sleeping.
When you are conquered by sleep
and numerous millions arrive
millions arrive to disturb you
millions will find you asleep.

SOUSSOU, AFRICA

82

Thapri Karam

Song for a dance at the end of the Karam festival

Cowherd boy,
Why do you cut a flute?
The cow does not come
And so I cut a flute
Cow
Why do you wait?
The grass does not sprout
And so I wait
Grass
Why do you not spring up?

The rain does not fall
And so I do not sprout
Rain
Why do you keep away?
The frog does not call
And so I do not come
Frog
Why do you not cry?
The snake does not bite me
And so I do not cry
Snake
Why do you not bite him?
His wail of pain
Winds in the ear
And so I do not bite.

URAON, INDIA

83

Rain Outside

Rain outside, drenches bracken;
Sea shingle white, fringe of foam;
Fair candle, man's discretion.

Rain outside, need for refuge;
Furze yellowed, hogweed withered;
Lord God, why made you a coward?

Rain outside, drenches my hair;
The feeble plaintive, slope steep;
Ocean pallid, brine salty.

Rain outside, drenches the deep;
Whistle of wind over reed-tips;
Widowed each feat, talent wanting.

EARLY MEDIEVAL WELSH

84

In the Chena Field

Sun, declined, come not in the noon;
Moon, declined, come not in the sky;
Muddiness, mix not with water clean;
To motherless us may no hunger come!

Out in the field two bulls are grazing,
One of those bulls, without tail, keeps swaying,
The bull with the tail keeps whisking at flies;
Like poverty there that bull without tail.

On a thorny twig platform while asleep in the field,
A pair of stags come to devour the plants;
Crouching cautious I crept to the plants,
And struck with my rod on the back of the stags.

A cry in my ear from the female frogs;
A wild boar I see near, eating the yams;
Terror prevents my descending to go there;
What grief to my body thus watching the fields!

SINHALESE

Dance Poem for the Karam Festival

From where are the black clouds rising?
Noise of the rain falling
Where is the rain falling?
In the east the clouds are massing
Noise of the rain falling
In the west the rain is falling
Whose is the red turban which the rain is wetting?
Noise of the rain falling
Whose is the long hair which the rain is wetting?
It is the red turban of the flirting boy which the rain is wetting
Noise of the rain falling
It is the long hair of the pale-skinned woman that the rain is
     wetting
Where shall I dry the red turban?
Noise of the rain falling
Where shall I dry the long hair?
I shall dry the red turban on the dead bushes
Noise of the rain falling
I shall dry the long hair in the body's core
Choose the cloth and tie the red turban
Noise of the rain falling
Comb and tie the long hair.

URAON, INDIA

The Amaranth

(Emigration song)

Look at the amaranth – what mountain does it bloom on?
It blooms at the fork of the road, on the stones, on the rocks.
Whoever cuts it, cuts himself; whoever eats it, dies.
Why didn't my mother eat it before she bore me?
If she bore me, why did she want me? If she has me, what does
      she want me for?
I who walk in foreign lands, who eat and drink in foreign lands,
      and foreigners wash and iron my clothes.

GREEK, FROM THE PELOPONNESUS

Saint Columba and the Flounder

Columba passing on his way
Came to the Sand-Eel Strand one day
And trod upon a flounder fair,
Hurting her tail a-trampling there.

The lovely little flounder cries,
And makes a sad loud voice arise –
'Thou Colum big, of clumsy gait,
With thy great crooked feet crosswise
The hurt thou doest me is great
When on my tail thy big foot lies'.

Columba, angry he replies –
'If I have crooked-footed tread,
Be thou wry-mouthed within thy head'.
And leaving her that way she lies.

GAELIC

88

Cut Short the Ills of Life

Come, friend and fellow, come – for sometimes is folly sweet!
  so come, let us greet our band of drinkers aglow with wine,
And wash from our hearts sour speech of wisdom with cups abrim,
  and cut short the ills of life with laughter and jest and joy!
Yea, when once a moment comes of rest from the whirl, be quick
  and grasp it: for time's tooth bites and quits not, and
  mischief waits;
And sure, if a bright hour lifts thy soul to a little peace, enough in
  thy path there lies of shadow and grief and pain.

ANCIENT ARABIC

4

Change and Mortality

Chant

In the time when Dendid created all things,
He created the sun,
And the sun is born, and dies, and comes again;
He created the moon,
And the moon is born, and dies, and comes again;
He created the stars,
And the stars are born, and die, and come again;
He created man,
And man is born, and dies, and never comes again.

DINKA TRIBE, SUDAN

The morning sun emerges,
It emerges gold-like.
The evening sun descends,
It descends silver-like.
Our lives pass away,
They pass away silk-thread-like.
We flow and go flowing-water-like.

CHEREMIS CHARM, FINLAND

Dance Song

The bed says to the carpenter, Do not make me,
For if you do, tomorrow or the day after, they will carry you
      upon me to your grave.
And there will be no one to help you.

The pick says to its proud maker,
Do not make me, for tomorrow or the day after, they will use me
      to dig your grave,
And there will be no one to help you.

The cloth says to the weaver,
Do not weave me, for tomorrow or the day after, I will be your
      shroud.
And there will be no one to help you.

GOND ABORIGINAL, INDIA

Sadness in Spring

Springtime, loveliest season,
Noisy the birds, new the shoots,
Ploughs in furrow, oxen yoked,
Green the sea, fields are dappled.

When cuckoos sing on comely tree-tops,
    The greater is my sadness,
Smoke bitter, loss of sleep plain,
Because my kinsmen are gone.

In mount, in meadow, in ocean isles,
    In each way one may take,
From Christ there is no seclusion.

EARLY MEDIEVAL WELSH

93

The Broken String

The singer mourns a friend, a magician and rain-maker

People were those who
Broke for me the string.
    Therefore,
The place became like this to me,
    On account of it,
Because the string was that which broke for me.
    Therefore,
The place does not feel to me,
As the place used to feel to me,
    On account of it.
    For,
The place feels as if it stood open before me,
Because the string has broken for me.
    Therefore
The place does not feel pleasant to me,
    On account of it.

BUSHMAN, AFRICA

94

Death

There is no needle without piercing point.
There is no razor without trenchant blade.
Death comes to us in many forms.

With our feet we walk the goat's earth.
With our hands we touch God's sky.
Some future day in the heat of noon,
I shall be carried shoulder high
Through the village of the dead.
When I die, don't bury me under forest trees,
I fear their thorns.
When I die, don't bury me under forest trees,
I fear the dripping water.
Bury me under the great shade trees in the market,
I want to hear the drums beating
I want to feel the dancers' feet.

KUBA, AFRICA

95

Take a golden comb
Bathe in shining water
Look at your body in the glass
The body is made of earth
It will be mingled with earth again
Were it made of bell-metal
You could change it for another

Were it made of copper
You could change it for another
But no man can change
His earthen body.

GOND ABORIGINAL, INDIA

96

Be not proud of your sweet body
The moon and sun were proud and met disaster
For eclipses catch them
Be not proud of your sweet body.

Be not proud of your young body
The fish in the water were proud
And they too came to trouble
For the net has covered them
Be not proud of your young body.

Be not proud of your swift body
The deer in the forest were proud
But they too came to trouble
For the Bahelia sets traps for them
Be not proud of your swift body.

Be not proud of your fair body
The birds in the wood were proud
And they too came to trouble
For a great wind came and blew them away
Be not proud of your fair body.

GOND ABORIGINAL, INDIA

97

Even the moon
Each time it rises
Is young.
What will become
Of my body so full
Of years?

JAPANESE, 12TH CENTURY

98

Summer is Gone

My tidings for you: the stag bells,
Winter snows, summer is gone.

Wind high and cold, low the sun,
Short his course, sea running high.

Deep-red the bracken, its shape all gone –
The wild-goose has raised his wonted cry.

Cold has caught the wings of birds;
Season of ice – these are my tidings.

IRISH, 9TH CENTURY

The Death of Cold

Cold in August is conceived
In the womb of earth received,
All September under-ground,
Lying hidden safe and sound.
One long month before his birth,
Being nourished by the earth.
At the sowing of the corn,
In October he is born.
In November fast he grows,
A lusty lad and apt to blows;
In December squares his back
To do battle and attack,
And when January is come
Sounds his horn and charges home.
Doomed alas! his death to meet
Slain at February's feet.
March puts ashes on her head
To lament the mighty dead;
April next with streaming eyes
Comes to do his obsequies;
But in May he's clean forgot
And in June the wind blows hot.

PUNJAB

At the Chapel of Saint Paraskevi

At the chapel of Saint Paraskevi
a girl is sleeping all alone.

She sleeps and she dreams
and she sees that she is being married.

She sees a tall tower
and two rivers with water.

'Mother, the tower is my husband,
the orchard my wedding,

and the two rivers with water
wine for the in-laws.'

'Daughter, the tower is your death,
the orchard your grave,

and the two rivers with water
the tears that I'll shed.'

GREEK, SPORADES ISLANDS

IOI

Song of the Aged

The body perishes, the heart stays young
The platter wears away with serving food.
No log retains its bark when old,
No lover peaceful while the rival weeps.

OLD ZULU POEM

Onokura Laments the Old Age which has Overtaken Him and his Wife

Alas, we are growing old, my love,
We two –

We two indeed together, O my love,
When we were children!
When we played together in the sea!

We two indeed together, O my love,
When we went inland – Oh yes, inland! –
In our years of growing wise.

We two indeed together, O my love,
When your girlish breasts were firm,
And when in motherhood they drooped.

We two indeed together, O my love,
When long hair floated down your back
And springy strength was in your arms.

We two indeed together, O my love,
When we both grew old and thin
Like two grey flatfish resting on the bottom.

We two indeed together, O my love,
When grown so frail, we sit apart
And only rest the hours away.

We two indeed together, O my love,
When our dim eyes stare at misty skies
And no more know their splendour –

Ah! Where is the god taking me?

MANGAREVA, POLYNESIA

103

If I had known
That old age would call,
I'd have shut my gate,
Replied 'Not at home!'
And refused to meet him.

JAPANESE, ABOUT 900 A.D.

104

The Old Man's Song

I have grown old,
I have lived much,
Many things I understand,
But four riddles I cannot solve.
Ha-ya-ya-ya.

The sun's origin,
The moon's nature,
The minds of women,
And why people have so many lice.
Ha-ya-ya-ya.

ESKIMO

Ulivak's Song of the Caribou

The singer was old, and inclined to weep for his lost youth, but sang this song instead.

Eya – aya
I call to mind
And think of the early coming of spring
As I knew it
In my younger days.
Was I ever such a hunter!
Was it myself indeed?
For I see
And recall in memory a man in a kayak;
Slowly he toils along in toward the shores of the lake,
With many spear-slain caribou in tow.
Happiest am I
In my memories of hunting in kayaks.
On land, I was never of great renown
Among the herds of caribou.
And an old man, seeking strength in his youth,
Loves most to think of the deeds
Whereby he gained renown.

CARIBOU ESKIMO

Kalahari hunters
BBC copyright

The Uncertain Life

To be spoken when suddenly in mortal danger

See, great earth,
these heaps
of pale bones in the wind!

They crumble in the air
of the wide world,
in the wide world's air,
pale, wind-dried bones,
decaying in the air!

IGLULIK ESKIMO

107

The Sun and the Moon and
the Fear of Loneliness

It's a fearful thing
to turn one's mind away,
and long for solitude
among a happy crowd of people.
    Ijaija-ja-ja.

It's a happy thing
to feel warmth
come to the great world,
and see the sun
follow its old footsteps
in the summer night.
    Ijaija-ja-ja.

91

Canadian Indian couple
National Film Board, Canada

It's a fearful thing
to feel the cold
return to the great world,
and see the moon –
now new, now full –
follow its old footsteps
in the winter night.
  Ijaija–ja–ja.

Where does all this go, I wonder?
For myself, I long to travel east!
But I'll never see
my father's brother,
whom my mind so longs
to open itself to.

COPPER ESKIMO

108

An Old Laragia Man Laments for Country which is no Longer His

Waves coming up, high waves coming up against the rocks,
Breaking, shi! shi!
When the moon is high with its light upon the waters,
Spring tide, tide flowing to the grass,
Breaking, shi! shi!
In its rough waters the young girls bathe.
Hear the sound they make with their hands as they play!

ABORIGINAL, AUSTRALIA

Far away I see the mist,
I see Ben Beg, Ben More as well,
I see the dew on grassy tips.
Heard ye how my woe befell?
The traveller broke, the sail was rent,
Into the sea the mast it went,
The gallant boatmen further fared.
O would my father's son were spared –
My mother's son 'tis makes my woe,
He breathes not in the wrack below,
No raiment now his body needs,
His foot no covering but the weeds.
Hearty fellows be ye cheerful,
Let us prove the tavern's hoard,
Fetch the glass and fill the measure,
Tossing bonnets round the board,
Banish sorrow unavailing,
The dead come not to life with wailing.

HEBRIDEAN WAULKING SONG

IIO

The Dead Man Asks for a Song

The original recorder of this song from Togoland says: 'After the corpse is buried, the mourners shout and sing and drum and make merry over the dead man. He takes all this with him on his journey to the underworld. Here is one such song.'

Sing me a song of the dead,
That I may take it with me.
A song of the underworld sing me,
That I may take it with me
And travel to the underworld.

The underworld says,
Says the underworld:
It is beautiful in the grave.
Beautiful is the underworld
But there is no wine to drink there.
So I will take it with me
And travel to the underworld
And travel to the underworld.

Sing me a song of the dead,
That I may take it with me.
A song of the underworld sing me,
That I may take it with me
And travel to the underworld.

TOGOLAND

III

The Lifting of the Head

To make straight the way of the dead into the land of their ancestors

I lift your head, I straighten your way, for you are going home,
    Marawa, Marawa.
Home to Innang and Mwaiku, Roru and Bouru,

You will pass over the sea of Manra in your canoe with pandanus
    fruit for food;
You will find harbour under the lee of Matang and Atiia and
    Abaiti in the west,
Even the homes of your ancestors.
Return not to your body; leave it never to return, for you are
    going home, Marawa, Marawa.
And so, farewell for a moon or two, a season or two.
Farewell! your way is straight; you shall not be led astray.
Blessings and peace go with you. Blessings and peace.

SPELL SPOKEN BY A GILBERT ISLANDER OVER
THE BODY OF THE GIRL HE HAD HOPED TO MARRY

112

She has gone from us; never as she was will she return.
Never more as she once did will she chop honey,
Never more with her digging-stick dig yams.
She has gone from us; never as she was to return.

Mussels there are in the creek in plenty,
But she who lies here will dig no more.
We shall fish as of old for cod-fish,
But she who lies here will beg no more oil;
Oil for her hair, she will want no more.

Never again will she use a fire.
Where she goes, fires are not.
For she goes to the women, the dead women.
Ah, women can make no fires.
Fruit there is in plenty and grass seed,
But no birds nor beasts in the heaven of women.

AUSTRALIAN EUAHLAYI TRIBE

A Vedic Funerary Hymn

... Betake thee to the lap of the earth the mother, of earth far-
    spreading, very kind and gracious ...

Heave thyself, Earth, nor press thee downward heavily: afford
    him easy access, gently tending him.
Earth, as a mother wraps her skirt about her child, so cover him.

Now let the heaving earth be free from motion: yea, let a
    thousand clods remain above him.
Be they to him a home distilling fatness, here let them ever be his
    place of refuge.

FROM THE 'RIG-VEDA', INDIA

*David's Lament over Saul
and his son Jonathan*

The beauty of Israel is slain upon thy high places:
How are the mighty fallen!
Tell it not in Gath,
Publish it not in the streets of Askelon;
Lest the daughters of the Philistines rejoice,
Lest the daughters of the uncircumcised triumph.

Ye mountains of Gilboa,
Let there be no dew, neither let there be rain, upon you, nor fields
    of offerings:
For there the shield of the mighty is vilely cast away,
The shield of Saul, as though he had not been anointed with oil.
From the blood of the slain, from the fat of the mighty,
The bow of Jonathan turned not back,
And the sword of Saul returned not empty.

Saul and Jonathan were lovely and pleasant in their lives,
And in their death they were not divided:
They were swifter than eagles,
They were stronger than lions.
Ye daughters of Israel, weep over Saul,
Who clothed you in scarlet, with other delights,
Who put ornaments of gold upon your apparel.
How are the mighty fallen in the midst of the battle!

O Jonathan, thou was slain in thine high places.
I am distressed for thee, my brother Jonathan:
Very pleasant hast thou been unto me;
Thy love to me was wonderful,
Passing the love of women.
How are the mighty fallen,
And the weapons of war perished!

THE SECOND BOOK OF SAMUEL, AUTHORISED VERSION OF THE BIBLE

115

A Speech to the Dead

Now this day you have ceased to see daylight.
Think only of what is good.

Do not think of anything uselessly.
You must think all the time of what is good.
You will go and live with our nephew.
And do not think evil towards these your kinsmen.
When you start to leave them this day you must not think
    backwards of them with regret.
And do not think of looking back at them.
And do not feel badly because you have lost sight of this daylight.
This does not happen today to you alone, so that you thus be
    alone when you die.
Bless the people so that they may not be sick.
This is what you will do.
You must merely bless them so that they may live as mortals
    here.
You must always think kindly.
Today is the last time I shall speak to you.
Now I shall cease speaking to you, my kinsman.

FOX INDIAN

116

Lament

*At the funeral of a New Zealand chieftain killed in war, the sight of the
rising moon prompted his sister to utter this poem.*

It is well with thee, O moon!
Spreading your light on the little waves. Men say,
    'Behold the moon reappears';
But the dead of this world return no more.

Grief and pain spring up in my heart as from a fountain.
I hasten to death for relief.
Oh, that I might eat those numerous soothsayers
Who could not foretell his death.
Oh, that I might eat the Governor,
For his was the war!

MAORI, NEW ZEALAND

117

The Earth does not get Fat

The earth does not get fat. It makes an end of those who wear the
    head plumes   [the older men]
We shall die on the earth.
The earth does not get fat. It makes an end of those who act
    swiftly as heroes.
Shall we die on the earth?

  Listen O earth. We shall mourn because of you.
  Listen O earth. Shall we all die on the earth?

The earth does not get fat. It makes an end of the chiefs.
Shall we all die on the earth?
The earth does not get fat. It makes an end of the women chiefs.
Shall we die on the earth?

  Listen O earth. We shall all mourn because of you.
  Listen O earth. Shall we all die on the earth?

The earth does not get fat. It makes an end of the nobles.
Shall we die on the earth?
The earth does not get fat. It makes an end of the royal women.
Shall we die on the earth?

Listen O earth. We shall mourn because of you.
Listen O earth. Shall we all die on the earth?

The earth does not get fat. It makes the end of the common
    people.
Shall we die on the earth?
The earth does not get fat. It makes an end of all the beasts.
Shall we die on the earth?

Listen you who are asleep, who are left tightly closed in the
    land.
Shall we all sink into the earth?
Listen O earth the sun is setting tightly.
We shall all enter into the earth.

OLD NGONI SONG, AFRICA

118

The Sleep-Prayer

I am now going into the sleep,
    Be it that I in health shall wake;
If death be to me in deathly sleep,
    Be it that in thine own arm's keep,
O God of grace, to new life I wake;
    O be it in thy dear arm's keep.
O God of grace, that I shall awake!

Be my soul on thy right hand, O God,
  O thou king of the heaven of heaven;
Thou it was who didst buy with thy blood,
  Thine the life for my sake was given;
Encompass thou me this night, O God,
  That no harm, no mischief be given.

Whilst in the sleep the body doth stay,
  The soul in heaven's shadow doth stray,
Red–white Michael to meet by the way,
  Amen, early, late, night and day,
    Early and late, and night and day.

GAELIC, BENBECULA

119

The Soul Speaks to the Body

Now there is nothing to link you and me together
Dumb corpse
When you and I were together how proudly you went about
Dumb corpse
Now why do you lie so still with gaping mouth?
Dumb corpse
When you and I were together what enormous joys you had
Dumb corpse
The tank was filled, the lotus bloomed, the boat swam to and fro
Now the tank is broken, the lotus withered, the boat has sunk in
    the mud
Dumb corpse.

CHATTISGARH, INDIA

Prayer before the Dead Body

The gates of the underworld are closed.
Closed are the gates.

The spirits of the dead are thronging together
like swarming mosquitoes in the evening,
like swarming mosquitoes.

Like swarms of mosquitoes dancing in the evening,
When the night has turned black, entirely black,
when the sun has sunk, has sunk below,
when the night has turned black
the mosquitoes are swarming
like whirling leaves
dead leaves in the wind.

Dead leaves in the wind,
they wait for him who will come
for him who will come and will say:
'Come' to the one and 'Go' to the other
and God will be with his children.
And God will be with his children.

HOTTENTOT, SOUTH AFRICA

121

Neighbours

Before the door of each and all a slumber-place is ready set:
    men wane and dwindle, and the graves in number grow from
        day to day;
And ever more and more out-worn the traces fade of hearth and
        home,
    and ever yonder for some dead is newly built a house of clay.
Yea, neighbours are they of the living: near and close their
        fellowship;
    but if thy soul would seek their converse, thou must seek it far
    away.

ANCIENT ARABIC

122

Slowly the muddy pool becomes a river.
Slowly my mother's illness became her death.
When wood breaks, it can be mended.
But ivory breaks for ever.
An egg falls to reveal a messy secret.
My mother went and carried her secret along.
She has gone far –
We look for her in vain.
But when you see the kob antelope on the way to the farm,
When you see the kob antelope on the way to the river –
leave your arrows in the quiver,
And let the dead depart in peace.

YORUBA, NIGERIA

123

A Funeral Song

The dew on the shallot,
How quickly it dries!
The dew that's dried
Will fall again tomorrow.
The man that's died
Will never return again.

CHINESE FOLK SONG OF THE HAN DYNASTY

124

If death were not there,
Where would the inheritor get things?
The cattle have been left for the inheritor;
Ee, how would the inheritor get things?
The iron-roofed house has been left for the inheritor;
Ee, if death were not there,
How would the inheritor get rich?
The bicycle has been left for the inheritor;
The inheritor is most lucky;
Ee, brother, tell me,
If the inheritor were not there,
Ugly one, whose daughter would have married you?
A wife has been left for the inheritor;
Ee, inheritor, how would you have lived?
The house has been left for the inheritor;
If death were not there,
How would the inheritor get things?

ACOLI PEOPLE, NORTHERN UGANDA

No lake is so still but that it has its wave;
No circle so perfect but that it has its blur.
I would change things for you if I could;
As I can't, you must take them as they are.

OLD CHINESE RHYMING PROVERB

5

Men and the Powers

Hymn of Creation

Non-being then existed not nor being:
There was no air, nor sky that is beyond it.
What was concealed? Wherein? In whose protection?
And was there deep unfathomable water?

Death then existed not nor life immortal;
Of neither night nor day was any token.
By its inherent force the One breathed breathless:
No other thing than that beyond existed.

Darkness there was at first by darkness hidden;
Without distinctive marks, this all was water.
That which, becoming, by the void was covered,
That One by force of heat came into being.

Desire entered the One in the beginning:
It was the earliest seed, of thought the product.
The sages searching in their hearts with wisdom,
Found out the bond of being in non-being.

Their ray extended light across the darkness:
But was the One above or was it under?
Creative force was there, and fertile power:
Below was energy, above was impulse.

Who knows for certain? Who shall here declare it?
Whence it was born, and whence came this creation?
The gods were born after this world's creation:
Then who can know from whence it has arisen?

None knoweth whence creation has arisen;
And whether he has or has not produced it;
He who surveys it in the highest heaven,
He only knows, or haply he may know not.

FROM THE 'RIG-VEDA', INDIA

127

Creation

The first period: of Thought
    From the conception the increase,
    From the increase the swelling,
    From the swelling the thought,
    From the thought the remembrance,
    From the remembrance the consciousness,
    From the consciousness the desire.

The second period: of Darkness
    The knowledge became fruitful;
    It dwelt with the feeble glimmering;
    It brought forth night:
    The great night, the long night,
    The lowest night, the loftiest night,
    The thick night, the night to be felt,
    The night to be touched, the night unseen,
    The night following on,
    The night of death.

The third period: of Light
From the nothing the begetting,
From the nothing the increase,
From the nothing the abundance,
The power of increasing,
The living breath;
It dwelt with the empty space,
It produced the atmosphere which is above us.

The atmosphere which floats above the earth,
The great firmament above us, the spread out space dwelt with
    the early dawn;
Then the moon sprung forth;
The atmosphere above us dwelt with glowing sky,
Forthwith was produced the sun,
They were thrown up above, as the chief eyes of Heaven:
Then the Heavens became light,
The early dawn, the early day,
The mid-day. The blaze of day from the sky.

The sky which floats, above the earth ...

MAORI, NORTH ISLAND, NEW ZEALAND

128

The Fulani Creation Story

At the beginning there was a huge drop of milk.
Then Doondari came and he created the stone.
Then the stone created iron;
And iron created fire;

And fire created water;
And water created air.
Then Doondari descended the second time.
And he took the five elements
And he shaped them into man.
But man was proud.
Then Doondari created blindness, and blindness defeated man.
But when blindness became too proud,
Doondari created sleep, and sleep defeated blindness;
But when sleep became too proud,
Doondari created worry, and worry defeated sleep;
But when worry became too proud,
Doondari created death, and death defeated worry.
But then death became too proud,
Doondari descended for the third time,
And he came as Gueno, the eternal one.
And Gueno defeated death.

FULANI, AFRICA

129

Chant to Io

Io dwelt within the breathing-space of immensity,
The universe was in darkness, with water everywhere.
There was no glimmer of dawn, no clearness, no light.
And he began by saying these words,
 That he might cease remaining inactive:
'Darkness, become a light-possessing darkness.'
And at once a light appeared.

He then repeated these self-same words in this manner,
That he might cease remaining inactive:
'Light, become a darkness-possessing light.'
And again an intense darkness supervened.
Then a third time He spake, saying:
 'Let there be one darkness above.
 Let there be one darkness below,
 Let there be a darkness unto Tupua,
 Let there be a darkness unto Tawhito,
 A dominion of light,
 A bright light.'
 And now a great light prevailed.
Io then looked to the waters which compassed him about, and
spake a fourth time, saying: 'Ye waters of Tai kama, be ye separate.
Heaven, be formed.'
Then the sky became suspended.
 'Bring forth thou Te Tupua horo nuku.'
And at once the moving earth lay stretched abroad.

TIWAI PARAONE, NEW ZEALAND,
1880

130

Introduction of the Child
to the Cosmos

Ho! Ye Sun, Moon, Stars, all ye that move in the heavens,
 I bid you hear me!
Into your midst has come a new life.
 Consent ye, I implore!
Make its path smooth, that it may reach the brow of the first hill!

Ho! Ye Winds, Clouds, Rain, Mist, all ye that move in the air,
   I bid you hear me!
Ho! Ye Hills, Valleys, Rivers, Lakes, Trees, Grasses, all ye of the
      earth . . .
Ho! Ye Birds, great and small, that fly in the air,
Ho! Ye Animals, great and small, that dwell in the forest,
Ho! Ye Insects that creep among the grasses and burrow in the
      ground . . .
Ho! All ye of the heavens, all ye of the air, all ye of the earth:
I bid you all to hear me!
Into your midst has come a new life.
   Consent ye, consent ye all, I implore!
Make its path smooth – then shall it travel
   Beyond the four hills!

OMAHA INDIAN

131

Rain Song

White floating clouds.
Clouds like the plains
Come and water the earth.
Sun, embrace the earth
That she may be fruitful.
Moon, lion of the north,
Bear of the west,
Badger of the south,
Wolf of the east,
Eagle of the heavens, shrew of the earth,
Elder war hero,
Warriors of the six mountains of the world,

Intercede with the cloud people for us,
That they may water the earth.
Medicine bowl, cloud bowl, and water vase,
Give us your hearts,
That the earth may be watered.
I make the ancient road of metal,
That my song may straight pass over it – the ancient road.
White shell bead woman,
Who lives where the sun goes down,
Mother whirlwind, mother Sus'sistumako,
Mother Ya-ya, creator of good thoughts,
Yellow woman of the north, blue woman of the west,
Red woman of the south, white woman of the east,
Slightly yellow woman of the zenith,
And dark woman of the nadir,
I ask your intercession with the cloud people.

SIA INDIAN

132

Give Thanks to Mother Earth

Behold! Our Mother Earth is lying here.
Behold! She giveth of her fruitfulness.
Truly, her power she gives us.
Give thanks to Mother Earth who lieth here.

Behold on Mother Earth the growing fields!
Behold the promise of her fruitfulness!
Truly, her power she gives us.
Give thanks to Mother Earth who lieth here.

Behold on Mother Earth the spreading trees!
Behold the promise of her fruitfulness!
Truly, her power she gives us.
Give thanks to Mother Earth who lieth here.

We see on Mother Earth the running streams;
We see the promise of her fruitfulness.
Truly, her power she gives us.
Our thanks to Mother Earth who lieth here!

PAWNEE TRIBE, OKLAHOMA

133

The Riches of the Earth

Bless the Lord, O my soul.
O Lord my God, thou art very great;
Thou art clothed with honour and majesty.
Who coverest thyself with light as with a garment;
Who stretchest out the heavens like a curtain;
Who layeth the beams of his chambers in the waters;
Who maketh the clouds his chariot;
Who walketh upon the wings of the wind;
Who maketh his angels spirits,
His ministers a flaming fire;
Who laid the foundations of the earth,
That it should not be removed for ever.
Thou coveredst it with the deep as with a garment;
The waters stood above the mountains.
At thy rebuke they fled;
At the voice of thy thunder they hastened away.

He causeth the grass to grow for the cattle,
And herb for the service of man:
That he may bring forth food out of the earth;
And wine that maketh glad the heart of man,
And oil to make his face to shine,
And bread which strengtheneth man's heart.
The trees of the Lord are full of sap,
The cedars of Lebanon, which he hath planted,
Where the birds make their nests;
As for the stork, the fir trees are her house.
The high hills are a refuge for the wild goats,
And the rocks for the conies.
He appointeth the moon for seasons;
The sun knoweth his going down.
Thou makest darkness, and it is night,
Wherein all the beasts of the forest do creep forth.
The young lions roar after their prey,
And seek their meat from God.
The sun ariseth, they gather themselves together,
And lay them down in their dens.
Man goeth forth unto his work
And to his labour until the evening.
O Lord, how manifold are thy works!
In wisdom hast thou made them all;
The earth is full of thy riches.

PSALM 104, 1–7, 14–24, AUTHORISED VERSION OF THE BIBLE

134

Prayer to the Young Moon

Young Moon!
Hail, Young Moon!
  Hail, hail,
    Young Moon!
Young Moon! speak to me!
  Hail, hail,
    Young Moon!
Tell me of something.
  Hail, hail!
  When the sun rises,
  Thou must speak to me,
  That I may eat something.
Thou must speak to me about a little thing,
  That I may eat.
  Hail, hail,
  Young Moon!

BUSHMAN, AFRICA

135

Khwa! Ye! O! Rainbow, O rainbow!
You who shine on high, so high,
Above the great forest,
Among the black clouds,
Dividing the black sky.

Beneath you you have overturned,
Victor in the struggle,
The thunder which growled,
Which growled so strongly in its wrath.
Was it angry with us?

Among the black clouds,
Dividing the dark sky,
Like the knife which cuts a too ripe fruit,
Rainbow, rainbow!

He has taken flight,
The thunder, the man-killer,
Like the antelope before the panther,
He has taken flight,
Rainbow, rainbow!

Mighty bow of the hunter on high,
Of the hunter who chases the herd of clouds,
Like a herd of frightened elephants,
Rainbow, tell him our thanks.

Tell him: 'Do not be angry!'
Tell him: 'Do not be provoked!'
Tell him: 'Do not kill us!'
For we are very frightened,
Rainbow, tell it to him.

GABON PYGMY

The Eagle and the Moon Goddess

A Song from the Fertility Rites

Under the sky the eagle, there he abides, there far above us.
Beautiful he appears.
In his talons he holds his world.
A gray garment he wears, a beautiful, living-moist garment of
    clouds.
There he waits for the words of Tetewan.
Bright-eyed he looks down upon his world.
Towards the west his eyes are turned.
Bright-eyed he looks down upon the waters of life.
His countenance radiates calamity.
Magnificent is his eye, the sun!
Red are his feet.

There he abides, far away, above us.
There he remembers those who live on this earth.
Wide he spreads his wings over the earth.
And beneath his wings the gods grant rain, the gods grant dew.
Dew of life comes forth here on earth.
His voice rises, above us.
It is we who hear it, lovely are the words . . .
Tetewan even hears them, she who abides in the underworld.
There the Mother hears him.
And she responds: here we listen to the words of Tetewan.
Here they meet with the words of the eagle, here they mingle.

The words of the eagle fade away, far above the waters of life.
There, the words of the Mother drift . . .
There they die away, far yonder, beneath the dome of the sky.
Far yonder the words vanish.

CORA INDIAN

Call to Sing While
Liquor Ferments

Come together!
You shall see this thing which we have always done
And what must truly happen.
Because we have planned it thus and thus have done.
Right soon, indeed, it will happen.
It will rain.
The fields will be watered.
Therein we shall drop the seed.
Seed which bears corn of all colours;
Seed which grows big.
Thus we shall do.
Thereby we shall feed ourselves;
Thereby our stomachs shall grow big;
Thereby we shall live.

FROM THE RAINMAKING CEREMONY OF THE PAPAGO INDIANS

Charm against Wens

Wen, wen, little wen,
Here thou shalt not build, nor stay.
But thou must go north to the hill hard by,
Where thou hast a brother in misery.
He will lay a leaf at your head.

Under the foot of the wolf, under the wing of the eagle,
Under the claw of the eagle, ever mayest thou fade.
Shrivel like coal on the hearth!
Shrivel like muck in the wall!
Waste away like water in a bucket!
Become as small as a grain of linseed,
And far smaller too than a hand-worm's hip-bone,
And become even so small that at last thou art nothing.

ANGLO-SAXON

139

Song of the Sky Loom

O our Mother the Earth, O our Father the Sky,
Your children we are, and with tired backs
We bring you the gifts you love.
Then weave for us a garment of brightness;
May the warp be the bright light of morning,
May the weft be the bright light of evening,
May the fringes be the falling rain,
May the border be the standing rainbow.
Then weave for us a garment of brightness,
That we may walk fittingly where birds sing,
That we may walk fittingly where grass is green,
O our Mother the Earth, O our Father the Sky.

TEWA INDIAN, NEW MEXICO

The great sea
Moves me!
The great sea
Sets me adrift!
It moves me
Like algae on stones
In running brook water.
The vault of heaven
Moves me!
The mighty weather
Storms through my soul.
It tears me with it,
And I tremble with joy.

ESKIMO

141

The War God's Horse Song

I am the Turquoise Woman's son.
On top of Belted Mountain
Beautiful horses – slim like a weasel!
My horse has a hoof like striped agate;
His fetlock is like a fine eagle plume;
His legs are like quick lightning.
My horse's body is like an eagle-plumed arrow;
My horse has a tail like a trailing black cloud.
I put flexible goods on my horse's back;
The Little Holy Wind blows through his hair.

His mane is made of short rainbows.
My horse's ears are made of round corn.
My horse's eyes are made of big stars.
My horse's head is made of mixed waters
(From the holy waters – he never knows thirst.)
My horse's teeth are made of white shell.
The long rainbow is in his mouth for a bridle,
    And with it I guide him.
When my horse neighs, different-coloured horses follow.
When my horse neighs, different-coloured sheep follow.
    I am wealthy, because of him.

Before me peaceful,
Behind me peaceful,
Under me peaceful,
Over me peaceful –
Peaceful voice when he neighs.
I am Everlasting and Peaceful.
I stand for my horse.

NAVAJO INDIAN

142

Song for the Sun that
Disappeared behind the Rainclouds

The fire darkens, the wood turns black.
The flame extinguishes, misfortune upon us.
God sets out in search of the sun.
The rainbow sparkles in his hand,
the bow of the divine hunter.
He has heard the lamentations of his children.

122

Navajo Indians
Edward Curtis; lent by Exeter University Library

He walks along the milky way, he collects the stars.
With quick arms he piles them into a basket
piles them up with quick arms
like a woman who collects lizards
and piles them into her pot, piles them up
until the pot overflows with lizards
until the basket overflows with light.

HOTTENTOT, AFRICA

143

Even in a little thing
(A leaf, a child's hand, a star's flicker)
I shall find a song worth singing
If my eyes are wide, and sleep not.

Even in a laughable thing
(Oh, hark! The children are laughing!)
There is that which fills the heart to overflowing,
And makes dreams wistful.

Small is the life of a man
(Not too sad, not too happy):
I shall find my songs in a man's small life. Behold them soaring!
Very low on earth are the frigate-birds hatched,
Yet they soar as high as the sun.

GILBERT ISLANDS

123

Taiwan religious ritual
Donald McCullin, Sunday Times

His Sacred Feet

Some think to find their God upon the hills,
And climb with weary feet. So some declare
He is beyond the sea. They sail afar
To find Him out. Oh ignorant and fools!
'Tis pride that prompts your work. His sacred feet
Are in your heart. If there you seek, your soul
Will find the Being that alone is real.

SOUTHERN INDIA

145

Orifusi, the father of Elu, wanted to overcome death,
so that he might not kill him with his wives and children.
Ifa said to him:
'If you do not want death to kill you,
you must sacrifice.
But if you do not add good character,
your sacrifice shall be in vain.
Free the fowls in your basket.
Do not kill anything from today on.
Anybody who does not want death to kill him
let him not kill anything either.'

YORUBA, NIGERIA

146

The Best Friend

One begs of others for a wife,
   On her bestows both rule and home,
He counts her half of all his life.
   But when death comes, he dies alone.

Chorus: Of all good things the best are three –
       Wives, lands and countless gain.
       Which is the dearest friend to thee?

One mounts the throne of mighty kings,
   His palace girds with fort and wall;
Of his great power the whole world rings.
   His lifeless corpse to dogs will fall.

King's grace, good luck, hard work and trade,
   May load with wealth of coin or land.
What tyrants leave, the moths invade;
   For riches fly like desert sand.

In vain wives mourn, in vain sons weep,
   Wealth helps e'en less in death's last scene.
Two things alone the gulf can leap –
   The sin, the good, our life has seen.

In this weak frame put not your trust,
   But think on him with inward calm.
Is your heart clean? For him you lust?
   Then Vishnu is a healing balm.

SOUTHERN INDIA

125

147

Hospitality

O King of stars!
Whether my house be dark or bright,
Never shall it be closed against any one,
Lest Christ close His house against me.

If there be a guest in your house
And you conceal aught from him,
'Tis not the guest that will be without it,
But Jesus, Mary's Son.

ANCIENT IRISH

148

Wisdom is the finest beauty of a person.
Money does not prevent you from becoming blind.
Money does not prevent you from becoming mad,
money does not prevent you from becoming lame.
You may be ill in any part of your body,
so it is better for you to go and think again
and to select wisdom.
Come and sacrifice, that you may have rest in your body,
inside and outside.

YORUBA, NIGERIA

Job Curses the Day of his Birth

Let the day perish wherein I was born,
And the night which said, 'There is a man child conceived.'
Let that day be darkness;
Let not God regard it from above,
Neither let the light shine upon it.
Let darkness and the shadow of death claim it for their own;
Let a cloud dwell upon it;
Let all that maketh black the day terrify it.
As for that night, let thick darkness seize upon it:
Let it not rejoice among the days of the year;
Let it not come into the number of the months.
Lo, let that night be barren; let no joyful voice come therein.
Let them curse it that curse the day,
Who are ready to rouse up Leviathan.
Let the stars of the twilight thereof be dark:
Let it look for light, but have none;
Neither let it behold the eyelids of the morning:
Because it shut not up the doors of my mother's womb,
Nor hid trouble from mine eyes.
Why died I not from the womb?
Why did I not give up the ghost when I came out of the belly?
Why did the knees receive me?
Or why the breasts, that I should suck?
For now should I have lain down and been quiet;
I should have slept; then had I been at rest:
With kings and counsellors of the earth,
Which build up waste places for themselves;
Or with princes that had gold,
Who filled their houses with silver:
Or as a hidden untimely birth I had not been;
As infants which never saw light.
There the wicked cease from troubling;

And there the weary be at rest.
There the prisoners are at ease together;
They hear not the voice of the taskmaster.
The small and great are there:
And the servant is free from his master.

THE BOOK OF JOB, AUTHORISED VERSION OF THE BIBLE

I 50

The Water of Kane

A query, a question,
I put to you:
Where is the water of Kane?
At the Eastern Gate
Where the Sun comes in at Haehae;
There is the water of Kane.

A question I ask of you:
Where is the water of Kane?
Out there with the floating Sun,
Where cloud-forms rest on Ocean's breast,
Uplifting their forms at Nihoa,
This side the base of Lehua;
There is the water of Kane.

One question I put to you:
Where is the water of Kane?
Yonder on mountain peak
On the ridges steep,
In the valleys deep,
Where the rivers sweep;
There is the water of Kane.

This question I ask of you:
Where, pray, is the water of Kane?
Yonder, at sea, on the ocean,
In the driving rain,
In the heavenly bow,
In the piled-up mist-wraith,
In the blood-red rainfall,
In the ghost-pale cloud-form;
There is the water of Kane.

One question I put to you:
Where, where is the water of Kane?
Up on high is the water of Kane,
In the heavenly blue,
In the black piled cloud,
In the black-black cloud,
In the black-mottled sacred cloud of the gods;
There is the water of Kane.

One question I ask of you:
Where flows the water of Kane?
Deep in the ground, in the gushing spring,
In the ducts of Kane and Loa,
A well-spring of water, to quaff,
A water of magic power –
The water of life!
Life! O give us this life!

HAWAII

129

The Judgement Flood

The great storm will come when Monday's a day,
    All the world of the air will outpour,
And through all its lasting we shall obey,
    We whose ears will be filled with its roar.

The freezing will come when Tuesday's a day,
    All pain to the heart and piercing fine,
Flecking from the cheeks, though pale of array,
    Blood as red as the red-pouring wine.

The wind it will blow when Wednesday's a day,
    Sweeping bare down the strath and the plain,
Sharp-showering the gusts that cut and slay,
    Thunderclaps and mountains split in twain.

The rain it will pour when Thursday's a day,
    Driving men into blind rushing flight,
Faster than leaves which scurry from the spray,
    A-shake like Mary's plant-leaves in fright.

The dark cloud will come when Friday's a day,
    The direst dread that ever was known,
Multitudes left with their reason astray,
    Grass and fish underneath the one stone.

The great sea will come when Saturday's a day,
    Full of anger, full of sorrow's pain,
As he hears the bitter words all men say,
    A red cross on each right shoulder lain.

GAELIC, NORTH UIST

152

The plough and yoke are in the forest
The bullock is yet in the womb of the cow
The ploughman is still unborn
But the girl who takes him food
Is standing in the field
The Mother gave no grain, no wealth
The Mother gave no child in her womb
The ploughman is still unborn
But the girl with his food
Is standing in the field.

GOND ABORIGINAL, INDIA

153

And I thought over again
My small adventures
As with a shore-wind I drifted out
In my kayak
And thought I was in danger.

My fears,
Those small ones
That I thought so big
For all the vital things
I had to get and reach.

And yet, there is only
One great thing,
The only thing:
To live to see in huts and on journeys
The great day that dawns
And the light that fills the world.

COPPER ESKIMO

SOURCES AND NOTES

Number
of poem

1   L. Van Der Post, *The Lost World of the Kalahari*, p. 226.

2, 3, 4   Willard R. Trask, *The Unwritten Song*, pp. 130, 195, 190.

5   C. H. and R. M. Berndt, *The World of the First Australians*, p. 315. With the Northern aboriginals the beginning of the monsoon season, when the air is charged with thunder and lightning, marks the start of the human courting time. 'Courtship becomes even more dramatic because it is associated with formidable natural powers and partakes of their strength and magnificence.' (C. M. Bowra)

6   Folk song translated by Blanaid Salkeld.

7   B. W. Andrzejewski and I. M. Lewis, *Somali Poetry*.

8   Okot p'Bitek, *Horn of My Love*, p. 15. Among the Acoli people poetry is important for the cultural and moral education of children, and because adults turn to it as a means of coping with the main events of life.

9   M. Lawrence, *A Tree for Poverty* (Somali Poetry and Prose) Nairobi, 1954.

10   Verrier Elwin, *Folk-songs of Chattisgarh*. Elwin went as a priest to live with the people; he stayed to become an Indian. Life there, he records, was hard, dusty and unrewarding: 'It might well be hopeless were it not for the happiness that song brings to the meanest hovel.'

11   L. Harries, *Swahili Poetry*.

12   René Bazin, *Charles Foucauld, hermit and explorer*, trans. Peter Keelan, p. 278. An ahal is a social gathering of young men and women, presided over by an older woman known for her beauty or skill at improvising poetry.

133

13 Verrier Elwin, *Folk-songs of the Maikal Hills*, p. 150. He reminds us that the Indian 'primitive', in whose life poetry was an important element, is 'not to be pitied and "uplifted", but rather to be respected and admired. Nothing in his life is more admirable than his flair for poetry, his sense of rhythm, his love of art.'

14 A nineteenth-century translation.

15 Verrier Elwin and S. Hivale, *Songs of the Forest*, p. 129.

16 *Penguin Book of Japanese Verse*, p. 107.

17 As No. 13. Cf. Donne 'Busy old fool, unruly sun' and other aubades.

18 W. G. Archer trans., *The Dove and the Leopard*, p. 90. See note on No. 82.

19 Bulletin 127 of the Bernice P. Bishop Museum, Honolulu.

20 Peggy Rutherfoord, *Darkness and Light*; also in Ulli Beier, *African Poetry*.

21 C. J. Lyall, *Translations of Ancient Arabian Poetry*, p. 68, 1885. Pre-Islamic, handed down by rawis (reciters); every poet had his rawi, to whom he committed his poems as they were composed.

22 A. S. Harvey, *Ballads, Songs and Rhymes of East Anglia*.

23 Ellen Frye trans., *The Marble Threshing Floor*, p. 284 (copyright of the American Folklore Society).

24 Collected in Somerset by Cecil Sharp; cf. his *English Folksong: some conclusions*.

25 As No. 16, p. 99.

26 As No. 24; see *English Folksong*, pp. 83, 98.

27 Ruth L. Tongue, *The Chime Child*, p. 59.

28 Margot L. Astrov, *The Winged Serpent*, p. 26. 'Individual songs are born out of the moment of lonely suffering ... a woman whose task it is to watch over the crops might be overwhelmed by loneliness and sorrow.'

30 D. Subotic, *Yugoslav Traditional Poetry*, p. 34.

31 Trask I, p. 114.

32 J. D. Frodsham, *An Anthology of Chinese Verse*.

33   As No. 18, p. 131.

34   As No. 13, p. 196.

35   C. M. Bowra trans., *Primitive Song*, p. 188.

36   As No. 18, p. 142.

37   Folk song, W. G. Archer trans., *The Blue Grove*, p. 136.

38   J. F. Stimson, *Songs and Tales of the Sea Kings* (Peabody Museum, Salem, Mass.).

39   R. P. Trilles, *Les Pygmées de la Forêt Equatoriale*, 1931.

40   Kwabene Nketia trans., 'Akan Poetry' *Black Orpheus* 3, 1958, p. 18 (Ministry of Education, Ibadan, Nigeria).

41   W. G. Ivens, *Melanesians of the South-East Solomon Islands*, 1927.

42   As No. 16, p. 144.

43   Willard R. Trask trans., II, p. 135.

44   Sir Arthur Grimble, *A Pattern of Islands*, p. 125. An islander told him to take his daughter to an eastern beach, and to repeat this spell three times as the sun appeared.

45   As No. 28, p. 216.

46, 47   Peter Freuchen, *Book of the Eskimos*, p. 276.

48   G. R. D. McLean, *Poems of the Western Highlanders*, p. 11. Alexander Carmichael collected in the course of his official duties 'the biggest sum of literature in any Western European language handed down by word of mouth', and published them in *Carmina Gadelica* (five volumes, 1900–1954). All aspects of life are covered by these Gaelic poems – lullabies, charms, spells (many medical, e.g. for toothache, others for recovering strayed cattle), and verses for spinning, weaving, making shoes and many other needs and occasions of life. Unfortunately there is no selection in print. This poem is a woman's prayer for the men of the house; a 'pillow-death' was rare among fishermen and rock-climbers.

49   Nineteenth century; *Journal of the Polynesian Society*, XXI, p. 59.

50   C. H. Berndt trans. An Australian woman of north-east Arnhem Land journeyed to Yirkalla, and on arrival her

small grand-daughter fell ill and died. 'The situation is presented just as it is, with an exact and loving care, but because it is infused with grief, none of the details is otiose or irrelevant, and the whole piece has a unity in its single, tragic occasion . . . her selection of what matters rises from the very intensity of her grief, and for this reason her song has its own pattern and completeness.' (C. M. Bowra)

51 As No. 10, p. 104.

52 W. G. Archer trans., *Man in India* XXII, p. 237.

54 E. Tregear, *The Maori Race*, 1904.

55 P. H. Buck, *Ethnology of Mangareva* (Bishop Museum Bulletin 157, 1938, Honolulu).

56 H. M. and N. K. Chadwick, *The Growth of Literature*, I.

57 Hugh Tracey collected this in the original Chizezuru in 1933; cf. his *Songs from the Kraals*.

58 C. G. Seligmann, *The Veddas*, p. 370, 1911.

59 J. C. Andersen, *Myths and Legends of the Polynesians*, p. 129.

60 As No. 5. For comment see Bowra, p. 252.

61 As No. 35, p. 44. The gods of the forest must be appeased, and the elephant must be addressed with magical incantations to bring it into the hunters' power. The main text is sung by the leader, and the refrain by his fellow-hunters.

62 *Report of the Canadian Arctic Expedition*, 1913–1918. This 'acute and revealing piece of self-examination' is discussed by Bowra, p. 133.

63 Folk song translated by Blanaid Salkeld.

64 Ruth M. Underhill, *Papago Indian Religion*, p. 94.

65 K. Birket-Smith, *The Eskimos*.

66 W. W. Skeat, *Malay Magic*, 1900.

67 Frank Russel, *The Pima Indians*, 26th Annual Report of the Bureau of American Ethnology, 1904.

68 N. B. Emerson, *Unwritten Literature of Hawaii*, Bulletin No. 38, 1909, Bureau of American Ethnology.

69 As No. 5, p. 314.

70   *Journal of American Folklore*, 7, p. 191, 1894. The Navajo
      had a great belief in the power of the word to maintain
      and prolong life and (as in this poem) to support the
      power of germination by sympathetic magic.

71   As No. 13.

72   Ulli Beier, *Yoruba Poetry*, p. 49. Poetry comes more
      naturally to the Yoruba people than prose.

73   As No. 48.

74   Ulli Beier, *African Poetry*; another version in Trask I,
      p. 111.

75   D. C. Osadebay trans. in Peggy Rutherfoord, *Darkness
      and Light*.

76   This savage song of exultation is said to have been a camp-
      fire number with Hebrew warriors for centuries.

77   Trask I, p. 113.

78   As No. 11.

79   Taken from Jacquetta Hawkes and Leonard Woolley,
      Pre-History: the Beginnings of Civilisation, p. 818.

80   *Penguin Book of Chinese Verse*, p. 2. The *Book of Songs* is an
      anthology of ancient Chinese poetry that seems to have
      been formed by the time of Confucius (557–479 B.C.),
      who urged his hearers to study it as a means of learning
      the practice of virtue.

81   Ulli Beier, *African Poetry*.

82   Dr Archer's note tells us that the Karam festival occurs in
      August at the climax of the monsoon when the paddy is
      standing in the fields but is not ready; it is thus a time of
      relaxation.

83   Joseph P. Clancy, *The Earliest Welsh Poetry*, p. 99.

84   Folk song translated by George Keyt.

85   As No. 37, p. 47.

86   As No. 23.

87   As No. 48, p. 201.

88   As No. 21.

89   Willard R. Trask trans., I, p. 110. This is said to have been
      a very old poem when it was noted by an Italian in the

Sudan in 1854.

90   *Anthropos*, vol. 48, 1953, p. 98.

91   As No. 15, p. 143.

92   As No. 83, p. 98.

93   W. H. I. Bleek and L. C. Lloyd, *Specimens of Bushman Folklore*, 1911. The dead man was believed to make himself known to his friends by sounding a string in the sky; 'though the presentation is extremely spare and selective, the poem is surprisingly dramatic and touching.'

94   Ulli Beier, *African Poetry*, p. 25.

95, 96   As No. 13.

97   As No. 16.

98   *Selections from Ancient Irish Poetry* translated by Kuno Meyer, p. 56, 1911.

99   C. F. Usborne, *Panjabi Songs and Lyrics*, 1905.

100   As No. 23.

101   As No. 20, p. 16.

102   As No. 55.

103   As No. 16, p. 80.

104   As No. 46, p. 275.

105   Knud Rasmussen, *Observations on the Intellectual Culture of the Caribou Eskimos*, Copenhagen, 1929.

106   Tom Lowenstein trans. *Eskimo Poems*, p. 95.

107   As No. 106, p. 13.

108   As No. 5, p. 319. The Australian Laragia once lived by the sea but were driven inland by white settlers. Water was thus a source and symbol of fertility to the aborigines; and the bathing by moonlight probably had a ritual and religious significance.

109   J. L. Campbell and F. Collinson ed., *Hebridean Folksongs*. In the Highlands and the islands the fulling of cloth used to be done by hand, invariably to the accompaniment of song, with the workers sitting round a table or a bench. Songs also lightened such tasks as cutting corn and grinding it in a quern.

110 Willard R. Trask trans., I p. 49.

111 Sir Arthur Grimble, *Return to the Islands*, p. 42, where the author gives a moving account of the circumstances that led to the speaking of this poem.

112 K. K. Parker, *The Euahlayi Tribe*, 1905.

113 R. T. H. Griffith trans.; original perhaps not later than 1500 B.C.

114 Original dates back to 10th century B.C.; translation published 1611.

115 Truman Michelson, *On the Fox Indians*, 40th Annual Report of the Bureau of American Ethnology, 1925.

116 F. E. Maning, *Old New Zealand*, 1884.

117 M. Read, 'Songs of the Ngoni People', *Bantu Studies*, 11, 1937. A very old poem, originally intended for performance at a marriage, but now sung on other occasions, including church meetings. The refrain refers to the way in which the earth is always receiving the dead, but is never satisfied.

118 As No. 48, p. 415.

119 As No. 10, p. 244.

120 As No. 74.

121 As No. 21, p. 53.

122 *Black Orpheus*, 22.

123 As No. 32, p. 3.

124 As No. 8, p. 143.

125 Arthur Waley, *The Way and its Power*, p. 73.

126 A. A. Macdonell trans.

127 Trask II, p. 106.

128 *Black Orpheus*, 19.

129 Tiwai Paraone, 'A Maori Cosmogony', *Journal of the Polynesian Society*, 16, 1907.

130 Collected by Ruth Fletcher, 27th Annual Report of the Bureau of American Ethnology, 1911.

131 Noted in 1894; from Margot Astrov, *The Winged Serpent*.

134 As No. 93, p. 415.

135   As No. 35, p. 109.
136   As No. 28, p. 323.
137   As No. 64, p. 45.
139   Trask II, p. 256.
140   As No. 46. Whenever the woman composer of this song repeated it, everyone who heard it became senseless with joy and cleansed their minds of evil.
141   Dane and M. R. Coolidge, *The Navajo Indians*, 1930.
142   As No. 74, p. 22.
143   As No. 11, p. 207.
144, 145 Charles E. Gover, *The Folk-songs of Southern India*, 1872.
147   As No. 98, p. 100.
148   As No. 72, p. 47.
150   As No. 68.
151   As No. 48, p. 428.
152   As No. 13, p. 120.
153   Trask I, p. 27.

ACKNOWLEDGMENTS

Permission to quote copyright items is gratefully acknowledged to the following translators, or their representatives, and publishers. It has not been possible to trace some copyright holders; the publisher and editor will be glad to rectify any such cases brought to notice.

No. 1: Laurens Van Der Post, *The Lost World of the Kalahari* (Hogarth Press).

Nos. 2, 3, 4, 43, 89, 110: Willard R. Trask, *The Unwritten Song*, Volumes 1 and 2.

Nos. 5, 60, 69, 108: R. M. and C. H. Berndt, *The World of the First Australians* (Angus and Robertson).

No. 7: B. W. Andrzejewski and I. M. Lewis, *Somali Poetry* (Clarendon Press).

Nos. 8, 124: Okot p'Bitek, *Horn of My Love* (Heinemann Educational Books).

Nos. 10, 51, 119: Verrier Elwin, *Folk-Songs of Chattisgarh* (Oxford University Press, India).

Nos. 11, 78: L. Harries, *Swahili Poetry* (Oxford University Press).

Nos. 13, 17, 34, 53, 71, 95, 96, 152: Verrier Elwin, *Folk-Songs of the Maikal Hills* (Oxford University Press, India).

Nos. 14, 91: Verrier Elwin and S. Hivale, *Songs of the Forest* (Allen and Unwin).

Nos. 16, 25, 42, 97, 80: Geoffrey Bownas and Anthony Thwaite, *The Penguin Book of Japanese Verse* (Penguin Books).

Nos. 18, 33, 36, 82: Dr W. G. Archer, *The Dove and the Leopard* (Orient Longman Ltd).

No. 19: J. F. Stimson, *The Legends of Maui and Tahaki*, Bernice P. Bishop Museum Bulletin 127 (Bernice P. Bishop Museum, Honolulu).

Nos. 20, 57, 75: Peggy Rutherfoord, *Darkness and Light* (The Faith Press).

Nos. 23, 86, 100: Ellen Fryє, *The Marble Threshing Floor* (University of Texas Press).

No. 30: D. Subotic, *Yugoslav Traditional Poetry* (Cambridge University Press).

Nos. 32, 123: J. D. Frodsham, *An Anthology of Chinese Verse* (Clarendon Press).

Nos. 35, 61, 135: C. M. Bowra, *Primitive Song* (Weidenfeld and Nicolson).

Nos. 37, 85: Dr W. G. Archer, *The Blue Grove* (Allen and Unwin).

No. 38: J. F. Stimson, *Songs and Tales of the Sea Kings* (The Peabody Museum, Salem, Mass.).

No. 41: W. G. Ivens, *Melanesians of the South-East Solomon Islands* (Routledge and Kegan Paul).

No. 44: Sir Arthur Grimble, *A Pattern of Islands* (John Murray).

Nos. 46, 47, 104, 140: Peter Freuchen, *Book of the Eskimos* (Weidenfeld and Nicolson).

Nos. 48, 73, 87, 118, 151: G. R. D. McLean, *Poems of the Western Highlanders* (The Society for Promoting Christian Knowledge).

No. 50: Dr Catherine M. Berndt, *Oceania* XX, No. 4, p. 317.

No. 52: Dr W. G. Archer, *Man in India* XXII, p. 237.

No. 57: Hugh Tracey, *Songs from the Kraals* (International Library of African Music).

No. 59: J. C. Andersen, *Myths and Legends of the Polynesians* (Harrap).

Nos. 64, 137: Ruth M. Underhill, *Papago Indian Religion* (Columbia University Press).

No. 65: K. Birket-Smith, *The Eskimos* (Associated Book Publishers).

Nos. 72, 145, 148: Ulli Beier, *Yoruba Poetry* (Cambridge University Press).

No. 80: Robert Kotewall and Norman L. Smith, *The Penguin Book of Chinese Verse* (Penguin Books).

Nos. 83, 92: Prof. Joseph P. Clancy, *The Earliest Welsh Poetry*.

Nos. 106, 107: Tom Lowenstein, *Eskimo Poems* (Allison and Busby).

No. 109: J. L. Campbell, *Hebridean Folksongs* (Clarendon Press).

Nos. 111, 143: Sir Arthur Grimble, *Return to the Islands* (John Murray).

No. 115: Truman Michelson, *Annual Report of the Bureau of American Ethnology*, 1925 (The Smithsonian Institute Press).

No. 125: Arthur Waley, *The Way and its Power* (Allen and Unwin).

No. 141: Dane and M. R. Coolidge, *The Navajo Indians* (Houghton Mifflin Company).

People, Progress, and Employee Relations

Publications of the Colgate Darden Graduate School of Business Administration of the University of Virginia.

Bank Expansion in Virginia, 1962-1966: The Holding Company and the Direct Merger. By Paul Foster.

Basic Research in Finance: Needs and Prospects. By Charles C. Abbott.

A Financial Planning Model for Private Colleges: A Research Report. By William J. Arthur.

Forty Years of Public Utility Finance. By Harold H. Young.

Management of Small Enterprises: Cases and Readings. By William Rotch.

A Selected Bibliography of Applied Ethics in the Professions, 1950-1970: A Working Sourcebook with Annotations and Indexes. By Daniel L. Gothie.

PEOPLE, PROGRESS,
and
EMPLOYEE RELATIONS

PROCEEDINGS OF THE
FIFTIETH ANNIVERSARY CONFERENCE OF
INDUSTRIAL RELATIONS COUNSELORS, INC.

The Colgate Darden Graduate School of
Business Administration
University of Virginia

June 9, 10, and 11, 1976

Richard A. Beaumont, Program Director
and General Editor

University Press of Virginia
Charlottesville

THE UNIVERSITY PRESS OF VIRGINIA

Copyright © 1976 by the Rector and Visitors
of the University of Virginia

First published 1976

Library of Congress Cataloging in Publication Data
Industrial Relations Counselors, inc.
  People, progress and employee relations.
  1.   Industrial   relations—United   States—Con-
gresses. I. Title.
HS8057.I426 1976   331'.0973   76-54797   ISBN
0-8139-0716-0

Printed in the United States of America

PREFACE

From June 9 to 11, 1976, some 125 employee relations practitioners and scholars met to commemorate the Fiftieth Anniversary of Industrial Relations Counselors and to participate in part of its rich history. From its beginnings, IRC has been an unusual organization. Designed to engage in research in employee relations before such a field existed, it has contributed much to the thinking and concepts that have shaped employee relations in the world today. But it could not have made that contribution were it not for a continuing interaction with such practitioners and scholars as were represented at this meeting.

This volume of presentations at the Fiftieth Anniversary conference is truly reflective of IRC's continuing role. It reviews the past, considers certain current issues, and looks to the future. The majority of the papers lead to a better current understanding of employee relations in private organizations. This is true especially of the report of the Committee on 1985, a unique attempt to examine the long-term forces in the field and to anticipate the problems and opportunities that may arise over the coming ten-year period. Other talks, in reporting on special developments in employee relations history and the evolution of employee relations systems, give a historical perspective to the field as it has developed in the United States.

The setting for the commemorative meeting, the Colgate Darden Graduate School of Business Administration at the University of Virginia, was a particularly appropriate one. It is the location where IRC has endowed a chair. But, more important, the school is modern in its outlook, though it takes its nourishment from a long and important history.

Thanks are due to many for their role at IRC's historic conference. The specific contribution of each of the speakers and members of the Committee on 1985 is amply represented in this volume. Not represented, however, is the valuable contribution of each participant to the group discussions. Special thanks must go to Dean Stewart Sheppard of the Darden School and his staff for their assistance and cooperation in making the meeting the success it was. Finally, nothing would have been accomplished had it not been for the great help and assistance of Ann Kennedy in handling the arrangements for the meeting and in assuring that the program was developed in a timely fashion.

Also, thanks to my friend and former colleague James W. Tower, who aided us in running the sessions.

There was much assistance in preparing the manuscript for publication by Eleanora Compton and Ellen Friedman. Mrs. Compton has been chief editor and colleague at IRC for many years, but her guidance and help continue to be more valued than she can realize.

Finally, it is appropriate to dedicate this volume to many who are legend today but who, as members of the IRC staff or board of trustees, or as management representatives of their companies, were pioneers in the development of the employee relations field. There are two from the past who should be cited in particular, not only for their contribution to the field but for their guidance to all who have been associated with IRC. The first is Maud B. Patten, who, as editor and staff member of IRC, guided so many of the IRC staff in developing an understanding of the need for systematic research and writing. The other is Carroll E. French, whose forceful views have challenged so many of us over the years and who was present at this meeting to reflect on the developing and evolving process of employee relations.

Richard A. Beaumont
Director of Research
August 15, 1976

CONTENTS

CONTENTS (Continued)

x

PART I: INDUSTRIAL RELATIONS COUNSELORS AND ITS BACKGROUND

IRC was incorporated fifty years ago as a nonprofit organization dedicated to the concept of advancing the knowledge and practice of human relationships in industry, commerce, education, and government. Even before that time, however, the members of its staff had worked together in the interest of promoting principles of sound management-employee relations. Because the organization was the first in this country to specialize in industrial or employee relations counseling, its early history was a significant phase in the development and character of the employee relations process as it exists today. The following papers describe those beginnings and place modern employee relations in its historical setting.

INDUSTRIAL RELATIONS COUNSELORS AT FIFTY YEARS

LEO TEPLOW

LEO TEPLOW has been president of Industrial Relations Counselors, Inc., since 1974. Over the years he has advised on many aspects of management responsibilities in the employee relations field, particularly occupational safety and health. He was a member of the Secretary of Labor's National Advisory Committee on Occupational Safety and Health and served as chairman of the Planning Committee for several of the President's Conferences on Occupational Safety. Mr. Teplow was vice president, industrial relations, of the American Iron and Steel Institute until his retirement from that organization in 1970. He is a member of the Columbia University Seminar on Labor, served on the executive board of the Industrial Relations Research Association and is a past president of its New York chapter. He is a trustee emeritus of the Industrial Hygiene Foundation. He holds B.S. and M.S. degrees from M.I.T., and L.L.B. and M.P.L. degrees from Washington College of Law.

It gives me great pleasure to welcome you to the fiftieth birthday party of Industrial Relations Counselors, Inc.

Fifty years in the life of man or institution is a milepost. Most of our program these three days will be devoted to looking forward. But to look forward intelligently, we need to know a little about how we got to the present. So you may find a bit of nostalgia in my remarks and in the remarks of two men—Chauncey Belknap and Carroll French—who had so much to do with IRC's birth in 1926 and its progress in subsequent years.

In addition to welcoming you here today, my function is to paint in broad strokes the origin and significance of IRC—and to give you a little background on its philosophy.

Like most enduring institutions, IRC was the result of a conjuncture of extraordinary events and individuals. The event was a disastrous, militant strike of 9,000 coal miners against the Colorado Fuel

3

and Iron Company in 1913—a strike of fifteen months that involved a pitched battle between strikers and deputy sheriffs, and later between miners and militia—battles that resulted in deaths not only of miners but of miners' wives and children. The incident became known in labor history as the Ludlow Massacre.

On April 30, 1914, six troops of U.S. Cavalry took over. The strike ultimately failed. But the expressed public concern following the Ludlow Massacre caused John D. Rockefeller, Jr., who had a majority interest in Colorado Fuel and Iron, to cast about for a better way to deal with employee relations. He had the good judgment to call in William Mackenzie King, a former Canadian minister of labour and a recognized student of industrial relations, who had recently written a book entitled *Industry and Humanity.* In that book, King endorsed the right of employees to be represented by fellow employees of their own choice in dealing with management.

King proposed an employee representation plan for the CF&I mineworkers, but before putting it into effect, Rockefeller and King personally visited each of the company's mines and talked at length with mine superintendents and miners' wives and children. Upon submission of King's plan to a secret ballot vote of the miners, over 80 percent of them voted to accept the plan. The man hired to administer the plan, Clarence J. Hicks, is today honored as one of the pioneers of industrial relations.

Thereafter, John D. Rockefeller, Jr., asked his law firm to set up a separate section that might advise him on employee relations policies for companies in which the Rockefellers had substantial interest. There were no employee relations consultants in those days—and almost no industrial relations practitioners as we understand that term today. Such a section was established in 1922 and became so effective in improving employee relations in specific Rockefeller companies that soon other, non-Rockefeller companies began to seek employee relations advice. In 1926 the consulting function was incorporated as Industrial Relations Counselors, Inc., with a budget underwritten by John D. Rockefeller, Jr., until such time as consulting revenues and research grants might make the organization self-supporting.

These days, when we are paying appropriate respect to the geniuses who wrote the Declaration of Independence and the Constitution of the United States, we can also respect the remarkable foresight of those who wrote into IRC's charter of incorporation that ". . . the objectives and purposes for which the corporation is formed are to advance the knowledge and practice of human relationships in industry, commerce, education, and government." The year was 1926 (a year I then considered extremely important because I was in the class of 1926 at M.I.T.). The term "industrial relations" was hardly known.

In 1926 the population of the United States was scarcely more than half of what it is today. Civilian nonagricultural employment was nearly 30 million, as compared with today's 80 million. Organized labor numbered hardly more than 3,500,000 members, including Canada, as compared with over 24,000,000 today. The year 1926 also marked the first piece of substantial labor legislation—the Railway Labor Act. Calvin Coolidge was president of the United States. It was not until the following year that Lindbergh soloed across the Atlantic. No one was worried about air pollution or noise pollution.

IRC was not designed—and has never pretended—to have a pat answer for every situation. It was solidly founded on basic concepts largely attributable to Mackenzie King, Clarence Hicks, and Bryce Stewart, its first Director of Research. It is not easy to boil down its governing concepts to fit within the parameters of these brief remarks, but I have tried to do so as follows:

1. IRC's concern is the long-term establishment and maintenance of sound employee relations through appropriate management structure and development and the application of appropriate employee policies and practices. (This principle has been applied even when IRC was called in because of a specific, urgent problem. Consequently, in most cases IRC's intervention resulted in far more serious attention on the part of top management to its employee relations responsibilities as a permanent aspect of corporate policy.)

2. Management's freedom to make decisions depends not only on responsible use of authority but also on full recognition of the needs and interests of employees. (This recognizes that employee relations is an integral part of the management process and that employee attitudes, motivations, and loyalties derive from the totality of corporate employee relations policies and practices.)

3. Decision-making must be solidly based on determinable facts. (Thus, a major part of every undertaking by IRC, whether in counseling or research, was the determination of the facts of each situation, whatever the aspect of employee relations involved.)

4. The determination of the facts in employee relations has to be undertaken by confidential interviews with substantial numbers of management people at all levels—and confidentiality must be preserved at all costs.

5. No consulting arrangement should be undertaken with any

company except at the specific request of its top management, and the IRC report must be made in person to high-level management. In this way, the report is most likely to lead to appropriate action.

6. The staff must consist of people of the highest competence and integrity. (Names like Arthur Young, T.H.A. Tiedemann, Bryce Stewart, Clarence Hicks, Murray Latimer, Albert Regula, Carroll French, Howard Kaltenborn, and Richard Beaumont, among others, are names to conjure with.)

The concatenation of extraordinary events and extraordinary individuals resulted in policies and actions that have made a notable contribution to modern industrial relations. The heavy emphasis that IRC places on research stems from its earliest years. Between 1927 and 1932 IRC maintained a branch office at the International Labour Office in Geneva, conducting monumental research, reflected in several published volumes on national employment exchanges and unemployment benefits in several European countries. In return, the ILO looked to IRC for help in responding to inquiries concerning United States employee relations.

The total number of IRC research studies includes not only explicit employee relations subjects but also such national policy issues as unemployment compensation and national labor policy. IRC has also demonstrated profound interest in retirement provisions for the aged, and it had a consulting role in drafting the unemployment compensation provisions of the original Social Security Act.

In 1962 IRC initiated its series of annual research symposiums in which business researchers and academic researchers meet to discuss their recent findings and tests of hypotheses. A number of significant volumes based on these symposia have been published, the subjects ranging from the application of behavioral science research to computer technology.

As I have noted earlier, IRC's charter expresses its purpose as, among other things, the advancement of the knowledge and practice of human relationships in education. IRC's love affair with academe is of long standing, and its role has been much more activist than merely being available for consultation. It was largely due to Mr. Hicks's involvement in what he perceived to be an unrealistic academic approach to the teaching of employee relations in courses usually labeled "labor economics" that industrial relations centers or departments were established, first at Princeton, and later at Michigan, Stanford, Queens in Canada, M.I.T., and Cal Tech. In 1954, after Mr. Hicks's death, IRC established Hicks Fellowships at each of these universities.

More recently—in fact, only three years ago—IRC established an

IRC professorship in industrial relations at the Colgate Darden Graduate School of Business Administration at the University of Virginia. This is a rotating professorship, filled each year by an outstanding practitioner with a business background. During the past two years this post was occupied with distinction by Robert Levitt of Western Electric and by John F. Simons of Continental Can, respectively. Both IRC and the Darden School believe that useful cross-fertilization is being accomplished, although it is much too early to savor the fruit thereof.

When IRC was organized in 1926, there was no recognized industrial relations profession nor any way for those coming into the practice of the profession to acquire background, knowledge, or skills, except through the school of experience. When the demand for industrial relations competence became a matter of high national priority during World War II, IRC organized what we modestly believe to be the best training course in industrial relations in the United States.

I was a student at that first training course (which then lasted for two weeks) in 1943. It opened my eyes and broadened my vision to such an extent that instead of continuing as a patent attorney detached on a temporary industrial relations assignment, I devoted the rest of my working life—preretirement as well as postretirement—to various phases of industrial relations.

That industrial relations course is still going strong; the next one is scheduled in Williamsburg, Virginia, for November 1976. I have been back repeatedly as a member of the faculty, and it always rekindles my interest and enthusiasm. Approximately five thousand men and women, from line and staff functions, have graduated from the IRC Management Course, and I am confident that the companies and government departments that sent them there have benefited greatly.

You will remember that IRC was organized and operated as a nonprofit, membership (nonstock) corporation, entitled to tax exemption. After the Rockefeller contributions ended in about 1936, it became more and more necessary for IRC to rely for support on the payments received to cover the cost of research that involved consulting with industrial and other contributors. Eventually in the mid-1950s, in order to avoid possible questions as to IRC's continuing right to tax exemption, it was decided to drop all of its consulting activities. The work in this field has since been carried on and expanded by a newly-organized business corporation, Organization Resources Counselors (ORC), whose income is subject to tax like that of any other profit-making organization. IRC originally held all of the stock of ORC, but nearly half of its shares have been subsequently donated to the University of Virginia to underwrite the IRC professorship.

The uniqueness of IRC is that it has pioneered in a field that has gained increasing recognition as being central to the health and survival of industrial civilization. It has contributed notably to constructive, responsible management approaches during a period in which the United States moved from the halcyon 1920s through the Great Depression, two world wars, the growth in numbers and political power of organized labor, and the proliferation of labor-related legislation ranging from the Norris-LaGuardia Act to the Occupational Safety and Health Act and the Employee Retirement Income Security Act. It has helped substitute reason for emotion, long-range planning for emotionalism, carefully elaborated policies for seat-of-the-pants decision-making.

It is my biased view that IRC made notable contributions to the stabilization of volatile pressures in a way that helped management retain a modicum of flexibility in meeting its increasingly heavy burdens; and IRC has carried out its educational-research-counseling functions in a manner that has served the interests of both employees and stockholders.

That, my honored friends, is the organization whose fiftieth anniversary you are helping us celebrate.

8

THE FORMATIVE YEARS

CHAUNCEY BELKNAP

CHAUNCEY BELKNAP is a partner in the New York law firm of Patterson, Belknap and Webb. Mr. Belknap began his distinguished career as an attorney by serving as legal secretary to Justice Oliver Wendell Holmes of the United States Supreme Court. He was admitted to the New York bar in 1916. His past directorships include American Steel Foundries and Lehn and Fink Products Corporation. He was a member of the visitors committee of Harvard Law School and a trustee of Princeton University. Mr. Belknap is a fellow of the American Bar Foundation, a member of the American Law Institute, served as president of the New York State Bar Association and vice president of the Bar Association of the City of New York. In addition, he was president of the Harvard Law School Association of New York. Mr. Belknap was an incorporating trustee of Industrial Counselors, Inc., and wrote the initial articles of incorporation. For a number of years Mr. Belknap's firm, then known as Curtis, Fosdick and Belknap, housed the industrial relations counsel of John D. Rockefeller, Jr., until it was separately established as a nonprofit research and educational institution in 1926. Mr. Belknap is a graduate of Princeton University and the Harvard Law School.

This meeting commemorates the Fiftieth Anniversary of Industrial Relations Counselors, Inc., but in fact its formative years, which I have been asked to recall, go back five years earlier. The organization did not spring full-fledged from some Jovian brow just fifty years ago. There was a period of gestation in what some may consider the unlikely medium of a New York law firm. If you will permit a personal reference, this was the firm where I was a very junior partner in 1921 and where I am a very senior partner in 1976. The firm was then known as Curtis, Fosdick and Belknap, and the key figure in this story was our partner Raymond B. Fosdick. He had recently returned to the practice of law after a brief period of service overseas as deputy

9

secretary of the newly organized League of Nations, a post he had resigned when the Senate refused to ratify the Treaty of Versailles.

One of the clients who turned to Mr. Fosdick for advice was John D. Rockefeller, Jr. I need hardly point out that I am referring to a time preceding the infancy of labor law, a time when labor law, as we know it today, had not even been conceived. The Wagner Act, the Taft-Hartley Act, the Labor Relations Board, came many years later. I am referring to a time only shortly after the steel strike of 1919, which had been marked by violence and bloodshed, a strike in which one of the major issues was the twelve-hour day and the seven-day week. For many American corporations of that day industrial relations hardly went beyond distributing a turkey at Christmas. Indeed, the term "industrial" or "employee" relations had little currency before it was used in 1922 to designate a section of the Department of Economics at Princeton University, newly organized with Mr. Rockefeller's support.

This was the environment in which Mr. Rockefeller one day asked Mr. Fosdick to check into a report that a corporation in which the Rockefellers were financially interested was operating on a twelve-hour day, seven-day week. Fosdick's investigation confirmed the report; as Mr. Rockefeller's representative he succeeded in bringing about a change for the better.

As similar assignments multiplied, Mr. Fosdick, with Mr. Rockefeller's approval, added to our staff George J. Anderson, a layman whose exceptional qualifications included wide experience in dealing with the complex industrial relations problems of the printing industry. George Anderson was immediately absorbed in surveys of the labor situation in the Consolidation Coal Company, the Colorado Fuel and Iron Company, and other enterprises in which the Rockefellers had an interest. As Rockefeller's emissary, Anderson had no difficulty in initiating these investigations by contacts with the chief executives of the corporations involved. He was never content with a worm's-eye view of the situation. He worked from the top down and insisted upon obtaining firsthand information as a basis for his evaluation and conclusions. Anderson's reports went first to Rockefeller and, after receiving his approval, were then usually sent directly to the chief executive of the corporation. When these reports included cautionary recommendations, Rockefeller's backing made them cautions with a clout.

Within a couple of years George Anderson's supporting staff had grown to six, and he had achieved such a reputation that the Consolidation Coal Company lured him away from our office with a vice

presidency, which soon led to his becoming president of that compa-
ny. Mr. Fosdick enlisted as his successor Arthur H. Young, who had
worked on labor matters for the International Harvester Company.
Young developed and expanded the activities that Anderson had
started. A number of the companies with which he established con-
tacts began to realize that his recommendations, aside from any ethi-
cal motivation, had important inherent business value. By following
the advice in his reports, they might avert strikes and other labor
crises. Young's assistance began to be sought by companies that were
independent of any Rockefeller ties. In short, what had started as an
exercise of power by a dominant stockholder was developing into an
agency responding to the call of enlightened corporate management.
The efforts of Messrs. Fosdick, Anderson, and Young were persuading
corporate executives that attention to industrial relations was not just
fuzzy-minded idealism but was, in fact, sound management policy
that paid off in dollars and cents.

At this point, early in 1926, Fosdick went to Rockefeller with
the proposal that the industrial relations staff be set up as an indepen-
dent entity, separate from our law firm, under the leadership of
Arthur Young. As approved by Rockefeller, the plan contemplated
organization of a nonprofit, tax-exempt research corporation which,
it was believed, would receive support in the form of contributions
from many business corporations and other sources. The initial prob-
lem was to define the corporation's nonprofit nature.

Scientific research in medicine was a familiar activity as conduc-
ted, for example, in the laboratories of the Rockefeller Institute for
Medical Research. Other laboratories were carrying on research in the
chemical and physical sciences. Entomologists could conduct labora-
tory studies of the relations between the workers in a beehive and the
queen bee. But how could scientific research on the relations between
the workers in a coal mine or an oil refinery and their employers be
conducted? There was no supporting precedent, but we decided that
it should be possible to show that for such research the laboratory
was the coal mine or the oil refinery itself. Accordingly, the corpora-
tion was organized with a charter stating that its purpose was "to
advance the knowledge and practice of human relationships in indus-
try, commerce, education, and government."

Arthur Young and his staff moved out of our law office into
quarters of their own, and Industrial Relations Counselors was born.
It soon became evident that the expectations of support in the form
of contributions from a wide variety of sources would be realized.
The new enterprise showed such promise that there was no difficulty

in enlisting as members of its board of trustees such representative industrial leaders as Owen D. Young, chairman of the General Electric Corporation, and Cyrus McCormick, Jr., of the International Harvester Company, and such leaders in the field of education as Harold W. Dodds, president of Princeton University, and Ernest M. Hopkins, president of Dartmouth College.

As time went on the value of the organization's research on the firing line of industry was continually demonstrated. Publications such as Murray Latimer's work on industrial pensions were recognized as authoritative. The knowledge and experience of the IRC staff was drawn upon by legislators and administrators in developing the federal government's plans for unemployment insurance, social security, and other legislation in this area.

In short, during these formative years the pioneering work of Industrial Relations Counselors, Inc., provided convincing evidence that research in the science and art of industrial relations could significantly help "to advance the knowledge and practice of human relationships in industry, commerce, education, and government."

A LOOK AT THE PAST

CARROLL E. FRENCH

CARROLL E. FRENCH is a former president of Industrial Relations Counselors, Inc. Before joining IRC he held a number of management positions in industrial relations at the Standard Oil Company (New Jersey) (now Exxon) and Colonial Beacon Oil Company. He first joined the IRC staff in 1935. During the following nine years he directed surveys for many companies in a variety of industries in the United States and Canada. For more than a year he was stationed in Hawaii as advisor to various managements, mainly in the sugar and pineapple industries. In 1943 he joined the Boeing Aircraft Company as industrial relations director, and in 1946, joined the National Association of Manufacturers as director of its industrial relations division. In 1951 he rejoined IRC and served as president until 1965. During 1951 and 1952 he also served as advisor to the United States Employer Delegation to the Conference of the International Labour Organisation in Geneva. He is a graduate of Monmouth College in Monmouth, Illinois, and received his Ph. D. in political economics from Johns Hopkins University. His latest publication is Management and Industrial Relations 1919-1970.

It is indeed heartwarming to have this opportunity to greet old friends and associates on this Fiftieth Anniversary of IRC. I well remember the day I was called over to 26 Broadway from the Bayonne Refinery of the Standard Oil Company (New Jersey) to discuss with T.H.A. Tiedemann and C.J. Hicks the question of IRC's future. Arthur H. Young had just recently resigned as its first director to take the position as vice president of the U.S. Steel Corporation. Mr. John D. Rockefeller, Jr., had asked C.J. Hicks, then assistant to W.C. Teagle, president of Standard Oil Company (New Jersey) for his counsel and advice on whether or not IRC should be dissolved or continued and, if continued, what provision should be made for its leadership and financial support. Mr. Tiedemann and I joined in stating that if the establishment of IRC in 1926 was justified then, there was even greater reason for its existence in 1933, and we urgently recommended that it be continued. And so it was that T.H.A. Tiedemann became the second director of the organization, charged with the responsibility for its proper staffing and administration and for generating adequate financial support by the companies it served.

I think it appropriate at this time to quote from a letter dated February 1, 1935 that I received from John D. Rockefeller III, chairman of the board of trustees when I joined IRC forty-one years ago: "As Mr. Tiedemann has pointed out to you, the finances of Industrial Relations Counselors are such that the future of the organization is at the present time uncertain. However, as I said to Mr. Tiedemann when he became director about a year ago, my personal feeling is that we can make Industrial Relations Counselors so important to industry that the industrial interests of the country cannot afford to let it terminate its activities."

In my reply I said: "I am amazed at the scope of its present services to industry and government and at the knowledge, practical experience, and technical ability it brings to bear upon economic and labor problems. Personally, I am very hopeful that in this day and age an organization so equipped and directed has ahead of it a career of steadily increasing usefulness."

And so here we are fifty years after IRC's incorporation, and the organization is still strong and viable. It is entirely fitting that at this time we should remember and pay tribute to some of those whose assistance and support through the years contributed so much to the survival, progress, and current strength of the organization. There was Clarence J. Hicks who, as chairman of the board of trustees, helped bridge the period from Arthur H. Young until T.H.A. Tiedemann took over. Thomas Roy Jones served as chairman of the board of trustees for many years. His counsel and assistance were readily given when asked for. Bryce M. Stewart served as director of research for many years and was a tower of strength. Emile DuPont, Theodore Petersen, and Howard Kaltenborn rendered invaluable assistance and support, as did Logan Johnson. We owe much to Chauncey Belknap whose friendly and wise counsel has helped us over many problems, large and small. Winthrop Rockefeller was a trustee for many years. I recall that once, at a critical time in our history, he volunteered, in case it should ever become necessary to terminate the organization, to guarantee a year's salary to each employee. But as you can see it never came to that. With the type of support from young men and women as those on the Committee on 1985, I feel confident it never will.

Among the staff who have contributed especially to the value of the services rendered by IRC over the years, I wish to mention Thomas G. Spates, Albert Regula, T.G. Ford, John Burr, Earl D. Hackett, and James Tower.

And now a word in conclusion. I have always been impatient with those who claim that service with an organization or corporation suppresses the personality and restricts the individuality of the employee. It is my observation and experience that exactly the opposite is true. Faithful service to an institution or organization permits the individual to expand and grow to the fullest extent of his abilities and capacities. This has been my own experience with IRC. I am proud to have had a small part in its survival and progress. For having had this opportunity and privilege I am eternally grateful.

PART II: EMPLOYEE RELATIONS — PAST AND PRESENT

Over the years a shifting pattern of problems and issues has characterized employee relations. In today's setting the professional needs a grasp of the changing directions in many areas—labor law, collective bargaining, and national manpower policy, as well as the techniques of modern-day approaches. These may include, among others, ways to deal with nonunion employee relations issues, as well as awareness of how a systems approach to employee relations can be usefully applied.

EMPLOYEE RELATIONS:
A HISTORICAL PERSPECTIVE
J. DOUGLAS BROWN

J. DOUGLAS BROWN is a leader in the field of personnel and industrial rela-
tions. He joined the Princeton faculty in 1921, and in 1926, shortly after Prince-
ton established the nation's first university industrial relations section, he became
director of that center and headed its operations for the next thirty years. From
1946 to his retirement in 1967, he served as dean of the faculty, and in his last
year before retirement he became the University's first provost. Dr. Brown has
served as consultant to various branches of the federal government and to state
governments. He is a fellow of the American Academy of Arts and Sciences and
a member of the American Economic Association. He was one of the founders
and later president of the Industrial Relations Research Association, vice presi-
dent of Princeton University Press, a director of the Fund for Adult Education, a
director of McGraw-Hill, Inc., a trustee of the University of Rochester and of the
Princeton Theological Seminary, and a member of the Research Advisory Board
of the Committee for Economic Development. He received his undergraduate and
Ph.D. degrees from Princeton. Dr. Brown's recent publications include The Liber-
al University, an Institutional Analysis; An American Philosophy of Social Securi-
ty: Evolution and Issues; The Human Nature of Organizations; *and* The Industrial
Relations Section of Princeton University in World War II.

The planners of this conference have taken a serious risk in assigning
"A Historical Perspective" to a college professor who has studied em-
ployee relations for over fifty years. I could start with the strike and
walkout of the children of Israel in Egypt some thousands of years
ago. That was a remarkable example of collective bargaining in which
the business agent used powers of intimidation scarcely approved by
the courts today. While the Egyptians were great builders, their art of
foremanship could be symbolized by the whip.

　　With the brief time allotted, I must skip along a few thousand
years to sketch briefly the kinds of industrial relations philosophies

that have underlain employee relations in modern times—particularly those philosophies which developed as corporations took over from small shops and services run by individual owner-managers. It is interesting, unfortunately, that every philosophy or pattern that has developed over the last two centuries is still found somewhere in America today. The old philosophy has not become extinct even though a newer philosophy has prevailed for a time, to be, in turn, overlaid by a still newer approach.

The reason for this overlay of succeeding philosophies of industrial relations over time is that they are the product of a complex amalgam of human attitudes, emotions, and cultures, as well as of intellectual, political, economic, and social reasoning. Anything to do with industrial relations is saturated with the factor of human response and is not based alone on a scientifically determined analysis or proof. Industrial relations are *human* relations, and human nature, thank God, is a more complex phenomenon than any computer can master—whether occurring in employers or employees. Our knowledge of science is cumulative from generation to generation. The ability to understand human relations must be gained by every individual in his lifetime, aided, but not predetermined, by the experience of his predecessors—even in the best-managed, perpetual corporations.

What are the succeeding, but accumulating, philosophies of industrial relations that have developed in modern times?

The oldest is *laissez-faire.* It was blessed by Adam Smith just two hundred years ago in his influential treatise *The Wealth of Nations.* Smith invented the concept that vigorous free enterprise and competition were regulated by an "Unseen Hand" and resulted in a condition of "Economic Harmonies." Labor was essentially a commodity to be bought and sold competitively. The resultant condition of the laborer was a fortunate or unfortunate by-product. The assumption was that the worker bargained as an individual and could take the job at the wage offered or look elsewhere.

In the mass production industries of America when immigration from Europe was bringing in millions of unskilled workers, laissez-faire was a common corporate philosophy of industrial relations. I can remember visiting the offices of the U.S. Steel Corporation in the mid-1920s when the only industrial relations unit in the corporation was called the Department of Safety and Sanitation, stimulated by workers' compensation laws.

The next philosophy or approach to corporate industrial relations in America can be called that of *paternalism* or *welfare.* It commenced in smaller companies like Dennison, Leeds and Northrup,

Endicott-Johnson, and Hershey Chocolate, but some larger corpora-
tions developed welfare funds. It was largely the inspiration of the
leader-owner of the corporation, who took a paternal interest in his
people. It did, however, carry the overtones of the master-servant re-
lationship, which did not satisfy the sense of self-reliance of a people
no longer uneducated or dependent.

The next philosophy to develop in corporate industrial relations
in America more or less paralleled the welfare approach but grew out
of the thinking of engineers rather than philanthropists. It emphasized
the use of labor as an instrument of production in the tradition of
Adam Smith, but was "scientific." It included time-study, work plan-
ning, and the use of mass production techniques. It greatly enhanced
productivity but did not answer the basic human problems of indus-
trial relations. In fact, by making work more machinelike, it planted
the seeds of rebellion, sit-down strikes, and industrial unionism.

Along with paternalism and scientific management a parallel phi-
losophy of industrial relations had grown up over many years in the
first American industry to form great corporations, the railroads. This
can be termed the *adversary approach.* Sparked by the key crafts that
operated the trains, the railroad unions, because of their ability to
halt transportation, put the employers (and the government) on the
defensive. There developed an elaborate jurisprudence of rules and
the interpretation of rules which, along with the conservatism of aging
managements, led to the decline of the industry.

In the 1920s when both the Industrial Relations Section at
Princeton University and Industrial Relations Counselors entered the
scene, a new approach to industrial relations was developing that may
be called the *company-cooperative philosophy.* The aim was to en-
hance the interest, respect, and sense of partnership of the employees
of a larger, progressive corporation in company affairs and to solve
problems within the "company family." The leaders of the movement
were such men as C. J. Hicks, and the companies associated with the
special conference committee he developed. On the financial side,
employee stock ownership and profit-sharing programs were devel-
oped. Within the plants, employee representation plans were formed
under definite rules of procedure, supported by stated company in-
dustrial relations policies and encouraged by company magazines.

With the depression of the 1930s and the coming of the New
Deal, the interest of labor in *organizations and collective bargaining
beyond the limits of the industrial corporation* introduced a philos-
ophy of industrial relations that has come to play a pervasive role in
our larger corporations today. Concentrated on wages, working rules,

and benefits, it has become a framing structure, but far from the whole of the industrial relations philosophy and practice within the corporation.

The last defined stage in the philosophy of industrial relations is what I will designate the *professional approach*. It involves a thorough understanding and willing acceptance of the basic economic, political, and social principles and conditions that surround the employment of people and, at the same time, embodies the sustained requirements of integrity, mutual respect, intuitive humaneness, and foresight in leadership in both management and labor to attain a viable and effective relationship. It overlies collective bargaining, labor legislation, and intracompany cooperation. It is an inclusive approach.

Since this conference exemplifies the *professional approach* to industrial relations, I will add but a few personal comments concerning it, after fifty years in encouraging its development.

1. The professional approach to industrial relations requires both an understanding of the individual employee and his aspirations and problems and an understanding of the way people function in organized groups.

2. It involves the recognition of the value of labor as a coequal resource along with all the other factors of production and awareness that labor is the most complex and sensitive resource in terms of human motivation and leadership.

3. It requires thorough and subtle analysis, courageous decisiveness, and patient and sustained powers of persuasion. In scientific and engineering design, a proposition can be proved right or wrong. In industrial relations policy, reason must be supplemented by intuition, and past experience must be constantly leavened by judgment, insight, and faith in weighing policy for the future.

4. Leadership in a professional approach to industrial relations is vital not only to a successful corporation, but to the welfare and happiness of a nation now two hundred years old. Its practitioners are truly members of a strategic and demanding *learned profession*.

Definition of a "Learned Profession"

A profession is man-centered in two ways: (1) a profession demands practitioners who are free and responsible individuals and who, through their personal integrity, dedication, and courage, can be depended upon to establish and maintain their personal standards of performance; (2) a profession, no matter how technical the procedures it employs, demands that its practitioners be primarily motivated by service to their fellowmen.

22

A *learned* profession is a still more demanding occupation. Two further ingredients are required: (1) a learned profession requires years of preparation of the whole person and one's knowledge and skills; (2) a learned profession requires the learning approach throughout life as a means of fulfilling one's responsibility to one's fellowmen through the ready application of new knowledge.

The central attribute of a learned profession is thus *responsibility*, not for a segmented detail of a total problem, but for an effective solution of the total problem.

EMPLOYEE RELATIONS
AND LEGISLATIVE TRENDS

WILLIAM G. CAPLES

WILLIAM G. CAPLES is president emeritus of Kenyon College and is of counsel in the firm Vedder, Price, Kaufman and Kammholz. He was admitted to the Illinois bar in 1933 and practiced law in Chicago for five years. Beginning in 1938 he served as general attorney with Continental Casualty Company and later joined National Casualty Company as vice president. His next move was to Inland Steel Company as manager of industrial relations, where he subsequently became vice president. He also served as president and a director of Inland Steel Container Company. In 1968 Mr. Caples became president of Kenyon College.
From 1954 to 1961 he was vice president of the National Association of Manufacturers. He has also served as chairman of the Industrial Relations Committee of the American Iron and Steel Institute and on the board of directors of the American Arbitration Association. Mr. Caples has been a member of the National Advisory Committee on the Manpower Development and Training Act and of the President's Advisory Committee on Labor-Management Policy. He is a graduate of Kenyon College and Northwestern University School of Law.

It was a pleasure to be invited to this Fiftieth Anniversary celebration of Industrial Relations Counselors and to have the opportunity to look back over that period just past, for it happens to have covered approximately the same period as my working life. My first job was in June 1924, there being no problem at that time in the District of Columbia of restriction by child labor laws. The job was as a laborer for Ross-Thompson Construction Company, which is still operating, and I joined the Hodcarriers' and Laborers' Union, which still prospers, its members working at considerably higher hourly wages and for fringes that did not then exist. A labor contract was usually written on one sheet of paper, if there was any written contract at all.

I was interested then, as now, in how work is best accomplished, how work can be a fulfilling human achievement, how work is best organized, and how one betters the human condition in the work environment. To me this interest requires constant reexamination as theory and practice change. Let us take a look back then at what we have tried to do legislatively in this area of human endeavor.

In 1924 the great industrial complexes were approximately twenty-five years old. U.S. Steel had been put together in 1900. The automobile companies, many more in number, were becoming giants, as were the oil companies. The antitrust laws were relatively new, the last one then but twelve years old. Employer representation schemes had grown as a result of Mackenzie King's studies. Scientific management was evolving from Taylor's and the Gilbreths' works. There was no such thing as an industrial union—John Llewellyn Lewis was just beginning his rapid rise in the labor movement. The first workers' compensation law was only thirteen years old. Yellow dog contracts were not long outlawed. Mr. Gompers was the dominant power in the union movement, which was purely trade and craft, and he had established the base for bread-and-butter unionism and made the statement that what labor wanted was "more."

It was indeed a much simpler society and economy. With the exception of oil, it was primarily narrow, or at most national, in industry outlook, with no questioning of the limitations of anything —energy, land, water, food, or forest. The concepts for what was to come were then laid. The integration of the industrial process from raw-material source to delivery of the product to the ultimate consumer had begun, the outstanding examples being the oil, steel, automobile, electrical, rubber, and chemical industries. The concept of industrial unions had emerged but attempts to organize industries had ended in disastrous strikes and had not furthered this concept.

It is well to remember this history, as well as the history of the failures to sustain unionization in the manufacturing sector of the economy.

When I served as a public member of the Pay Board in Phase II of President Nixon's economic controls program, I was impressed that the union people on the board knew the history of their movement thoroughly and the background against which it evolved. Their judgments were made constantly against the long-term objectives of the union movement. I was equally surprised that management's representatives often did not know that history and, in many cases, the history of their own particular industry, although both are current histories, as time is measured. When I talked to some of them about it, they did not seem to think it mattered.

To review recent history matters a great deal, for looking backward is 20/20 vision and may lead us to correct the course in which we are moving. J. Douglas Brown's latest book, *The Industrial Relations Section of Princeton University in World War II*, vividly enforces my opinion in this regard.

In 1921 we had an agricultural depression in this country that is often forgotten because in spite of it, industrial growth was such that the GNP moved steadily upward until 1930. But the movement away from the land had begun, and mechanization and chemical use came on such a scale that the production figures of industry, impressive as they are, suffer by comparison. The migration to the cities accelerated with the Great Depression and the war economy that followed, and only now appears to have stopped. It is really one of history's great mass migrations, far greater in numbers of people than the number who came from Europe and Asia when the country was industrializing in the late 1800s and early 1900s and needed people in great numbers.

The Great Depression created problems with which no industrialized nation knew how to cope. Each in its own way tried to meet the problem of feeding parts of its population when jobs were not available to them and when, economically, they had become nonproductive. Great Britain experimented with aspects of socialism; Germany and Italy with state control; and so on. In the United States we tried through a variety of methods, almost entirely by legislation or law-created mechanisms, to seek solutions aimed at preserving a free society. It is to those solutions in the industrial or labor sector that I will address myself.

These are most of the main ones:

1926	The Railway Labor Act
1931	Davis-Bacon Act
1932	Norris-LaGuardia Act
1933	National Industrial Recovery Act (NIRA) (from a labor viewpoint, Sec. 7(a))
1935	Social Security Act
1935	National Labor Relations Act (Wagner Act)
1938	Fair Labor Standards Act (FLSA)
1947	Taft-Hartley Act
1963	Equal Pay Act
1964	The Civil Rights Act of 1964
1967	Age Discrimination in Employment Act
1970	Occupational Health and Safety Act (OSHA)

1974   Employee Retirement Income Security Act (ERISA)

1941 ⎫
1952 ⎬   Wage Controls—2 wars, 1 peacetime
1971 ⎭

The Railway Labor Act was created to codify what in effect had grown up in the railway industry, beginning in 1845, as a method of bargaining and thus an accommodation acceptable to both sides to "maintain agreements concerning rates of pay, rules and working conditions" and to give an employee due process under agreed procedures in matters covered by agreement. It also called for a fact-finding board and a cooling-off period before a strike could be legal. The theory behind this legislation was that railroad transportation was essential to the U.S. economy. The Act was designed therefore to meet the problems of a particular industry; it carefully spelled out the scope of bargaining, the craft or class of employees covered, and the procedures for administration. It also distinguished between different kinds of disputes and differences, "interest" and "rights," and the principles which underlay them. To quote a publication of the National Mediation Board: "These principles, methods and agencies, evolved through years of experimentation, provide a model labor relations policy, based on equal rights and mutual responsibilities." It worked well until an outsider, in this case the president of the United States, interfered. Air carriers were brought under the Act in 1936.

John Llewellyn Lewis, who was a man of considerable vision, conceived the idea that if the union movement was to expand in size and economic and political power, it would have to do so through industrial unions, a union for each major manufacturing industry, and the amalgamation of all crafts within that union. Expansion could not and would not come about through the American Federation of Labor. The concept is the opposite of the separate works councils in the British system, where the crafts remain separate. Lewis could not sell his idea to the other unions in the AF of L and ultimately took the United Mine Workers, which he headed, out of the Federation to form the Congress of Industrial Organizations (CIO).

In 1933, in the National Industrial Recovery Act (NIRA), an act designed to allow for codes of fair competition, or how to legally collude on prices, Lewis successfully pushed for insertion of what became Section 7a, which declared the policy of the United States to allow freedom of employees to organize. He exploited the section to the limit before the NIRA was declared unconstitutional.

The NIRA experience, the insecurity of the industrial worker,

27

and the continuing political pressure exerted by organized labor, which had a strong advocate and friend in Senator Wagner of New York, resulted in the law ultimately known as the Wagner Act. The Act was said to be modeled to a degree on the Railway Labor Act, to a degree on Section 7a of NIRA, and to a degree upon the naive notion that the "door be open to the boss's office so the worker could have entry to discuss his problems." It gave employees the free and protected right to organize, and defined the matters to be discussed as "wages, hours and conditions of employment." The National Labor Relations Board was created as the agency to oversee proper administration of the law.

It is interesting more than forty years later to see what these "wages, hours and conditions of employment" have become. One concept enunciated in the Act was that of the bargaining unit; a second, the scope of the unit. Neither, however, was debated as a part of legislative intent. There are countless other concepts that have been adopted in the same way. Conditions of employment, for example, have become a variety of work rules, pay, hours, and fringes defined in book-length contracts, which now, by administrative and court decision, have become the statute law of industrial establishments, with enforcement generally subject to review by arbitration.

I am not trying to imply that any or all of this is necessarily good or bad. My main thesis is that when a legislature tries to cure social illness by passing a law—in effect, *a decree of cure*—without carefully defining the extent of the jurisdiction and the procedural rules by which it will be administered, the result is at best unpredictable and sometimes surprising, particularly if one reads the legislative debates and statements of intent as predictive.

The Fair Labor Standards Act was designed as a depression device to spread work, the theory being that if an employer were forced to pay a premium to workers for work over forty hours in a workweek, more people would be hired to work at the regular rate. I know of no case or cases where this happened. I do know that we have premium pay for hours over six or seven in a day, premium pay on Saturdays and Sundays, and a variety of other variations. What has been determined is a "normal" workweek. The economics of the minimum wage I leave to the economists, with the caveat that there must be some minimum to protect against exploitation. However, the figure is otherwise speculative.

The Davis-Bacon Act was designed to raise construction wages by means of what is in effect a federal standard, though it was established locally.

Wage controls have now been tried three times: World War II, the Korean War, and in 1971-72. The different economic backgrounds of the control periods are interesting. In World War II and the Korean War, we had shortages of goods and productive capacity for civilian consumption but plenty of market. In Phase II, we had an excess of goods and production, and an insufficiency of market. In no case is the evidence persuasive that we know much about controlling wages, but it is quite persuasive that a rational pay system and method is desirable at any time, and particularly in time of controls.

The National Labor Relations Act, as now amended, has become in forty years the base for a fairly predictable body of law supplemented by the law of the workplace as determined by arbitration decisions which, too, are fairly predictable. But beginning in 1963 with the Equal Pay Act, employee relations and labor trends took on new dimensions, which have been expanded with Title VII of the Civil Rights Act, Executive Order 11246, the Age Discrimination in Employment Act, the Occupational Safety and Health Act (OSHA), the Vocational Rehabilitation Act, the Vietnam Era Veterans' Readjustment Act, and the Employee Retirement Income Security Act. We now have come to the point where employment relationships are determined by statute, and the union-management relationship of collective bargaining is diminishing as the major determining factor. Union-management decisions, jointly or separately, cannot be made without consideration of the government as a partner or, in some cases, as the sole determinant of rules or course of action.

The law, of course, is very unsettled in regard to all the new areas—EEO, OSHA, ERISA, equal pay, age, and disability. It is probably fair to say that unions, management, and the numerous administrative agencies with their overlapping jurisdictions are equally unsettled and unsure. In fact, all seem to be groping toward a solution or solutions which, I predict, will again be far from what was anticipated in the period shortly before and at the time of the enabling legislation.

Industrial unionism in the late 1930s started to bring to the attention and consciousness of many the gross inequities that existed between the rights and privileges of whites and those of other skin color. This awareness was accelerated by World War II, when our nonwhite citizens were called upon for the same commitment to country as whites. At this time many first pledged themselves to remedy that condition and to insure there was in fact equal opportunity for all in our society. I was one, and I know it was not an easy road. For instance in Illinois, in endeavoring to have a Fair Employment Practices Act enacted, only two businessmen could be found who were willing

29

to testify: Charles Percy, then president of Bell and Howell and now a U.S. Senator, and myself. There are now forty-nine state fair employment practices laws.

Many believed, among them President Lyndon Johnson, that the first answer to discrimination was a federal law giving equal employment opportunity without regard to race, religion, or national origin. In the debate in the House on what ultimately became the Civil Rights Act of 1964, a congressman from northern Virginia, in a sense of ridicule, added the word "sex" to race, color, creed, and national origin, hoping to confuse the issue and defeat the measure. This insertion added a whole new dimension to the world of employment to the degree that sex-discrimination cases, including those under the Equal Pay Act, now are the majority of EEO cases. If I were still in academe I could, from this, draw "Caples Law," which is that the results of legislation written or amended on the floor are neither foreseeable nor predictable.

The state of the law today regarding equality of opportunity can, in my view, be well summarized as follows: Good intentions are not enough in the field of equal employment opportunity. Many laws, regulations, and other legal restrictions exist to safeguard the employment rights of minorities and women. These laws can be easily violated by employers with the best of intentions. Such violations, whether willful or not, can have severe and far-reaching consequences for the operation of any company, in terms of both money damages and future ability of management to structure its own hiring and employment practices.

For the foreseeable future we shall be concerned in all employee relations matters, whether employees are organized or unorganized, exempt or nonexempt, professionally licensed or unlicensed, with a series of standards (still in the process of formulation) and record-keeping systems that, for the record, will establish compliance with the standards.

To give a few examples:

1. In hiring we must be sure our advertisements do not indicate any preference for, or limitation on, race, color, sex, or national origin, and in some cases age. Certain language is prohibited or specified by federal and state laws.

2. Title VII of the Civil Rights Act does not require an employer to give preference to any individual or group because of race, color, religion, sex, or national origin; it in fact prohibits such treatment. Thus, an employer has no legal obligation to hire a member of a minority group who is less qualified than another applicant. But if dis-

crimination has produced an imbalance of persons of any race, sex, etc., quotas or preferential treatment can be ordered to remove the imbalance.

3. A variety of devices must be used to increase recruitment of minority groups.

4. The employment of "qualified handicapped individuals" by government contractors is a new dimension.

5. The question must be resolved of what, if any, preemployment inquiries can be made and, if so, what is the job relationship to the inquiry. This will require the formulation of hiring standards that are reasonable, objective, and uniform. (Here I believe the most difficult problems will be formulations that do not discriminate against females with respect to marriage, pregnancy and motherhood.)

6. The utilization of tests as a method for screening job applicants and for determining employee promotion qualifications is a well-established employer practice. Because the results of these tests may significantly affect management's decision to hire a job applicant or approve an employee's promotion, and since the testing, grading, and interpretation of test results is entirely under the control of the employer, it is important that all elements of testing that have a disparate effect on persons of a given race, color, religion, sex, or national origin be eliminated. Title VII specifically recognizes the usefulness of testing, but from 1964 there is a tortuous administrative and judicial trail which leaves what is legal testing much in doubt. In August 1972 the Equal Employment Opportunity Coordinating Council (EEOCC), made up of EEOC, OFCC, the Civil Service Commission, the Civil Rights Commission, and the Department of Justice, announced its intention to issue new joint federal regulations under Title VII and Executive Order 11246 to replace the existing Guidelines on Employee Selection Procedures. To date the new guidelines have not been issued and the guidelines of 1970 remain in effect. Thus, the problem remains largely unanswered. What we do know is negative. But the problem, including the validation of tests, is an interesting challenge and is having great impact on hiring, placement, and progression.

I could go on giving examples through plant rules, scheduling work, seniority and layoff, fringes, employment conditions, equal pay, recordkeeping, reporting and communicating in general, safety, and health, but I will stop here.

The conclusions which I draw and think are valid are:

First, this is a time to reexamine and think through personnel policies, programs, and procedures, and to know why we do what we do.

Second, it is a time in which there must be in organized plants a type of cooperation between union and management that is a far different behavior pattern from the adversary roles of the past. I need not dwell on the difficulty of changing habit patterns that are long-established and comfortable for the parties.

Third, no longer can one person be the complete industrial relations expert. The need was never greater for a high degree of cooperation between the industrial relations expert and the specialists needed to supplement his basic discipline, whether it be formal industrial relations training, industrial engineering, psychology, statistics, safety, chemistry, physics, health care services, law or any other, including work experience and common sense.

If there is neither a major military conflict nor an economic depression, the next ten to twenty years will be ones of continuing change as the new triple function of union-management-government develops and changes the dual union-management relationship that has basically shaped industrial relations in the last half century.

There is a Chinese saying which, I suspect, may be a curse, "May you live in interesting times." The immediate future in industrial relations will be "interesting times."

THE EVOLVING COLLECTIVE BARGAINING STRUCTURE

ROY B. HELFGOTT

ROY B. HELFGOTT joined IRC in 1960. He served with the United Nations from 1966 to 1967, rejoining IRC in 1968 as director of economic research. He is chairman, Department of Organizational and Social Sciences, New Jersey Institute of Technology. He was a senior Fulbright Scholar; a member of the United States delegation to the Conference on Human Relations in Industry, European Productivity Agency, Rome, Italy (1956); and a fellow, Inter-University Institute in Social Gerontology, Berkeley, California. He served as research direc-tor, New York Cloak Joint Board, International Ladies' Garment Workers' Union from 1949 to 1957, was an industrial relations analyst with the Wage Stabiliza-tion Board in 1952, and an economist with the New York Metropolitan Region Study from 1957 to 1958. He was adjunct associate professor, the City Univer-sity, New York, and assistant professor economics, the Pennsylvania State Uni-versity. He is co-author of Management, Automation, and People *and author of* Labor Economics. *He is a graduate of City College, New York, and received M.A. and Ph.D. degrees from Columbia University and the New School for Social Research, respectively.*

The structure of collective bargaining in the United States is quite diverse. Labor and management in each bargaining relationship utilize the type of structure that best suits their needs—craft or industrial, local, regional, national, or variations of any of these.* Once estab-lished, however, collective bargaining relationships are not easily or quickly changed, for this requires the consent of both parties. Only as the circumstances in which they operate change, do the parties seek, or are forced, to alter existing collective bargaining structures.

---

*We are, of course, discussing the actual negotiating units, not the so-called "ap-propriate bargaining units" as determined by the National Labor Relations Board, which are really election districts.

THE TYPICAL BARGAINING STRUCTURE

There is a tendency to think of the individual plant as the prevalent form of bargaining structure, but only a minority of workers under collective bargaining today are covered by this type of bargaining. And, except for some industries such as chemicals, it is declining.

The typical bargaining unit is large, covering one thousand or more employees.[1] In manufacturing, it is multiplant though not multiemployer.[2] Multiemployer units are typical of nonmanufacturing, where two-thirds of the agreements involve more than one firm. Certain issues, however, generally noneconomic, are subject to local plant or separate craft bargaining, even where multiplant or multicraft bargaining exists. The master agreement covering broad economic issues is supplemented by separate subsidiary agreements on plant or craft working conditions and the like. Thus, it appears we are evolving a dual structure of collective bargaining.

TREND TOWARD CENTRALIZATION

Although decentralization is at present one of the most significant characteristics of the American collective bargaining system, the trend is toward greater centralization—a change from plant to company-wide bargaining, from individual to multiemployer, from craft to multicraft, and from local to regional or national. This trend is not new—it has been going on for some time—nor does it ultimately mean a uniform pattern for all. Moreover, there are counterforces that tend to slow the movement. Overall, however, the impact of techno-economic factors and the influence of public policy are spurring both managements and unions to exercise preferences for greater centralization.

Impact of Techno-Economic Factors

To begin with, the very nature of industrial organization promotes centralization, largely because of the economies of scale made possible by technological advance. As a result of these economies the business unit has grown, and since the union attempts to parallel the employer organization, the bargaining unit also grows. As mergers and vertical and horizontal expansion of companies continue, further widening of bargaining units is encouraged.

According to the Commons-Perlman theory of union behavior,[3]

---

[1] Only 20 percent of the workers covered are in units of less than five hundred.

[2] In manufacturing, only one-fifth of the units are multiemployer, and even these tend to be multiplant.

[3] Selig Perlman, *A Theory of the Labor Movement* (New York: Augustus M. Kelley, 1949).

which to me is an accurate description, the aim of American unionism has been to take labor out of competition. Techno-economic developments often necessitate the expansion of existing bargaining units in order to achieve that goal. For example, technological advances in transportation and communication have made possible the spread of product markets from local to regional and national, and unions, in order to maintain competitive control over labor, have had to seek wider bargaining units. This has already occurred in such industries as trucking and baking.

Often the spread of product markets also leads to greater economic concentration and inevitably greater centralization of bargaining. To illustrate, forty years ago brewing was a local market industry and there were 750 beer companies. But in time the product market widened to a broad region, and the number of brewers is now down to seventy. Now that market is in the process of becoming national, and the prediction is that within a few years it will be dominated by only eight major companies. In terms of collective bargaining, do not be surprised if eventually there is one national brewing agreement.

Such forces operate to widen bargaining units even in industries that remain highly competitive. An excellent example is the women's garment industry. Here it is the relevant competitive labor market, the area in which garments are competitively produced, rather than the product market per se that has widened.

Originally design, selling, and manufacturing of garments all took place within a concentrated area, in particular Manhattan's garment center. Collective bargaining took place, therefore, between the International Ladies' Garment Workers' Union (ILGWU) joint board (composed of a number of occupational locals) and the association(s) of Manhattan manufacturers of that product. With the rise of the motor vehicle, production spread to Brooklyn and New Jersey, and it was the metropolitan area that became the bargaining unit. Later, with the spread of the highway system and increases in truck speed, production moved further from the center to Pennsylvania and Massachusetts, and collective bargaining units became regional.

Today the garment industry is headed toward still wider bargaining units. Garments are now being produced competitively all over the country, particularly in the South. Recent years have seen the emergence of a few large national firms and also a blurring of traditional differences among products. Sportswear, for example, now substitutes for dresses and suits. Thus, garment industry bargaining units are spreading geographically, to deal with interregional competition, and industrially, to deal with the rise of substitute products.[4]

With the standardized products and mass production techniques that modern technology makes possible, some industries, such as automobiles, are vertically integrated. Multiplant companies in industries with integrated production systems prefer centralized bargaining because they cannot afford local strikes that can shut down all operations. (Industries with product diversification tend not to be vertically integrated and can stick to plantwide bargaining, such as chemicals. Even when the product is standardized but each production unit is independent, bargaining can be kept local if management so desires, as is the case in the petroleum industry.)

New technology also sometimes wipes out existing union jurisdictions or dilutes skills and thus necessitates wider bargaining units. This has happened in printing and publishing and with the railroads.

Management and Union Preferences

Aside from technological and economic developments, there are many other agents of change. In some cases the major force stems from management decisions and initiatives. Employers who bargain separately with a given union may decide that it is preferable to bargain together in order to avoid whipsawing. Where benefit plans are companywide, employers often insist that bargaining on these subjects be on a companywide basis, even when wage bargaining remains local. Employers in small-scale industries generally prefer to bargain through employer associations in order to counter union power and to standardize labor conditions. This is especially important where labor costs are a high proportion of total costs, and it is facilitated where firms are near one another. Sometimes, as has occurred with the New York newspapers and the railroad firemen, the force for change is simply the breakdown of existing bargaining processes. In those industries the breakdown of existing processes obviously can be linked to techno-economic developments.

More often union desires and initiatives are influential. Where unions perceive a centralization of labor relations policies in some multiplant companies, they may decide that the only way to get to the real decision-makers is to negotiate directly with headquarters on a companywide basis. Or a change in union structure may prompt a desire to change the structure of bargaining. There has been a trend

---

[4]Product substitutability also leads to union mergers in some cases, as, for example, between the aluminum workers and Steelworkers. The Oil, Chemical and Atomic Workers (OCAW) rose out of the merger of the old Oil Workers and the United Gas, Coke and Chemical Workers.

to mergers among unions, spurred by the fact that small ones are finding it difficult to survive financially because they cannot enjoy administrative economies of scale. The merger of the Steelworkers and the Mine, Mill, and Smelter Workers led, in 1967, to greater centralization of bargaining structures in nonferrous metals. Similarly, the merger of the Packinghouse Workers and the Amalgamated Meat Cutters further facilitated companywide bargaining in meatpacking.

How successful unions are in forcing employers into adoption of new structures depends, of course, upon their strength vis-à-vis the employer. The entrance of the Steelworkers into the chemical industry, as a result of a merger with District 50, led to a new attempt to achieve companywide bargaining in that industry, which so far has met with only limited success. Similarly, the Oil, Chemical and Atomic Workers (OCAW), despite continued efforts, has been unable to achieve centralized bargaining in the petroleum industry. In other industries, however, the unions have been successful in forcing centralized bargaining. Examples are first the regional and then the national bargaining achieved in trucking, and the systemwide bargaining now practiced between the Communications Workers (CWA) and the Bell System.

Wider bargaining units have also resulted from coordinated bargaining, as in electrical manufacturing. Where a company formerly negotiated with each union separately, it now, in effect, deals with them as a group. The union motivation for forcing coordinated bargaining was to overcome the problem of multiunionism and to reverse the shift in relative bargaining power of the parties.

International developments may be pushing toward collective bargaining structures that go beyond national boundaries. There have been sporadic attempts by unions to force some multinational companies to bargain on a global scale. While some coordination of bargaining is a possibility in the European Economic Community, my own research in this field leads me to conclude that transnational bargaining is not likely to occur, certainly not on a worldwide basis, by 1985.

Resistance to Broader Units

Despite the constellation of forces pushing toward greater centralization of bargaining, there are counterforces tending to slow the movement, and they emanate from within the ranks of both labor and management.

One is the desire of the rank-and-file union member to have a voice in decision-making concerning the terms of a collective bargaining agreement. The larger the unit, the harder for the individual union member to influence the content of bargaining. Similarly, individual employers often resist multiemployer bargaining, fearing they will lose control over their own destinies if they bargain as part of a group of employers. The NLRB policies of requiring consent of both parties to change and of allowing withdrawals from multiemployer groups by both unions and employers also facilitate resistance to wider units.

The emergence of local issues, which have become more important relative to national economic ones, is another factor that operates against wider bargaining units. Even where centralized bargaining takes place, special agreements must be reached over local issues. The wider the unit, however, the more local plant working condition issues tend to be submerged and lost in the shuffle of reaching agreement on the broad economic package.

Craftsmen in industrial unions, who are the minority within these groups, frequently oppose centralization, believing that their interests are being subordinated to those of the majority of semiskilled workers. Their discontent with the erosion of differentials between the skilled and unskilled continues to threaten existing bargaining structures. Only recently, for example, the craftsmen in the rubber industry attempted to break away and form a separate bargaining unit of their own. In the automobile industry the UAW has tried to assuage the craftsmen's threats to seek a separate bargaining unit by giving them veto power over the agreements to be reached with the companies in 1976 negotiations.

Finally, regional differences may slow centralization. The West Coast paper workers, for example, split off from the existing unions to form their own union in 1964. Although this did not significantly alter existing bargaining structures, it illustrates a case in which differences prevented the establishment of wider bargaining units.

Dangers from Centralization

In many ways the movement toward greater centralization of bargaining structures presents dangers or at least problems for labor, management, and government:

1. With wider units, a breakdown in negotiations automatically leads to larger strikes, and possible tie-ups of an entire company or industry. Thus, there is increased danger of emergency disputes, which, in turn, could bring about further government intervention in labor-management relations.

2. For the individual firm, multiemployer bargaining implies loss of freedom in labor relations. Since groups tend to be more cau-

tious and tradition-bound, this could mean, for society, less innovation in labor-management relations. Formal employer associations, moreover, sometimes become more interested in their own institutional survival than in the well-being of their members.

3. Multiemployer bargaining can also result in a squeezing of marginal firms, as all are locked into a standard wage/benefit package regardless of differences in demand for their products, in their productivity, and in their profits. The demise of some firms increases the danger of further economic concentration within an industry.

4. Similarly, disputes may arise over issues that are not germane to a particular firm but lead anyway to a shutdown of its facilities. This happened in the famous steel dispute of 1960 over Clause 2B, which had no relevance to some of the companies involved in the bargaining. The very recent New York City building service employees strike lasted longer than had been expected because the owners of rent-controlled buildings could not afford the same agreement as the other landlords. (At one time there were separate wage scales for different types of buildings, but they were all combined into one, thus increasing the possibility of disputes over issues not pertinent to some of the landlords.)

5. Greater bargaining centralization dilutes communication with the plant level and, as the hammering out of a national economic agreement proceeds, may foster disregard for plant-level issues. In the case of multicraft bargaining, items of importance to a single craft may be ignored. For management this often creates acrimonious labor relations at the operating level, bad morale, and poor productivity; for unions it can lead to a revolt of the locals, the formation of opposition groups, and general internal turmoil. Experience along these lines is already well known.

CENTRALIZATION IN
THE CONSTRUCTION INDUSTRY

Construction offers an excellent example of a very competitive industry in the process of significant change in bargaining structure. Historically it has had highly decentralized bargaining structures, basically local labor market bargaining between individual craft union locals and various contractor associations. But now, notwithstanding the clamor over President Ford's veto of the common situs picketing bill, which was tied in with structural reform, the industry is heading toward multicraft, regional, and even national bargaining on economic issues. Indeed, benefit bargaining is already more centralized than wage negotiations.

Among the major developments fostering more centralized bargaining are (1) the rise of national contractors, with heavy capital investment, which has resulted in national agreements between them and the national unions, and (2) the desire of employers to reduce whipsawing as each craft tries to outdo the other in negotiations. Another factor is the desire to deal with jurisdictional disputes (which have always been endemic to the industry), particularly as new technology creates new job classifications and blurs existing demarcations between crafts.

The construction unions, for their part, have their own motivations for favoring reform of the bargaining structure. With the skyrocketing wage rates that result from the present system of individual craft bargaining, the unions, particularly national headquarters, are seeking some device to restrain wage rates in order to prevent further growth of nonunion competition.[5]

Transportation developments are another factor pushing for greater bargaining structure centralization. The craft unit has tended to be coextensive with the relevant labor market, but virtual universal automobile ownership has seen the spread of the labor market over a wider area.

Unlike the locals, which try to outdo each other in negotiations regardless of the consequences, the national unions can cope better with economic realities. However, the locals too want to reduce the rivalries among themselves that so often lead to leapfrogging settlements and ultimately reduce job opportunities. For this reason we are witnessing the creation of more craft councils to act on a unified basis in negotiations, and on the employer side, more coordination among contractor associations, with support from large customers, as has occurred in the Dallas-Fort Worth area.

A final important factor in the movement to wider bargaining units in construction has been government intervention to stop wage escalation. This was evidenced in the special stabilization program and, when that came to an end, the attempt to directly legislate new bargaining structures. It is to this last factor—public policy—that I want to turn my attention in concluding this discussion of the forces operating on collective bargaining structures.

PUBLIC POLICY

Public policy has always had an impact on the structure of collective bargaining. As Arnold Weber points out, the NLRB policy of

---

[5]Up from 20 percent of construction to 50 percent in the last seven years.

the 1930s of certifying plantwide units paved the way for company-wide and marketwide bargaining.[6] NLRB policy, in fact, continues not to favor decentralization.[7] By 1985 new public policy will be pushing the structure of collective bargaining further toward centralization but without being designed to do so.

Daniel Bell, in his most recent book, identifies better management of the "public household" as a major need in the coming period. Underlying inflation is "a basic change in the character of society which makes it difficult for any polity to use the traditional modes of restraint or 'discipline' . . . to hold down demand, to increase unemployment, or to reduce government expenditures."[8] Attempts will be made, therefore, to establish rules to govern the public household and to reduce unemployment without incurring high rates of inflation. These attempts will include, whether it works or not, renewed movement toward "incomes policy," regardless of ideology or of which party is in office. The Democrats may be more inclined to intervene in order to restore full employment, while the Republicans will do so in order to hold down inflation, but the net result will inevitably impact on the structure of collective bargaining.[9]

Experience elsewhere has shown that a highly centralized union movement and bargaining structure facilitate incomes policy because consideration of the wider ramifications of wage policy becomes easier.

In Sweden centralized bargaining in the private sector has amounted to a privately operated incomes policy. In the Netherlands centralized bargaining has resulted from an incomes policy.[10]

Events in the United States tend to confirm this experience. By treating claims on a consolidated basis for a firm or industry, the War Labor Board during World War II fostered companywide bargaining in meatpacking and multiemployer bargaining in steel. This was in-

---

[6] Arnold R. Weber, "Stability and Change in the Structure of Collective Bargaining," in *Challenges to Collective Bargaining* (Englewood Cliffs: Prentice-Hall, 1967), p. 20.

[7] This was shown in the recent decision to bar a separate unit for the skilled workers in the rubber industry.

[8] Daniel Bell, *The Cultural Contradictions of Capitalism* (New York: Basic Books, 1976), p. 239.

[9] The Humphrey-Hawkins bill, HR 50, is probably indicative of what lies ahead, and even though incomes policy has been deleted from its current version in deference to the AFL-CIO, it will undoubtedly come back if there is any serious attempt to implement the proposed legislation.

[10] Lloyd Ulman and Robert J. Flanagan, *Wage Restraint: A Study of Incomes Policies in Western Europe* (Berkeley and Los Angeles: University of California Press, 1971), pp. 234-235.

evitable, for, as George Taylor pointed out, when national wage policy is developed, it is applied on a formula instead of on a case-by-case basis, and this is the very nature of national planning.[11]

We discovered during World War II price controls that it was much easier to control concentrated industries than highly competitive ones. Under President Nixon's New Economic Policy, we actually had different price control requirements for firms of different sizes, with the most stringent for the large ones. Similarly, it is easier to control wage settlements in large bargaining units than in small ones, as the experience under the Kennedy/Johnson wage/price guideposts showed.

Construction is the perfect example of this trend in public policy. The whole movement toward greater centralization of bargaining has been promoted by government, particularly under the leadership of John Dunlop, from the stabilization program through legislation that was specifically designed toward that end. It has been asserted that Dunlop also targeted the cement and supermarket industries for restructuring toward wider bargaining units,[12] and the Joint Labor-Management Committee operating in food retailing is moving in that direction.

Thus, in addition to the other forces pushing toward centralization, public policy pressures to ameliorate inflation while pursuing high employment will force greater centralization of bargaining on economic issues, while other issues will be left to continued decentralized bargaining.

---

[11] Arnold R. Weber, editor, *The Structure of Collective Bargaining* (Glencoe: The Free Press, 1961), pp. 195-196.

[12] Herbert R. Northrup, "Reflections on Bargaining Structure Change," *Proceedings of the Industrial Relations Research Association*, 1973, pp. 142-143.

A POSITIVE MANAGEMENT-EMPLOYEE RELATIONS SYSTEM

WALTON E. BURDICK

WALTON E. BURDICK is vice president, personnel plans and programs, at International Business Machines Corporation. He joined the company in 1955. He subsequently held personnel and personnel management positions in Endicott, New York; Dayton, New Jersey; New York City; and Greencastle, Indiana. In 1962 he became administrative assistant to the IBM director of personnel, corporate headquarters; and in subsequent years was manager of personnel planning, manager of personnel programs and services, and director of personnel relations, corporate headquarters; director of personnel, IBM World Trade Corporation; and Data Processing Group director of personnel. He became IBM director of personnel plans and programs in November 1970 and was elected a vice president in June 1972. Mr. Burdick holds a B.S. degree in industrial and labor relations from Cornell University. He is a member of the Advisory Council of Management and Personnel of the Conference Board, the board of trustees of the National Manpower Institute, and the Commerce and Industry Council of the National Urban League, Inc.

The essence of IBM's employee relations philosophy is to work on the basics. There are regrettably no secrets about the company's employee relations program. The emphasis is on requiring managers to understand the company philosophy and the company's principles and programs, and to apply policies and programs appropriately and equitably to all employees. The standards set for management performance make clear to all the importance of employee relations in IBM.

THE EMPLOYEE RELATIONS APPROACH

The approach to employee relations at IBM consists of five basic elements: (1) philosophy, (2) principles and policies, (3) capable management, (4) professional personnel management, and (5) diligent application of effort.

Philosophy

There must be a commitment to philosophical beliefs regarding the treatment of people. Researchers at Harvard who have studied the evolution and status of nonunion companies report that typically the philosophies of such companies result from the beliefs of the founders. The founder of IBM, Thomas J. Watson, Sr., had strong philosophical beliefs based on respect for the dignity of the individual. From this flows most of the other beliefs, philosophies, and principles of the company's employee relations approach. The Harvard researchers also report that after the passing of the founders, professional management becomes doctrinaire in its commitment to the same philosophies and beliefs, and this is the case in IBM.

Principles and Policies

Principles must be consistent with philosophical beliefs, must flow from those beliefs, and must be the vehicles through which beliefs and philosophies are promulgated to the organization.

Capable Management

Management must be well informed so that communications with employees can be open, thorough, and regular. Management must be sensitive and responsive to employee needs, issues, and complaints and have sufficient authority to resolve employee problems. Management must be well disciplined to implement corporate policies and practices consistently.

Professional Personnel Management

Personnel management must have all the qualifications and characteristics necessary for success in any organization. However, in the nonunion setting, personnel management must be especially influential—influential enough to cause programs or practices to be undertaken in the corporation and, perhaps more important, influential enough to prevent action from being taken that might be detrimental to the company's employee relations posture.

Diligent Application of Effort

At IBM, effort is needed for the training of managers so that they execute and apply the policies, principles, and beliefs uniformly and equitably.

PRINCIPLES UNDERLYING
EMPLOYEE RELATIONS PROGRAMS

The basic principles on which the various IBM employee relations programs are based can be grouped into seven categories: (1) individualism, (2) competitive incentives, (3) communication, or appeal, channels, (4) open communication, (5) egalitarian environment, (6) quality management, and (7) social responsibility.

Individualism

The first and perhaps most important principle in guiding IBM policy development and management is individualism—that is, an individual approach to employees. IBM holds managers responsible for the management of individuals, not only in terms of the mission of the department but also for all personnel aspects associated with an employee.

Participation in the performance plan is an individual process. And the merit pay concept rewards individual performance, achievement, and contribution. The entire awards program, in fact, is highly individual, ranging from innovation awards and outstanding contribution awards down to instant individual recognition with a dinner, a night on the town, or a sincere thank-you.

Interest in the individual goes much further than just the employee, extending to his or her family. Because of IBM's family picnics and Christmas parties and because employees' children compete for company-supported Watson Scholarships and Watson Trophies, many people think that the company approach is paternalistic. I suggest that the approach is an extension of the company's concern for the individual.

Company action in times of crisis is, perhaps, the best reflection of IBM's concept of individualism. For example, if the company learns that an employee or member of an employee's family was a passenger on a plane that has crashed, it will provide whatever assistance it can. In the event of an international disaster, such as an earthquake, the company will aid the country and the affected community or village as well as discharge its human relations responsibility to any employees in the area—locating employees, assisting them with housing, feeding their families, and so forth.

Competitive Incentives

A second principle underlying IBM's employee relations approach is the concept of competitive incentives. Incentives can, of course, be economic, the most common being compensation plans, merit pay, and benefits. In addition, IBM has established several programs—special care for children, adoption assistance, nondeductible dental coverage, orthodonture coverage, total and permanent disability coverage, military service benefits—most of which are unique.

Noneconomic competitive incentives are possibly even more important. IBM's promotion-from-within policy has created motivation and incentive within the company for decades. The job development program takes account of the structure of jobs and the degree of satisfaction employees receive from their jobs. The concept of job development can be traced to Thomas Watson, Sr., and his concern during World War II about production workers and the expansion of their jobs to include the setting-up of production equipment, the calibration of the equipment, and the inspection process. Today managers are trained in the principle of job development, job enlargement, and the application of those principles.

IBM is still experimenting in this area. The Austin, Texas, plant has experience with the one-person-one-machine concept. The facilities in Amsterdam and Berlin are experimenting with minilines. There have been problems, of course, but job development and job satisfaction are areas of continuing concern and interest.

Another important noneconomic incentive considered by IBM (and some may argue that it really is economic) is full employment. The training and retraining of people and the transfer of people from surplus areas to areas where skills are needed is a major rebalancing program. The company's use of banked employee vacation in order to balance manpower with work load was quite effective in the past. And the use of the special early retirement program has been effective in continuing full employment in the 1970s.

Leadership in the management of personal information is another example of a noneconomic incentive. Of course, it could be concluded that a company such as IBM would be concerned about the management of personal information because of the nature of its business, but our concern is a natural extension of a concern and respect for the individual. A real attempt is made to acquaint the individual with the nature of the information collected about him or her, why it has been collected, how it is disseminated, and to whom it is available.

Communication, or Appeal, Channels

The next principle is that of internal appeal, or communication, channels. Many companies have internal communications systems similar to IBM's: quick turnaround, impartial investigation, anonymity when required, no retribution, a check-and-balance system, and good promulgation. But there are few organizations that pursue internal appeal systems with enough discipline. The use of the open-door program, the responsiveness to employee appeals coming through the open door, the responsiveness to questions and complaints coming through IBM's "speak up" program all contribute toward the company's success. The employee opinion surveys that IBM conducts and uses as guidelines are also valuable communication vehicles.

Open Communications

The next principle also concerns communication, specifically open communication. IBM has not only those communications programs that are traditional in industry—house organs, video, and so on—but also several singular ways of maintaining open communication: manager-employee meetings four times a year, skip-level interviews, and executive interviews.

Egalitarian Environment

The fifth principle behind IBM's employee relations approach is the maintenance of an egalitarian environment. The company attempts to treat all groups similarly. For example, the chairman of the board and the "lowest skilled employee" enjoy precisely the same benefits program. All employees are on salary, and the absence of hourly employees avoids a class distinction. Offices are generally functional; they are, in fact, rather spartan. And, lastly, wherever appropriate, perquisites are avoided.

Quality of Management and Personnel Function

A sixth principle is the quality of management and of the personnel function. Managing in IBM's setting is a difficult job. Administering a merit pay plan, for example, is challenging; administering a fixed-rate plan is simple. Therefore IBM continually attempts to train managers on a centralized basis. Emphasis is on subject matter, and there are training modules to assure consistency and high standards.

The nature of IBM's business and the setting in which it operates require that the personnel function be influential. In addition, it must maintain a difficult role in its management approach—a pure, classical, traditional staff role. Personnel does not become directly involved in the management of people but only in the training of managers to better manage people and in giving advice and counsel to managers.

Social Responsibility

Only recently has a seventh principle been included in the employee relations area—the principle of social responsibility, which is difficult to define. I think social responsibility is important by itself and that it is an obligation of the company. From a personnel point of view, the activities in which the company engages reflect social responsibility and contribute a great deal to the pride employees feel for, and their identity with, the company.

The two programs that have been most successful in terms of the company's social responsibility are consistent with the company's beliefs. Under the social leave program more than four hundred IBM employees in this country have been "loaned" to worthwhile social projects during the decade 1965-75. The company feels it is contributing to society its most valued product, its people. The other highly successful program is the Community Service Fund, which motivates employees to become involved in organizations and in projects within those organizations and provides monetary contributions through those employees.

CONCLUSION

I believe these seven principles that have guided IBM's employee relations approach in the past are sufficient to guide the company in the future. It is clear, however, that the important element in the management approach at IBM is the first-line manager — the manager who is interfacing with each individual employee. In any organization, employee interests or concerns can emerge from the employee directly, through a third-party representative, or as a result of the initiative of management. Initiating through management is the IBM system, and that is the system the company attempts to earn the right to preserve.

NATIONAL
MANPOWER STRATEGIES

CHARLES A. MYERS

CHARLES A. MYERS is Sloan Fellows Professor of Management and director of the Industrial Relations Section at the Massachusetts Institute of Technology's Sloan School of Management. From 1949 to 1964, he was professor of industrial relations in the Department of Economics at M.I.T. He is a member of the National Manpower Policy Task Force and served as chairman from 1969 to 1971. From 1960 to 1962 he was a public member of the Presidential Railroad Commission. He was a member of the Committee on Labor Market Research; the Social Science Research Council, New York; and served as technical advisor to the Special Policy Committee on Collective Bargaining, the Committee for Economic Development, New York. He is a fellow of the American Academy of Arts and Sciences, is a charter member of the National Academy of Arbitrators, and is a member of the Industrial Relations Research Association. His most recent publications include Industrialism and Man Reconsidered *(with Clark Kerr, John T. Dunlop, and Frederick H. Harbison);* Personnel Administration *(with Paul Pigors), 7th edition;* Management of Human Resources *(with Paul Pigors and F. T. Malm), 3d edition; and* The Role of the Private Sector in Manpower Development. *He is a graduate of the Pennsylvania State University (A.B.) and the University of Chicago (Ph.D.).*

Since 1962 federal funds have been allocated for training people who are unemployed and have labor market disadvantages associated with poor education, lack of regular employment experience, minority status, and related characteristics. How have these programs operated over the years? Have they helped people find jobs? What about public service employment? How are employee relations managers and other managers affected by the programs? What are the prospects for the future?

I hope to cover some of these questions by focusing on (1) experience under the Manpower Development and Training Act of 1962 (MDTA); (2) the first public service employment program in the

Emergency Employment Act of 1971 (EEA); (3) dissatisfaction with earlier programs that led to the bipartisan passage of the Comprehensive Employment and Training Act of 1971 (CETA); and (4) preliminary experience under CETA, particularly as seen from the study of Eastern Massachusetts areas now underway in the Industrial Relations Section at M.I.T. I should note that the term "manpower" was supplanted in 1975 when the U. S. Department of Labor changed the name of the Manpower Administration to Employment and Training Administration.

Much of what I have to say is drawn from my participation in the National Manpower Policy Task Force, an advisory group in Washington of which I was chairman during 1971-73 and still remain a member. This group also was recently renamed the National Council on Employment and Training. Over the years it has issued a number of position papers, and it had a role in the development of the CETA approach.

The significance of the training programs, especially CETA, for employee relations managers and others in management is that they are funded by federal taxes and are operating in states, counties, and cities where firms are located—they are part of the external environment that affects management. Managers should interest themselves in the efficacy of these programs and get involved so that they benefit from improved preemployment and job-preparation training programs and from "job creation" in public service employment, which might lead later to jobs in the private sector. Other groups are interested in these programs; why not management?

MANPOWER DEVELOPMENT AND TRAINING ACT (MDTA)

The initial emphasis of MDTA was on those assumed to be structurally unemployed, usually as a result of technological change or automation. Automation and its presumed impact on employment got a lot of attention in the early 1960s. Subsequently attention turned to those variously called "economically disadvantaged" or "hard-core unemployed," who frequently were members of minority groups, particularly young people whose rates of unemployment were double-digit. Training programs were conceived and developed by the Manpower Administration, which became the largest group within the U. S. Department of Labor. Funds for each program were allocated on the basis of specific proposals from cities, counties, and states on how the funds would be used during a fiscal year.

Among the so-called categorical programs were institutional training, usually classroom and skilled training; on-the-job training (OJT), usually in private firms and later expanded into the National Alliance of Businessmen's Job Opportunities in the Business Sector (NAB-JOBS) under the direction of leading top executives and staffed by business volunteers; in-school and out-of-school youth job programs and summer jobs to keep young people off the streets, under the National Youth Corps (NYC); Operation Mainstream for employing older people on useful projects in cities and in rural areas; and the Job Corps, which removed seriously disadvantaged youths from poor home environments and provided remedial education, vocational training, counseling, health care, and other services to give them a better chance for productive employment. All these programs were developed and administered within the Department of Labor. But there were other programs, such as vocational rehabilitation (for those with physical and mental handicaps), administered by the Department of Health, Education, and Welfare (HEW). In 1964 all of these programs required a federal expenditure of $400 million; by 1970 the budget was $2.596 billion.

A number of studies were made to determine whether these centralized and categorical programs were effective. The findings generally showed that gains in earned income after training were greater than those of a matched group without the benefit of training programs. A recent large-scale study of persons in classroom (institutional) and on-the-job training programs during the first six months of 1969, 1970, or 1971 showed that in the year before they entered a training program, participants earned an average of $400 a year less than the comparison group's earnings, but that in the year after training, they earned an average of $220 more than the comparison group.[1]

EMERGENCY EMPLOYMENT ACT (EEA)

The nation's first experience with a public service employment program since the Great Depression was the Emergency Employment Act, which was passed by Congress and signed into law by President Nixon in 1971. The EEA was rapidly implemented by a federal agency established for the purpose of making grants directly to state and local

---

[1] U. S. Department of Labor, Office of Information, news release May 11, 1976. For a careful review of other evidence on the costs and benefits of employment and training programs, see Sar A. Levitan and Robert Taggart, *Promise of Greatness* (Cambridge: Harvard University Press, 1976), chapter 7, "Manpower Programs."

governments, which then determined the services they considered most vital and hired workers to perform them.

Only unemployed or underemployed workers could be hired; there was to be no substitution for other expenditures for personnel; and 90 percent of the funds was to be used for wages and salaries. The people hired for jobs were similar to those already employed by state and local governments—teachers, social workers, policemen, maintenance men, road crews, secretaries, and aides to a variety of occupations, including some of those just listed.

Needed work was done that could not otherwise be funded locally because of tight budgets and pressure to avoid tax increases; unemployed workers got jobs and later often moved to other jobs; and the costs of the program were offset by reduction of welfare and unemployment compensation costs as well as by taxes paid by the new jobholders on their earnings. About 160,000 jobs were provided at the peak of the program in 1972, a year in which some 2.6 million (4.9 percent) were unemployed. The evaluations of this program were generally favorable, and public service employment provisions were included in subsequent legislation.

COMPREHENSIVE EMPLOYMENT
AND TRAINING ACT (CETA)

The EEA provided that direct grants would be made to states, counties, and cities to be used as they saw fit. Other programs under MDTA did not permit this; they were still centrally administered, and funds were provided by contract under certain categories of programs. The Nixon administration had pushed the revenue-sharing idea widely and suggested it was appropriate for manpower programs. At the same time, governors and big-city mayors had been complaining about the red tape and strict control of manpower funds in Washington. These two factors led to a bipartisan effort for a comprehensive manpower program, federally funded but locally administered. Congress passed such a bill in 1970, with a public service employment component, but President Nixon vetoed it because of his objection at the time to public service employment. But when the EEA was passed in a period of rising unemployment, the Comprehensive Employment and Training Act of 1973, with provision for public service employment, was signed by the president in December 1973.

The CETA has a number of provisions. Title I covers all the manpower services that have been decentralized to the states and cities or other units of government with over 100,000 population, called "prime sponsors." They get federal funds under a formula that takes into account a number of factors, including unemployment rates, for a system of manpower services including classroom and on-the-job training, counseling, testing, and placement. Title II provides decentralized public service employment in areas of 6.5 percent unemployment or more. Title III retains certain national programs for Indians, migrant farm workers, offenders, youths, and others with special labor market disadvantages. Title IV retains the Job Corps, which was an earlier MDTA program. An independent National Commission on Manpower Policy was established under Title V. A subsequent Title VI was added by the Emergency Jobs and Unemployment Act of 1974, which provides for a larger public service employment program to ease the higher unemployment resulting from the most severe economic downturn since the 1930s.

The amounts appropriated by Congress for these programs, for continuing programs under HEW, for the Employment Service and federal administration, were $4.6 billion in fiscal 1974, down from nearly $5 billion in fiscal 1973. There was an increase to $6.2 billion in fiscal 1975, but in real terms this amount was less because of the double-digit inflation rates that year. If we consider only the Title I manpower programs under CETA, which are decentralized to the prime sponsors, the amounts are much smaller: $2.4 billion in fiscal 1973, $2.1 billion in fiscal 1974, and less than $2 billion in fiscal 1975—a reduction each year since 1973, despite rising inflation over that period. Considering the need for training of those with labor market disadvantages, these amounts seem too small. As we come out of the recession, there is a real need for subsidized or unsubsidized on-the-job training in the private sector, similar to NAB-JOBS, and an opportunity for managers to provide jobs for those in the disadvantaged groups.

PRELIMINARY EVALUATION OF CETA

There have been a number of preliminary evaluations of the operation of CETA, most of them generally favorable to its decentralized and decategorized approach to manpower services for training and placement. The Industrial Relations Section at M.I.T. has been conducting a three-year study of the experience with CETA compared with earlier programs in six Eastern Massachusetts prime sponsors, under a research contract from the Office of Research and Development of the Employment and Training Administration of the U. S. Department of Labor. Graduate students have been out in the field under faculty direction, and the second year of research has been completed. Some tentative conclusions can be mentioned briefly.

First, it is clear that mayors and city manpower officials have more control over the use of funds for programs they consider to be most important for the disadvantaged and unemployed people in their localities. *Second,* the manpower planning councils established in each prime sponsor provide an opportunity for representatives of business and labor, program managers, minority community representatives, and others to discuss proposed employment and training programs for the next fiscal year and then to monitor them. At least that was the intent behind the councils. But not all members attend meetings, and staff help is often insufficient.

Third, programs are changed by manpower planners with the approval of the councils and the elected officials as conditions change in the local labor market. For example, in New Bedford, Massachusetts, which has the highest unemployment in the state, work experience programs predominate. In Lowell, on the other hand, with somewhat lower, but still high, unemployment, on-the-job training contracts have been written with some private employers. *Fourth,* the generally higher-than-average unemployment rates in Massachusetts have meant that public service employment funds help a wider group of "economically disadvantaged" (for instance, those laid off from prior jobs) to find useful and needed work to tide them over the recession period.

Fifth, large cities, especially Boston, have lost employment and training funds relative to the suburban and rural areas. The CETA allocation formula means that existing Title I funds are better distributed among all cities and towns than they were under MDTA. Central cities under that program were favored with more funds; as a consequence some of the more affluent Boston suburbs have had some difficulty spending all their public service employment funds under CETA's Title VI, as well as struggling to develop training programs with available Title I funds for those with labor market disadvantages, especially minority groups. One suburban area, for example, is 98 percent white.

Sixth, planning for program changes in the prime sponsors is hampered by the inadequacy of local labor market information about prospective occupational trends and entry-level job openings, especially in private employment. Local offices of the public employment service are not always effective, and not all employers list their openings with this publicly supported service. The lack of labor market information makes planning for relevant classroom and vocational training difficult. Here is where private employers could be more helpful than they have been in many localities, and not only in Massachusetts.

54

CONCLUDING COMMENTS

Training programs help those who otherwise have difficulty finding jobs, even as general employment expands. This is particularly true of minority groups, and also of whites with lower levels of education and job experience. Teenagers in both cases have much higher unemployment rates than adults and, whether graduates or dropouts, need help in the transition from school to work. There is room for local management initiative here.

Public service employment helps former jobholders subject to chronic unemployment, and some disadvantaged, particularly in high unemployment areas. It is not helpful to condemn this as "useless make-work." Despite some abuses, the evidence is that *useful* work has been done by people who otherwise would have been drawing unemployment compensation, financed by employers, or have been on public relief rolls.

Continued interest and support of these types of programs by business managers will possibly head off or modify such sweeping proposals now before Congress as the Humphrey-Hawkins bill, the proposed full employment and balanced growth act, which would establish "the right of all adult Americans able, willing, and seeking work to opportunities for useful paid employment at fair rates of compensation." "Adult" was extended to include those aged 16 and over in the House version and may possibly include those aged 18 and over in the Senate version. The "full employment" goal is 3 percent unemployed by 1980.

The bill has come under attack from economists (including a number associated with the Kennedy and Johnson administrations) who contend that achieving such a goal by 1980 would result in double-digit inflation, especially since the wage provisions state that public service jobs shall be at "prevailing wage rates," which could be higher than some private sector jobs. As Dr. Sar A. Levitan, a widely recognized expert on manpower programs and former chairman of the National Manpower Policy Task Force, has said: "We can do much to reduce unemployment . . . but not this way." Expansion of existing employment and training programs and of present public service employment in areas of high unemployment is more realistic and certainly less inflationary.

A SYSTEMS APPROACH TO MANAGING HUMAN RESOURCES

STEPHEN H. FULLER and WILLIAM B. CHEW

STEPHEN H. FULLER is vice president, General Motors Personnel Administration and Development Staff. His expertise in personnel relations and general management has resulted in more than twenty years of service as a consultant to companies in the electrical, paper, automobile, airline, banking, communications, and clothing industries in the United States and Canada. He has been active in a number of management development programs overseas and has a special interest in and knowledge of the Philippines. Since 1973 he has been a member of the Council of Economic Advisors' Advisory Committee on the Economic Role of Women. Dr. Fuller is a graduate of Ohio University and received the M.A. and Ph.D. degrees from Harvard. For a period in 1947 he was an assistant professor at Ohio University. That same year he became a member of the faculty of business administration at Harvard Business School and was named a full professor in 1961. From January 1964 until 1969 he served as associate dean of external affairs. Dr. Fuller took a leave from Harvard to serve as president of the Asian Institute of Management from 1969 until 1971, and then joined General Motors.

WILLIAM B. CHEW is director of human resources management activity on the General Motors Personnel Administration and Development Staff. This position encompasses manpower planning programs for all levels of salaried employees, career planning programs, and studies of future managerial and professional requirements. He first joined GM in 1942 as an inspector with the Delco-Remy Division in Anderson, Indiana. Following his college education, he again joined the company as a personnel evaluation specialist on the staff of the GM Institute. In 1957 he transferred to the employee research section of the Central Office Personnel Staff and remained there until 1959, when he was assigned to the Salaried Personnel Activity. He was named assistant director in 1968 and director of the Salaried Personnel Activity in 1969. He served in that capacity until assuming his present assignment during 1973-74. Dr. Chew served on a temporary assignment as management liaison between the Labor/Management Advisory Committee and the Cost-Of-Living Council in Washington. He holds a B.S. degree in mechanical engineering and the M.A. and Ph.D. degrees in industrial psychology, all from Purdue University. He is a member of the American Psychological Association, the Midwestern Psychological Association, the American Statistical Association, and the Psychometric Society.

In 1973 General Motors recognized a need to further refine and integrate a number of existing personnel programs in order to better meet critical human resource needs. A task force of divisional personnel executives worked in concert with the personnel administration and development staff to develop a corporatewide human resources management system. The HRM system, as approved by the executive committee of the corporation, has three major objectives:

1. To improve the overall effectiveness of the salaried workforce, and

2. To assure an adequate supply of management talent for the future, and

3. To accelerate the upward mobility of minorities and women.

The individual elements of the HRM system are inventory, appraisal, forecasting, selection, acquisition, and career planning development. While many of these elements existed in some, they had not been applied consistently in each division and staff nor had they been fully integrated. Under the HRM system, the elements were integrated into a total systems approach, and responsibility for implementation and uniform application was assigned to a human resources management committee in each employing unit.

A graphic portrayal of the Human Resources Management System is shown below. The structure of the system generally

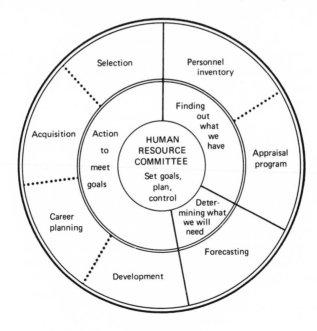

parallels the process of managing any resource. It involves the four basic steps of finding out what is available, determining what is needed, setting goals, and initiating the action required to meet the goals. For finding out what is available, the system contains a personnel inventory and an appraisal program. A forecasting model is used to project short- and long-range needs, and four elements—selection, acquisition, career planning, and development—are action-oriented processes used to meet the goals.

Functions of the HRM Committees

The HRM committees in each employing unit of General Motors are the major force behind the successful operation of the HRM system. Each committee includes the unit's chief operating executive and key members of the executive's staff, including the personnel director and the personnel administrator responsible for the coordination of the unit's equal employment opportunity activities. While much of the day-to-day administration of the HRM system is accomplished through the personnel department and the operating management, the HRM committee has the major responsibility for overall management and direction.

The HRM committees are responsible for assuring that all system elements are installed and operating within the employing units. Additionally, HRM committees use the system elements to formulate and carry out human resource plans for the employing unit. Such plans typically describe the amount and type of development, career planning, acquisition, and recruiting that are necessary to meet human resource goals. Goals are determined by comparing forecasted needs with the inventory of talent currently in the organization.

Personnel Inventory

The personnel inventory element of the HRM system maintains standard and current data elements on all salaried employees. This inventory is a computer-based system designed for application on a corporatewide basis to collect, record, and retrieve essential information on the human resources for each employing unit and the total corporation. The inventory produces numerous commonly used personnel reports and periodic special studies, thus relieving operating units of costly manual clerical work. Even more important, the inventory is used to identify candidates for openings, to monitor career plans, and to maintain appraisal data.

Appraisal

The appraisal element assures that appraisals are conducted according to established policy in a fair, nondiscriminatory manner, that current appraisal data are available on each salaried employee, and that all appraisals are based on the combined judgment of at least two levels of supervision to prevent arbitrary judgments from being made. The appraisal element contains a number of unique features. First, the developmental aspects of the process receive special emphasis by providing for a large degree of employee involvement. Employees have the opportunity to complete an appraisal worksheet, which becomes a part of their personnel file. They may list the key elements of the job, as they see it; make note of their accomplishments and performance obstacles; and register specific career goals, which can later be used when forming selection pools. Second, standardized forms, procedures, and supervisory training are used to assure consistency of approach. And, finally, methods of rating are designed to yield a rich supply of performance, potential, and promotability data for use in personnel administration decisions. A major consideration in incorporating these features was to have an appraisal system that was totally job-related and responsive to employee needs as well as management needs.

Forecasting

The forecasting element aids in determining what human resources will be required by the corporation. A fundamental building block is a computer model that facilitates projections of future outcomes of various personnel strategies when applied to the salaried workforce. The model is used in the preparation of affirmative action programs at the operating level and is used extensively in determining human resource strategies at the corporate level.

Selection

The selection element has brought about highly visible changes from earlier procedures and impacted heavily on day-to-day operations. For example, the following requirements have to be met company-wide: (1) a standard requisition that must indicate the job duties and skills required, (2) the establishment of "selection pools" with an adequate representation of minorities and women, (3) the review of all requisitions by the EEO coordinator, and (4) review and approval by the personnel department of selection decisions.

Acquisition

The acquisition element of the HRM system is a specialized staff service to operating units to assist them in locating qualified employees, primarily minorities and women, outside the corporation, for positions typically above the entry level. A corporate managerial recruiting activity has been established to carry out this mission. Operating units are required to use this service when a qualified minority person or woman is not available locally to fill a higher level position that has been earmarked to be filled by such an individual.

Career Planning

The career planning element establishes the practice of programming the development and advancement of selected employees, using inventory, forecasting, and other types of human resources data. Career planning includes two major segments: career pathing and career information.

The management-directed career pathing segment requires employing units to identify annually employees with the greatest potential for increased responsibility and to plan their development and mobility. Employees selected for such treatment, as well as the specific career path and development plans, are reviewed and approved by the HRM committees. The number of employees selected is consistent with the employing unit's upward mobility goals and other human resource needs. A career tracking system, contained in the HRM inventory, monitors the progress of career-pathed employees at both the divisional and corporate level.

The employee-oriented career information segment establishes a range of programs and activities designed to assist interested employees in making career decisions. Research, as well as practical experience, suggests that to be successful, such efforts should be directed in three ways. First, employees need information about the content and availability of typical jobs within functional areas of the business, examples of career paths within functional areas, and an understanding of the basic skills and background needed for entry to various positions. Second, methods are needed by which employees can assess their interests, capabilities, and developmental needs relative to various career options. Finally, employees need to be aware of alternatives for acquiring knowledge and skills required to become eligible for a desired position or career path. Based on this framework, a number of projects have been undertaken:

1. Publication of a career information booklet provides basic information about jobs, career paths, and qualifications.

2. Preparation of a video-cassette program that is a self-assessment device aims at helping employees determine their interests and developmental needs relative to supervisory positions.

3. Employing units maintain and communicate current information on useful educational and training programs available in the community or within the corporation.

4. Appraisals emphasize action planning for increasing effectiveness on the job and include a discussion of employee career interests and goals.

5. Data on employee career interests are maintained in the HRM inventory, and the capability will be present to conduct candidate searches along this dimension.

It is anticipated that additional employee-oriented programs and activities will be developed and implemented to supplement these first steps.

Development

The development element establishes a salaried employee-in-training classification to provide a framework for the intensive development of selected employees. This special classification allows employing units to carry extra headcounts for the purpose of meeting urgent developmental needs which must be satisfied to accelerate the upward mobility of minorities and women. The staff provides assistance in identifying employees qualified for intensive developmental treatment and counsel in the preparation of development plans. It is recognized that various development objectives are amenable to different methods. As a consequence, in providing counsel to employing units, an effort is made to explore what can be accomplished through job rotation, special assignments, internships, and other on-the-job possibilities, as well as through formal education or training programs. Additionally, studies have been initiated, using the forecasting model, to predict the numbers and types of employees eligible for formal programs at future points in time. Results will be useful in deciding the range and number of formal programs to be made available, and in making "make-or-buy" decisions. Through such efforts, appropriate supervisory, managerial, and technical skill-development programs will be developed and used in the least costly manner.

The development element also requires that all newly appointed supervisors receive training in supervisory job content and responsibilities. The education and training staff has developed programs that meet this requirement and provides guidance to operating units in the development of local programs. Effort is also directed toward the more systematic use of external executive development programs, and the early identification of candidates for such programs.

Summary

Each element of the HRM system has been designed to interface with the others to form an integrated management system responsive to the needs of management and the expectations of the salaried workforce. The complexity of installing this total systems concept is underscored by the fact that previously each of General Motors' divisions and staffs carried out the personnel function on a semiautonomous, highly decentralized basis. These divisional managements have now adopted a uniform, comprehensive personnel system which is administered consistently across the corporation. Naturally, this total systems approach will be modified and refined in response to changing needs. Progress in accomplishing affirmative action program commitments, changing technology, new expectations in the salaried workforce, and operating experience in using the HRM system are a few of the variables being monitored to determine what these needs will be.

PENSION ISSUES AND THE CORPORATE DECISION-MAKING PROCESS

ROGER F. MURRAY

ROGER F. MURRAY is S. Sloan Colt Professor of Banking and Finance at the Graduate School of Business Administration of Columbia University. After twenty years with Bankers Trust Company, he headed the Institutional Investment Advisory Services from 1952 to 1955. In addition, he served the Teachers Insurance and Annuity Association and College Retirement Equities Fund as vice president and economist and as executive vice president, and was chairman of the CREF Finance Committee. In 1956 Dr. Murray was appointed associate dean of the Graduate School of Business Administration, Columbia University, and in 1958 he became the first holder of the S. Sloan Colt Chair. He is currently a director of the Alliance Bond Fund; a member of the Advisory Committee of Bankers Trust Company; a public director of the Chicago Board Options Exchange; a director of the Lincoln National Life Insurance Company of New York; a trustee of the New York Bank for Savings; a member of the Investment Policy Panel, Pension Benefit Guaranty Corporation; and a member of the Securities and Exchange Commission Advisory Committee on Public Disclosure. He is the author of Economic Aspects of Pensions: A Summary Report. *Dr. Murray graduated from Yale University and received M.B.A. and Ph.D. degrees from the New York University Graduate School of Business Administration.*

In order to consider the future role of the business corporation in providing retirement income and related benefits for its employees, we must reexamine some long-held presumptions. It seems like only yesterday that the Old Age and Survivors Insurance system was intended to provide basic protection on which other benefit programs might be built. Comment and discussion now concern the system's adequacy as a presumed total income replacement program. The indexing of benefits accounts for another explosive element in the system.

63

THE FUTURE OF PRIVATE PLANS

The first and central issue, then, is whether private pensions will be subjected to further limitations and partially displaced by the expanding social insurance system. Perhaps concern over benefit plans will diminish as a result. The outcome depends in large measure on whether new developments such as IRA accounts and Keogh plans can rapidly enough extend private coverage to a major portion of the large number of employees who currently have no prospect of coverage under group private plans. This is the only effective way to forestall further increases in the public system's level of benefits. Recourse to general revenues financing to meet such higher payments is closer than ever before, and the size of the payroll tax will no longer act as a discipline.

These trends, if they persist, will affect the business corporation through the saving and investment process in the capital markets. The redistribution of income through the social insurance system will depress savings below the levels to which they would otherwise fall. Private pension plans, on the contrary, act to sustain the level of personal savings. The net effect of current trends will be to raise the cost and limit the availability of capital generated from savings. The likely consequence is that the basic objective of healthy economic growth without inflation will be more difficult to achieve.

A higher cost of capital is only one aspect of the problem faced by the employer. The case for the present deferment of the individual's income tax liability until she or he draws retirement benefits rests on the public policy decision to encourage voluntary private group plans. This determination is progressively weakened as the social insurance system carries more of the total responsibility. In order to preserve the private system by extending coverage, should more employers press for industrywide plans? Would it be productive for large firms to provide pension planning services for suppliers and distributors without cost to them so as to facilitate their extension of coverage? What other missionary work can be done?

A final question about the future role of private pensions in the economy is whether or when postretirement benefits will become indexed. This is, however, only one of the many specific questions that the individual firm must face in the period ahead. Let us now turn to some of those problems because they will affect the corporate decision-making process in various dimensions.

A NEW ROLE FOR THE EMPLOYER

As the 1960s ended, corporations gave increased attention to the selection of investment managers, began to measure performance more systematically, and adopted the multiple manager concept as funds increased enough to make it economical. Selecting managers became a principal activity of corporate financial officers. Complete delegation of investment decision-making was the order of the day. Rising expectations regarding the earning power of the assets were dampened in 1969-70, but the recovery to the end of 1972 was reassuring. The new profit centers were becoming more productive, and raising the interest rate assumption seemed the most reasonable basis for keeping contributions under control.

The third calendar quarter of 1974 saw the events that drastically changed this environment. The passing of the Pension Reform Act was enough of an event by itself, but the sharpest decline in corporate bond prices in the century eroded what was supposed to be the stable component of trusteed funds and made previously negotiated insured contracts look absurd. The devastating decline in stock prices was the sharpest since the second quarter of 1932. Cumulative rates of return for a decade or more turned negative. Whatever the previous tolerance of variability, the panic atmosphere of 1974 was most pervasive just as a new law seemed to demand more diligence and prudence of the employer's executives and directors.

The effects of ERISA and the capital market panic of 1974 cannot be separated. The "comfort level," or willingness to accept exposure to the variability of returns, was about to change with or without ERISA, but its passage reinforced and accelerated the reaction. As the corporate board faces up to the realities of its fiduciary responsibilities and to the inadequacies of past notions of delegation, it has to redesign its decision-making process to make specific decisions regarding each pension plan. The steps in this process that should not be delegated are as follows:

1. Precise definition of objectives expressed in quantitative terms, not vague statements about "highest return consistent with appropriate levels of risk."

2. Careful study of the strengths and weaknesses of potential managers with a view to giving them the assignments they are likely to perform best, not expecting a manager to be all things to all people in all seasons.

3. Systematic allocations of funds to one or more managers under precise guidelines and with limitations on the exercise of discretion.

65

4. Careful evaluation of performance in relation to defined objectives with a view to improving the process.

SHARING INVESTMENT DECISIONS

Managing a manager or managers, which is what the current definition of employer responsibilities demands, represents a wholly new experience for many business firms. The function should not include the selection of specific securities, but it must involve active participation with professional investment managers in formulating asset management strategy and in setting the range of possible shifts between different types of assets. This process places the corporate executive and his board of directors in a position of directly sharing with professional investment managers the decisions relating to:

1. The rate of return and variability level expected for the future.

2. The types and diversification of assets to be eligible for investment.

3. The degree of reliance to be placed on economic and capital market analysis in attempting to time shifts in the asset mix.

4. The extent of reliance on the manager's ability to select under- and overvalued securities and the acceptable level of turnover in the portfolio.

5. The length of the time horizon for planning investment strategy and measuring performance.

When listed in this manner, the agenda for the corporate decision-making process does not sound so abstruse or difficult. A moment's thought, however, makes clear the new demands they entail:

1. Returns to be expected in the future, both the level and variability, are extraordinarily difficult to forecast. No investment manager, after recent experiences, will not promise less in order to produce more.

2. The abundance of data about past history disguises but cannot conceal the flimsy structure on which expectations for the future must be built.

3. We know a great deal about diversifying a stock portfolio. The number of issues and the variability of returns are part of the current measurement methods that can be carried from past to future periods with some confidence.

4. The beta coefficient is supposed to indicate what the variability level of the stock portfolio will be relative to the market. Even

when it is conveniently stable, however, it begs the question of how stable the market as a whole will be. Forecasting the market's variability is notoriously unreliable.

5. How to diversify the total fund as ERISA requires is difficult to do because the law is not specific for enough of what is meant. Investing a fund in a single company's debt, commercial paper, sale and leasebacks, and common stock would satisfy those who think diversification means simply spreading assets among different types of assets. A more rational approach, it seems to me, is to look at the economic base for the investment, regardless of its form, and to spread assets across a broad range of activities not affected by similar economic, financial, political, and social factors. But it is by no means clear that the law sees diversification in this light.

6. The decision whether to rely on forecasts in order to time major shifts between assets of different variability characteristics is extraordinarily difficult to reach because the record of consistently well-timed decisions is virtually nonexistent. Perhaps formula timing plans, which have been out of style for the last dozen years or more, should be revived.

7. The efficient market hypothesis, beloved in academe, questions whether there are positive returns, after transaction costs, from attempting through security analysis to select undervalued securities. True believers recommend holding a market portfolio in the form of an index fund for most or all of an equity investment. Others suggest owning such a passive portfolio while also owning an actively selected and managed group of additional positions. The proportions to be allocated to the active and passive components are other difficult decisions.

8. Finally, can the corporate decision-makers stand still and hold to a basic investment strategy when values are subject to drastic shrinkage? Can the time horizon be kept firmly in place now that market values really matter in reporting and in measuring potential liabilities?

Such is the catalogue of decisions to be reached by the corporation. Advice and counsel can be used, but the decisions cannot be delegated. Furthermore, diligence and expert prudence are essential. Being wrong is still permissible, of course, but not being casual or negligent. This seems like an invitation to endless amounts of busy-work of writing memoranda and reports that rehearse the obvious and elaborate the irrelevant. To avoid such wasteful and ineffective activity, corporations will have to develop a decision-making structure that matches or parallels that of the best organized professional investment managers, even in the absence of any intention ever to buy or sell a security.

PART III: THE INDIVIDUAL EMPLOYEE AND CORPORATE ORGANIZATIONS

In the attempts of management to cope with legislation or in the drama of the collective bargaining process, we frequently lose sight of the individual and his place in corporate organizations. Yet the heart of employee relations as a management art is the individual employee. Kenneth B. Clark, a distinguished social scientist and philosopher, reviews the corporate framework and the role of the individual in modern systems.

THE ROLE OF THE INDIVIDUAL IN THE MODERN ENTERPRISE

KENNETH B. CLARK

KENNETH B. CLARK is president of Clark, Phipps, Clark and Harris, Inc. He has served as consultant to a number of foundations, private corporations, educational institutions, and branches of the federal government. Dr. Clark received his Ph.D. in social psychology from Columbia University. He is a distinguished professor of psychology, emeritus, of the City College of the City University of New York and recently retired as president of the Metropolitan Applied Research Center, Inc. He is author of several books and articles, including Prejudice and Your Child, *the prize-winning* Dark Ghetto, *and* Pathos of Power. *He is co-author of* A Relevant War against Poverty *and* The Negro American. *His work on the effects of segregation on children was cited by the United States Supreme Court in Brown v. Board of Education (1954). He is a past president of the American Psychological Association, a member of the board of regents of the State of New York, a member of the board of trustees of the University of Chicago, and a member of the board of directors of Harper & Row and the Lincoln Savings Bank.*

As I tried to organize my thoughts about the role of the individual in the modern enterprise, I thought that what I really wanted to talk about was the responsibility of individuals in assuring corporate social responsibility. The more I thought about this presentation, the more I became obsessed with disturbing and random ideas concerning the role of the individual, the responsibility of the individual, the obligations and the limitations of the individual in a social collective setting. My past as a social psychologist intruded and dominated my present role as a management consultant. I found that I could not avoid a key concern of social psychologists—to attempt to understand the nature and dynamics of interaction between individuals and groups.

One aspect of the problem of individual-group interaction concerns itself with the socialization process. In attempting to understand

71

socialization, one must try to understand the ways in which groups influence the values, attitudes, patterns of behavior, and of course, language of the individual. A basic premise in social psychology is that no individual is isolated from the social group of which he is a part. In fact, the individual is generally seen as a product of his family, his peers, and the overall culture in which he participates. According to some social psychologists the only inherent capacity of the human species is the capacity to be modified—to be socialized —by external influences. The ability to learn language is one of the most obvious and concrete examples of the socialization process. In the acquiring of language, the group's influence and impact upon the individual affect and determine the individual's ability to communicate with other members of the group who have this influence upon him. The socialization process, therefore, is revealed as a circular phenomenon. It is interactive.

Some social scientists in their attempt to understand the individual-group interactive process tend to emphasize the role of certain individuals upon the group. The social scientists who are particularly concerned with the phenomenon of leadership must necessarily have this emphasis because it is assumed that the leader is not only a product of his group but also influences the group. Outstanding leaders tend to build upon group norms, modifying the perspectives of the group, increasing the efficiency of the group, and, if they are constructive leaders, contributing to the progress of the group as defined in terms of its more constructive, positive, and effective functioning.

As already indicated, social scientists differ in their approach to this deceptively simple and complex problem. For example, sociologists tend to concentrate on the impact of the social group upon the individual as the primary aspect of the phenomenon of individual-group interaction; while the psychologists tend to concentrate on the possible impact of individuals on group patterns, or on the problem of individual differences in spite of common social group influences and common socialization. But the fact remains that whatever the emphasis, the individual exists with his values and perspectives—and he exists and functions within the context of a social group. The group exerts its influence upon the individual by rewarding or punishing or ridiculing or ignoring or excluding—or offering status or prestige to the individual in terms of the group's judgment about the contribution of the individual. The phenomenon of individual-group interaction remains a basic and elusive phenomenon of social science concern.

As I was thinking about this aspect of the problem, it occurred to me that these ideas are rather general, abstract, and theoretical and that they do not deal directly with the title of my presentation. "The Role of the Individual in the Modern Enterprise" sounds concrete. Nonetheless, specific insights continued to elude me.

As I tried to become more specific in dealing with this problem, I started recalling my earlier undergraduate years when I first became seriously interested in social philosophy and social psychology. When I was an undergraduate, one of the most provocative concepts for me was the fact that corporations were considered individuals before our courts. I learned from one of my courses that in the 1920s and 1930s our federal courts operated on the assumption that the equal protection clause of the Fourteenth Amendment was appropriately used to protect the rights and privileges of corporations. If I remember correctly, my professor pointed out that while the initial intent of the Fourteenth Amendment, and particularly that of the equal protection clause, was to protect the rights of the newly freed slaves, the federal courts had up to that time systematically ignored this initial intent. Instead, the courts were at that time using the Fourteenth Amendment almost exclusively for the protection of the rights and the laissez-faire freedoms of corporations. At the time I thought this was a rather odd legal perversion, which tended to support my youthful cynicism. I justified my undergraduate rebellion by the beliefs that our democratic safeguards could be easily perverted to serve the interests of the men of corporate and political power—and that there was little possibility that they would be used to protect the rights of minorities and other lower status individuals.

Since that time my involvement in various struggles for social and racial justice have brought me around to a broader and, I hope, more balanced and accurate perspective. I have now come to see that corporations and individuals are in fact indivisible. I have come to understand that social institutions, including corporations, educational institutions, government agencies, and churches, consist of individuals; that corporate and institutional decisions are decisions made by individuals; that these corporate entities are not isolated from the interactive processes and dynamics of the individuals who comprise them and who are charged with the decision-making responsibilities.

The French school of sociology, sparked by the ideas of LeBon in the early part of the twentieth century, argued strenuously that there existed a crowd-mind or a mob-mind, which had authority and responsibility and responsive dynamics independent of the individuals who comprised the crowd. I was fortunate as an undergraduate and graduate student to have been influenced by tough-minded professors who were critical in their discussion and analysis of the crowd-mind theory of social interaction. They argued persuasively that crowds, mobs, and other social groups consisted of individuals and that the social behavior of groups had to be understood in terms of factors influencing the behavior of individuals. It is true that in a social setting the individual's behavior tends to be reinforced by the group—or that the motivations and basic characteristics of individuals may be obscured by the passions and the emotions of the group. The fact remains, however, that even in the most passionate and emotional group situations, individuals are behaving. There is no such thing as a group's behavior isolated from the individual components that comprise the group. Individuals bear the responsibility for the actions of the groups of which they are a part.

Within this perspective, the role of individuals in a modern corporate enterprise tends to emerge with disturbing clarity. One sees that corporate decisions, corporate ethics, corporate social sensitivity, and the corporate sense of community responsibility cannot be isolated from the ethics, the sensitivity, and the responsibility that are found in the individuals who have the power to make the corporate decisions. It would, therefore, follow that corporate insensitivity, corporate immorality, and corporate irresponsibility are in a very basic sense indicative of the insensitivity, irresponsibility, and, in the extreme cases, the immorality of the individuals who comprise the corporate decision-making apparatus.

These thoughts then forced me to reexamine some of my earlier thoughts about Machiavelli. It became evident that I would not continue to organize my thoughts on the role of the individual in the modern enterprise without thinking about the momentous and influential classic moral treatise *The Prince*. Again I must confess that in my youth I tended to see *The Prince* as providing a rationalization for the amoral behavior of the state and the officials who are responsible for its governance. My initial view of Machiavelli—which I believe was shared by most of my fellow students who were serious readers of *The Prince*—was that, without question, he advised the prince that national ethics should not be confused with personal, individual ethics. Machiavelli's thesis was that the pragmatic amorality of a state, which was geared to power, national dominance and effectiveness, had to be distinct from the importance attached to the personal morality of an individual. To be specific, I thought that Machiavelli was, in effect, saying that in the interest of the state the leaders could lie in their relationships with other nations. Even the term "lie" was not to be construed as having the same meaning in international relations the term has when one is concerned exclusively with interpersonal relations.

In understanding Machiavelli, one cannot dismiss him as providing only immoral or amoral advice to a leader. One must understand that he was dealing with the problem of national or governmental power. He was, in fact, a moralist to the extent that he reserved moral and ethical concerns for interpersonal relations and interaction among individuals. He warned, however, that these ethical concerns should not interfere with the obligations and the responsibilities of national leaders in dealing with international problems of power and competition. I conclude that what Machiavelli was arguing was not by any means to be understood as total immorality, but rather a form of moral dualism; a dualism in the sense that moral and ethical concerns were valuable and valid in the interaction among individuals, but they should not be permitted to interfere with efficiency and effectiveness among nations.

In recent years I have come to understand or interpret Machiavellian moral dualism as not only accepted and utilized in international relations—cross-national power negotiations and diplomacy— but also as the basis for a pragmatic definition of effectiveness in the competition among a variety of groups, including corporations. In the corporate world Machiavellianism manifests itself in the apparent moral flexibility and pragmatism that seem to dominate many, if not all, corporate perspectives and decision-making. Few would argue that a successful corporate executive must give priority to efficiency, growth, profits, fiscal stability, and the competitive power of the corporation for which he is responsible. A tough-minded corporate board of directors can address itself to moral and ethical concerns only to the extent that these do not interfere with the inviolable priorities of a positive balance sheet.

If this perspective is valid, it makes it necessary if not imperative to try to understand the essential Machiavellian dualism if one is to understand the responsibilities and the role of individuals in modern corporate enterprises. To what extent is normative Machiavellianism unavoidable as an aspect of the corporate board members fulfilling their fiduciary responsibilities to their shareholders and to themselves? In seeking an answer to this question at this period of history, one has to understand that the Machiavellian perspective was articulated in a preindustrial, pretechnological, and, certainly, a prenuclear age. In fact, Machiavelli was advising the prince during

Renaissance times, when the development of national states required rather simple, pragmatic, flexible, and amoral measures, concerns which were necessary for the building of the power and the prestige essential for the stability, the strength, and the survival of these states.

The problem of national and group morality and survival is a critical problem today. Today one is required to reexamine the consequences of a pragmatic amorality in the context of an industrialized, technological, nuclear age. The simplistic perspectives of a Machiavelli and, indeed, a Karl Marx, may not be as consistent with the imperatives of social and national survival today as they might have been one hundred years ago. In this, the twentieth century, we are confronted with the realities of instantaneous communication, supersonic transportation, technological and electronic advances that have made for a dramatically shrunken world. We are confronted with the fact that the moral obscenity of one human being putting a gun to the head of another human being in Southeast Asia or in Dallas, Texas, is immediately communicated to millions of Americans in their living rooms as a part of their personal experience. We are confronted with the overriding reality that each of the major nuclear powers has nuclear warheads stockpiled sufficient to destroy all forms of life on this earth within a matter of hours, if not minutes.

These contemporary realities demand a major reexamination of Machiavellian dualism. It is my considered judgment that such a reexamination will lead to imposing upon individuals with major decision-making responsibilities the necessity for including moral and ethical concerns in everything that affects their decisions. The ironic fact is that, in a nuclear age, morality and ethics are to be defined pragmatically in terms of what is essential for the stability, the solidity, the effectiveness, and the survival of human civilization. Specifically, individuals charged with the responsibility of corporate decisions must in this period of human history take into account the extent to which their decisions, their role, their personal perspective contribute and go beyond the isolated power of the corporation for which they are responsible.

In fact, one of the new realities of today is that there is no such thing as isolated benefits to major corporations any more than there is any such thing as isolated rewards for one nation at the expense of the other. Corporate decision-making must take into account the interrelated consequences of decisions: What is the effect of the decisions of General Motors, AT&T, Lockheed Aircraft, or our major oil companies on the stability or instability of our cities, the stability or instability of our nation, the stability or instability of nations throughout the world and, indeed, of human civilization? These are difficult questions that individuals with decision-making power must begin to answer. If they attempt to deny the validity and importance of these questions and remain insensitive to them, they unfortunately will be contributing to the increase in our contemporary and future problems.

From this perspective, then, the contemporary imperative is to recognize and accept, no matter how difficult and painful, the pragmatic ethical reality of this, the late twentieth century: namely, in a nuclear age the ethics of individuals, the ethics of corporations, the ethics of institutions, of states and nations, are inextricably interlocked. The mere verbalization of this fact will not help us deal with the problems that remain and now confront our cities, our nation, and our world. There are very difficult and complex problems that we must face and mobilize our intellectual resources to solve.

The most obvious of the problems, of course, are the many residues of the Machiavellian dualistic past. A disturbing fact is that the Machiavellian dictum of national and corporate amorality has been successful in the past. This approach has been conducive to an effective power competition among states and corporations. This is a historic reality that cannot be brushed aside or resolved by mere moral preachments and verbalizations.

The logical consequence of successful collective amorality is sometimes seen in our newspapers, which describe near national catastrophies wherein individuals use the rationalizations of national security as the cover for intolerable personal immorality. The Nuremburg Trials, the Lieutenant Calley crimes, and, more recently, the Watergate obscenities have not yet driven home the lesson that individuals can no longer use the cloak of the group's pressures as an excuse for personal or collective immorality. The painful lesson is now clear: Individual morality and immorality and group morality and immorality are one. This personal burden is difficult for the individual to accept.

There is another important problem which interferes with the ability to develop a modern, pragmatically moral role for individuals. When one examines the decision-making process of states and corporations, it becomes more and more apparent that dominant individuals usually play a major role in determining the decisions and actions of the group. These dominant individuals are generally called leaders. They may be the nominal and visible leaders, or they may be anonymous or shadow leaders. Whether visible or in the shadows, such individuals generally, if not invariably, set the moral tone and standards by which their associates tend to conform.

77

The dominant leaders generally are permitted to operate in such a way as to determine the degree of genuine concern with moral or ethical questions, the degree of sensitivity, the degree of fundamental morality that will or will not be permitted to affect the decisions of the group. They tend to maintain their own dominant positions by selecting or rejecting individuals who are compatible with their level of morality. They tend to require, overtly or subtly, agreement ranging all the way from critical peer-level involvement in the decision-making process to subservience or sycophancy among their subordinate associates. The dominant leader tends also to cause subordinates to behave and express opinions and attitudes and values that are likely to be accepted by him. One must assume that a wise leader provides the opportunity and the social atmosphere whereby it is possible for his senior associates to provide independent and critical contributions to the decision-making process with impunity. This type of relationship with some of his advisors might have saved President Nixon from some of his anguish and tragedy.

Another subtle, probably quite important problem that must be faced in trying to deal with the realities of conditions under which individuals can fulfill a positive role in ethical and moral responsibilities in corporate and collective decision-making has to do with the problem of affability. In a group situation, the question of the extent to which the individual demonstrates that he is part of the group rather than an irritant is determined by the degree to which he and the group not only share common goals and aspirations and values and perspectives but also demonstrate this commonality by easy interaction and warm and friendly relations. The individual in the group who expresses personal and individual values that may be inconsistent or not totally compatible with the values of the dominant leader and his associates will, in fact, run the risk of breaking the unwritten rule of affability and compatibility. Unless extremely skillful, he will lose any possibility of influence by being dismissed as a chronic irritant, a dissenter, abrasive and irascible. If he persists in this role, his contributions, without regard to their solidity or substance, could be eliminated from the decision-making process on the grounds of social insensitivity and interpersonal irresponsibility.

The reality of this extremely important factor must be taken into account, but, at the same time, the individual must find some way in which his contributions to the collective decision-making process of the group can be accepted without his succumbing to passive compliance and opportunistic conformity. Stated another way, the pitfall of giving the priority to affability above that of making contributions to the solidity of the group's decision must be avoided as much as the pitfall of having the individual's contributions rejected or ignored because of chronic irascibility, chronic dissent, or attention-getting ego performance. The balance is a delicate one and clearly requires skill if the individual is to contribute to the group's moral and ethical sensitivity.

As I look back on these ideas, it becomes clear that the role of the individual in a modern decision-making enterprise is clearly not an easy one. There are no pat answers. There are no Dale Carnegie instant formulas for individual corporate responsibility. This observer can only offer certain guidelines concerning certain characteristics that seem essential to a positive, morally sensitive role for an individual in a group decision-making setting:

1. Such an individual must be clear about the objectives or the operation of which he is a part. His presence in the decision-making process indicates the acceptance of these objectives. Certainly no individual can be made an involuntary member of a decision-making group whose objectives or means or approaches he does not share or in some way identify with.

2. Such an individual must have consistent and realistic moral and ethical values that are important aspects of his total being—his style of life, his personality, and his reputation. These values must be so important to him that he remains sensitive to any violation of them.

3. Such an individual must not only perceive the possible violations of his values but must also have the courage and integrity to react to such violations. He must be able to communicate to his associates his ideas concerning the importance of these values in ways that do not alienate others through the aura of unctuous self-righteousness. And, probably most important, in order to be effective, he must be able to demonstrate the extent to which the violation of these values would be to the disadvantage of the group.

It is possible that this is asking too much of any single individual. Such an individual must be willing to assume the risk of rejection by a dominant leader who does not share his values, his style, or his methods of communicating them. Such an individual would be assuming the risk of rejection by his peers for confronting them with their own moral limitations and weaknesses. It is a fact that the human conscience is protectively pliable. It is only the unusual individual whose moral and ethical values are of such strength and of such priority that he would assume the risk of rejection by his peers or by those with whom he would like to be accepted. We must take into account the fact that a price of acceptance by the group is conformity.

Since the ethical and moral burden that an individual in a group situation will be required to bear is so great, a more realistic approach probably should be that of seeking to institutionalize the role of ethical sensitivity in the modern corporate enterprise. A few months ago I gave a paper at the City University of New York dealing with the social responsibility of corporations, and in that paper I suggested that such responsibility could be increased or strengthened by providing in the corporate executive structure a high official parallel to the chief executive officer of the corporation. His primary, if not exclusive responsibility would be to examine the decisions, the methods of operation, the approaches, and the day-to-day processes of the corporation in order to determine the extent of their conformance to the stated ethical images and the moral goals of the corporation. I suggested that this person could be designated as the corporate moral ombudsman who would be the personification of the corporate conscience. This executive would be the filter through which all corporate activities would be screened.

To be realistic, such an ombudsman must be given corporate power with a clear understanding of the complexities, burdens, and demands of this role. He must have the integrity and independence to fill this role and the clarity and strength necessary to see that it meshes with the realistic objectives of the corporation. This person must certainly have the ability to demonstrate that ethical and moral concerns are not inconsistent with the practical objectives of the corporation, but tend to strengthen and reinforce the power and the contributions of the corporation to the society as a whole.

Such an individual has to be backed by not only the chief executive officer but also by a standing committee of the board of directors itself. Almost all corporate boards that I know of and those few that I serve on have standing committees on investment, standing committees on audit and fiscal policies, standing committees on personnel practices, benefits, and incentives, but, unfortunately, I do not know of any board of directors with a standing committee on moral and ethical concerns. It would seem to me that if we are to avoid the pitfalls of known and unknown scandals of bribery, price-fixing, and other indications of faulty executive decision-making, which are Machiavellian amoral if not flagrantly immoral, some apparatus to provide the power for ethical and moral infusion in the corporate decision-making process must be created and used.

In addition to the suggestion of a high-level corporate officer charged primarily, if not exclusively, with the responsibility of moral monitoring of corporate decisions and practices, and in addition to a standing board committee to reinforce and evaluate the performance of such an officer, I would also like to suggest that at least in the initial stages of such an approach there be independent outside ethical consultants responsible to the board of directors, the chief executive officer, the moral and ethical executive officer, and the appropriate standing committee. The advantage of such a moral consulting firm would be that it would be outside the interpersonal, intrasocial affability dynamics, and therefore could bring a more objective approach to this important and complex problem.

Such consultants would serve in the moral and ethical sphere in a role similar to that now generally accepted as the monitoring and supportive roles of outside legal and outside financial auditors employed by corporations. Such an objective moral consultation group would address itself to such specific problems as the quality of personnel practices, interpersonal relations within the corporation, the role and possible contributions of the corporation in such specific socially responsible areas as public education, race relations, affirmative action and community relations and urban stability. Indeed, the whole question of the contributions of corporations in enhancing and solidifying the quality of life not only for their employees but also for the community as a whole is an area for future serious corporate discussion and decisions.

I now conclude by returning to my basic thesis that the individual and the group of which he is a part are inextricable. Corporate decisions are made by individuals. Individuals are responsible for determining whether corporations with which they are identified will or will not be socially sensitive, will or will not contribute to the stability of the community, the society, and the nation. Individuals and their corporations will determine the future direction, survival or extinction of human civilization.

I am optimistic that in this, the nuclear age, the alternative to the extinction of human civilization as we know it will be an awareness, hopefully quite soon—because the nuclear electronic age has compressed time—that the most pragmatic survival determinant is an immediate increase in the social, moral, and ethical sensitivity and responsibility by those individuals, groups, nations, and institutions that have the power to make those decisions that affect the destiny of their fellow man.

At this point in human history and the evolution of the human species, the ethical and the moral are now inextricably intermeshed with the practical and the efficient. Moral pragmatism is the contemporary determinant of human survival. We will do what is necessary for us to survive. Individuals will perform morally and ethically and responsibly in order to survive. This is the contemporary imperative that influences the behavior of individuals and which will, in turn, influence the behavior of modern corporations and modern nations. It is upon this that I base my optimism.

PART IV: LOOKING AHEAD – EMPLOYEE RELATIONS IN 1985

The following projections by the Committee on 1985, a group of outstanding young employee relations practitioners, represent a broad look at where the field is now and where it might be in the next ten years. Following this report six leading professors of economics and labor relations examine the conclusions of the Committee. Members of the Committee were:

Chairman: *Richard A. Beaumont*
Director of Research
Industrial Relations Counselors, Inc.

David D. Byrne, Assistant Director, Personnel Department, Inland Steel Company

Eugene E. Harris, Assistant Manager, Labor Relations, Fabrication, U. S. Steel Corporation

Michael J. Hickey, Manager, Employee Relations, U. S. Production, Del Monte Corporation

Richard L. Huber, Director, Human Resources Management, General Motors Corporation

Steven E. Kane, Union Relations Representative, The B. F. Goodrich Company

William E. Lambert, Division Head, Employee-Employer Relations, The Procter & Gamble Company

C. M. "Martin" Medford III, Employee Relations Manager, Chemicals and Plastics, Union Carbide Corporation

JoDare W. Mitchell, Vice President, CITIBANK

Roberta K. Peters, Career Management Specialist, Office of Civilian Manpower Management, U.S. Department of the Navy

The Committee was assisted in its efforts by Anthony K. Farina and Charles A. Hurley of Organization Resources Counselors, Inc.

Roger H. Rines, Labor Management Relations Specialist, Employee Relations Division, Patent and Trademark Office, U. S. Department of Commerce

Thomas E. Robinson, Personnel Manager, Akron Tire Plants, The Firestone Tire & Rubber Company

Edward J. Rutowski, Negotiations and Preparations Research Supervisor, Labor Affairs Planning Department, Labor Relations Staff, Ford Motor Company

Michael R. Schiavoni, Relations Representative, Lamp Business Division, General Electric Company

Joseph G. Stepich, Jr., Manager, Employee Relations, Whiting Refinery, Standard Oil Company (Indiana)

Nicholas C. Stevens, Personnel Planning Manager, Western Electric Company, Inc.

Joseph V. Thompson, Manager, Compensation and Management Development, International Harvester Company

Dennis V. Ward, Jr., Benefits Analyst, Standard Oil Company of California

Ross J. Williams, Regional Personnel Manager-CE, General Systems Division, IBM Corporation

REPORT OF THE COMMITTEE ON 1985

The idea for the Committee on 1985 grew out of the strong sense that too much time in employee relations is spent in grappling with current problems. The literature and performance of practitioners and scholars demonstrate the overwhelming concern with the present. It seemed that there would be value in having a small group take a broad look at where the field is now and where it might be in the next ten years.

Industrial companies and government agencies were solicited for nominations, and an impartial committee of recently retired employee relations executives selected the twenty members of the Committee on 1985. The organizations from which these young executives were drawn graciously made them available for the discussions, review, and analysis that provided the framework for the Committee's report.

The Committee was charged with the responsibility of establishing a conceptual framework within which employee relations may be practiced in 1985 and projecting what the employee relations opportunities and problems will be at that time. It first met in July of 1975 and during the subsequent year researched, through subcommittees, areas identified as significantly affecting the field of employee relations: (1) economic and demographic forecasts; (2) technology and natural resources; and (3) education, health law, the media, and government, labor, and management.

Through research of written materials and interviews with practitioners and academics, a series of questions was developed which the Committee then used to interview more than one hundred leaders in the fields under study. The results of the interviews provided the material from which the Committee developed a scenario for 1985 and identified the major issues that will confront the employee relations function in the coming decade. *

---

* See Appendix C for bibliography and interview guides used by the Committee.

DEFINITION OF EMPLOYEE RELATIONS

The definition of "employee relations" the Committee used for the purposes of our work is a broad definition, encompassing labor relations, human resources management, personnel relations, and the many other labels used to describe the functions being performed today:

> Employee relations is the interaction between
> the needs of an organization and the needs of
> the organization's employees. Since these needs
> are different, and, in fact, sometimes divergent,
> the objective of the employee relations function
> is the management of this interaction so as to
> best achieve the purpose of the organization.

In our view, the employee relations function contributes to the achievement of the purpose of the organization in three primary areas: (1) the maintenance of management flexibility; (2) the maintenance of an effective workforce; and (3) the maintenance of labor costs. The Committee has studied the emerging trends and has identified critical issues for employee relations in each of those areas.

The following discussion puts this definition in perspective through the identification of five basic characteristics that the Committee feels have molded and shaped the employee relations function in the past and in the present.

FUNDAMENTAL CHARACTERISTICS
OF EMPLOYEE RELATIONS

Confluence of External Forces

The Committee believes that the primary characteristic of employee relations is that it *functions at the confluence of the social, legal, legislative, and political forces that confront the organization.* We further conclude that this is true not because the employee relations field is structured to include responsibility for diverse disciplines—such as law and government relations—but because the employee relations process involves making accommodations between the organization's internal needs and the demands of outside forces.

If that is true, it should follow that employee relations exerts considerable influence in the management process. But this is usually not the case. In many instances, management is reluctant, for a variety of reasons, to give employee relations the authority it needs to operate effectively. In other instances, traditional employee relations executives and staff are themselves not ready or willing to assume the stronger role that would be required. Employee relations practitioners often tend to cling to historical practices, and they are not generally regarded as being aggressive risk-takers. The questions to consider here are: As the world changes, how will people in the field keep pace? If additional involvement in the management process is desirable, how can the needed authority be acquired?

The Nature of Change

The second fundamental is that *change is a continuous process and, for employee relations, has almost always been brought about by actions outside the organization.* There are two general classes of change: *dramatic* and *cumulative.* For example, consider the immediate and drastic impact that the Wagner Act had on management's obligation to participate in collective bargaining and the labor relations processes. As for cumulative change, equal employment opportunity and the changing workforce provide clear examples of how changes occur gradually through a system of continuous interpretation.

Because change is a constant process, it is necessary to consider whether the employee relations function is organized and oriented to change and at what point in the evolutionary or revolutionary process it will be prepared to respond.

In *Future Shock*, Alvin Toffler presents many examples of change, but one that stands out is his thumbnail account of the progress in transportation: Between the dawn of man and A.D. 1825, methods of travel had seen many changes, but the rate of travel had not increased appreciably, and it usually did not exceed more than 15 to 20 miles per hour. By 1880, with steam locomotion, speeds had increased to approximately 100 miles per hour. Toffler writes, "It took only fifty-eight years, however, to quadruple the limit, so that by 1938 airborne man was cracking the 400-mph line. It took a mere twenty-year flick of time to double the limit again. And by the 1960s rocket planes approached speeds of 4,000 mph, and men in space capsules were circling the earth at 18,000 mph. Plotted on a graph, the line representing progress in the past generation would leap vertically off the page."[1]

The Rate of Change

While dramatically illustrating the continuity of change, Toffler introduces the important concept that the rate of change has accelerated.

---

[1] Alvin Toffler, *Future Shock* (New York: Random House, 1970) page 26.

And we contend that *management's employee relations requirements and responsibilities are growing at an increasing rate.* Two external agents responsible for the rate of change are government and society.

Similar to the technological changes, as expressed by Toffler, the most dramatic and rapid employee relations developments have occurred in the recent past—equal opportunity, OSHA, ERISA. These changes result from government legislation and regulation and are partly the result of changes in the way government views itself as a regulator and as a partner in the social balance, partly the result of the government's requirements and expectations of how other organizations will respond.

Changes can occur also because society imposes requirements on an organization's employee relations, particularly where there is a continually changing societal perception of what the institution's social responsibilities are.

But government and society are not the only agents governing the rate of change. There are also internal elements. Requirements for talent are ever increasing, because qualitative improvements in technology or improvements in productivity are required. Also, managers themselves change as they review their own personal and social managerial responsibilities and as they interpret what they believe to be the organization's social obligations.

Dealing with so many changes at so fast a pace can be a frightening prospect, especially when also attempting to deal with the changing balance between the external forces and the internal needs of the organization. How will the employee relations process be able, in the future, to satisfy outside requirements while at the same time addressing the needs and expectations of the employees and the management?

Tradition

The fourth characteristic identified by the Committee is that *traditions and past accommodations of the employee relations field limit the capacity of practitioners to respond to new requirements and to evolve new systems.* This point can perhaps be best illustrated by the present state of labor relations, where managements and unions have evolved a reasonable accommodation for resolving differences. Imagine how difficult it would be to change that process now.

What we want to emphasize is that at any given moment the circumstances limit what can be done to bring about change. Relationships and programs established over a long period, especially when they have worked well, undergo change slowly. A business organization reacts normally when it is conservative in changing direction, even though a new direction is indicated. Thus, at any given time the employee relations effort is a peculiar mixture of tested and accepted methods, current needs, and programs for change. Change is impeded in this set of circumstances by past traditions, which make it difficult to introduce revision and obtain the administrative apparatus to be responsive to new needs.

The Social Balance

The fifth and final characteristic is that *the social balance between society, the individual, and the various institutions, with their constantly changing interrelationships, is so complex as to make proscriptive statements about employee relations difficult and prediction uncertain.* Before assuming this to be the Committee's disclaimer for all that follows, consider the following statement, which appeared in a *New York Times* article, "Physicists Face Idea That Nature is Ever Complex": "After 25 centuries of search for an overlying simplicity in nature, it may turn out . . . that natural phenomena, even at their most fundamental level, are as complex as a painting by Jackson Pollock."[2]

Even people in a hard scientific field are questioning the idea that there are simple solutions. What, therefore, can we think about a field like employee relations, where much is still not known about individual behavior either as an employee or as a member of society. Yet management has historically been oriented toward searching for the single, logical, simple solution. Manpower planning, for example, was frequently touted as the method that was going to solve management's problems. But the concept did not work out in practice quite as expected.

Should employee relations practitioners, like physicists, begin to question the idea that there are simple solutions? Should they instead recognize that they are dealing with probabilities and make their decisions based on relative probabilities?

Concluding Comments

Those, then, are the five fundamental characteristics that the Committee believes have shaped, and probably will continue to shape, the employee relations function. And the Committee believes that the ability of employee relations professionals to properly relate to the future will, in large measure, depend upon their ability to understand and deal effectively with these characteristics.

---

[2] April 28, 1976, page 44.

IMAGE OF THE EMPLOYEE RELATIONS PROFESSIONAL

In the course of considering an approach to the subject of employee relations in 1976, the Committee on 1985 was acutely aware of a basic reality: historically, many of those in employee relations have dutifully borne a passive role.

Herbert F. Meyer has suggested in a recent *Fortune Magazine* article that the personnel function may finally have "come of age."[3] While this is perhaps comforting, there is a certain opportunistic note to Meyer's rationale that laws and the imposition of new government programs have forced this new-found "respect" rather than given birth, within management, to a clear understanding of potential employee relations contributions and functions. It seemed to the Committee that it was important to determine how employee relations stands in terms of several organizational ideas, or functional areas.

Corporate Hierarchy

As Meyer so bluntly states in the *Fortune* article, a transfer to the personnel department has too rarely been viewed as a step up the promotional ladder. Although many organizations, both public and private, consider employee relations to be one of the key staff functional areas, a distressingly large percentage of organizations still view it as being in the minor leagues. Employee relations experts are usually called in only when specific problems have arisen. They participate only slightly in the planning process and contribute minimally in the councils of management (unless there is an urgent labor negotiation).

Executives responsible for the employee relations functions are often titled "vice presidents" in companies top-heavy with group and executive "VPs." Representation on executive committees and corporate boards of directors is frightfully rare. The realities of the situation are made even more apparent in the bread-and-butter areas where compensation, benefits, and bonus awards for leaders in the employee relations field are frequently a cut beneath their contemporaries in operations, marketing, finance, and engineering, regardless of individual contribution to organization success. While many perfectly valid reasons may be offered for the status problem (it should be emphasized that exceptions do exist in some corporate hierarchies), employee relations is seldom accorded a full partnership in the management system.

---

[3] February 1976, page 84.

Subject Matter

A second functional area is the *subject matter* to which the profession has addressed itself. The subject matter of employee relations is characterized as "soft" and imprecise. The impact of employee relations is not easily determined, except in those functional fields where laws dominate, such as labor relations, equal opportunity, OSHA, ERISA, etc. This absence of certainty plus low visibility make it difficult for employee relations functions to compete with finance, engineering, manufacturing, or marketing—the "full partners" in a typical management setting.

Payout in employee relations is *not* in terms of the income statement in near years. Rather, contributions to the organization must be measured in terms of impact over a prolonged period. Because of the imprecise nature of employee relations concerns and its inability to influence bottom-line results clearly and directly, employee relations issues are put off, or debated on a gut-feel level, which too often buys long-term problems in the interest of short-term solutions.

Line-Staff Relationship

Tradition suggests that employee relations, as a staff function, is destined to support line management's goals and plans. And it is no surprise that employee relations specialists are seen as troubleshooters rather than as part of the strategic planning organization.

Then there are the difficulties faced by the employee relations staff in those organizations which adopt strongly autonomous, decentralized profit centers. What is the role of the corporate expert, or the divisional specialist, or the plant-level employee relations supervisor who answers to the line plant manager? It has too often been clarified only when unions or legislation have forced an issue up to corporate headquarters. But even in labor relations, equal opportunity, OSHA, and others, there is considerable confusion and even competition about what "being in charge" of those problems really means. Indeed, employee relations professionals have spent much money and time managing the integration of an organization's workforce in accordance with the laws, while only occasionally attacking the need for genuine integration of the employee relations function itself into the management entity. Further complicating these relationships is the strain created by the apparently antagonistic role the professional must occasionally assume when representing employees wronged by line managers pursuant to organization policy or legislated rights.

91

Without debating its propriety, there is also a belief that it is the role of line management to "act and assume responsibility," while staff functions carry out second-echelon support. Where this theory exists, it is exceedingly difficult for an employee relations staff to anticipate, reshape, and reorient management practices.

Because of the line-staff relationship, it is difficult to see how (with the reality of increased centralization of certain management decisions on major issues) employee relations can influence major policy matters in a unified, thoughtful, and forceful fashion.

Career Development

The subject of career development is of considerable interest to the Committee on 1985. With certain notable exceptions, career paths in employee relations are unclear and ill-designed to attract and keep highly talented individuals. While many people in the field have directly and successfully attacked this problem, too often the top jobs are filled with highly competent men and women from fields other than employee relations because there are few broadly trained executives in the employee relations chain of command. The prestige of the field may be reflected by some recent Harvard Business School statistics, which revealed that fewer than 150 of that institution's 39,000 graduates were engaged in industrial relations or personnel. Of the 1,500 who attended the Harvard Advanced Management Program, only 37 were from employee relations.

Healthy debate continues over the need for employee relations specialists versus generalists with line and staff experience. Both categories of talent are no doubt required. While employee relations should not be maintained in a pure stream of specialists, total employee relations requirements must be more clearly understood, and career development processes that will relate more specifically to meaningful employee relations functions must be instituted.

Government Relations

In the course of time a series of "relations" have fallen, for better or worse, within the employee relations functional authority: government relations, human relations, and labor relations. In the case of government relations, legislation regarding the health and welfare of employees and pensioners has been plagued by gross uncertainty. During the wage board era just passed, many managements looked to their employee relations staffs for resolution of what governmental policies *seemed to be*. But the employee relations staffs, through no real fault of their own, were unable to perform this interpretative role. Unfortunately, one of the characteristics of current governmental initiatives is that, despite usually clear overall objectives, implementing the regulations is difficult. Understanding and compliance can only occur when all the parties have a chance to participate in fabricating the rules and regulations.

Similar uncertainties occur in relation to equal opportunity, OSHA, and ERISA. To the extent that line management assumes that staff is there to help reduce the uncertainty, and to the extent that staff cannot reduce that uncertainty because of the performance and behavior of government, that staff function as represented by employee relations loses credibility and faces still greater barriers in assuming a positive role within management.

Human Relations

The function known as human relations has taken a considerable beating in management circles. Over recent decades employee relations specialists have tended to support new "human relations techniques." Unfortunately, the packaged programs often failed to recognize true organizational needs.

The theory that "happy hands are busy hands" is far too simplistic a principle of human relations. Employee relations has too frequently argued, sometimes with no concrete, dollar-oriented evidence, that human relations approaches could be great morale builders which, in turn, would lead to high levels of motivation and therefore productivity.

The difficulty of this philosophy was great, the barriers substantial, and the results unprovable. While the enthusiasm of the "behaviorists" (who claim to have superseded the human relations specialist) has been infectious, too many opportunities exist for outsiders (line management and sometimes academics) to characterize employee relations practitioners who have opted for human relations approaches as "do-gooders." Partially as a result of the soft nature of the field, employee relations has been slow to recognize that high morale does not necessarily lead to high productivity or to the economic requirements of the enterprise itself.

Have employee relations practitioners perhaps permitted themselves to see human relations as a panacea for all their problems? The current research seems to indicate that while human relations techniques do have a place in employee relations, such techniques do not constitute a cure-all approach that will answer the many complex motivational questions. No one disputes that a better understanding of human behavior and motivational techniques is a proper objective in employee relations; employees will not perform well at what they fail to perceive as a benefit, in some fashion, to their own self-interest. But no one approach is likely to provide all the answers.

Labor Relations

Labor relations has long been the one relatively "hard" specialty, at least within the private sector, in the generally soft field of employee relations. The constant stresses and strains in the labor relations area and the complex changes in the power relationships, needs, and interests of the directly involved parties and the government and public are part of a dynamic and changing system. But numerous weaknesses exist in any labor relations pattern, and unhappiness with the system is apparent when strikes are costly to employees and settlements are highly inflationary.

The cyclical nature of the process too often leads people to approach bargaining in the "same old ways." Labor relations staffs in many organizations can rarely lead the way for change in employee relations, generally because they are in many ways committed to the accommodations and patterns of the past. This is neither improper nor wrong, but the fact remains that labor specialists are usually traditionalists. Their behavior has helped to evolve the system as it now is. And the nature of that system evokes an image that is seen by line managers as less dynamic than other aspects of the business.

Compensation, Benefits, Manpower Planning

The final focus of our functional review is on the classic roles of compensation, benefits, and manpower planning. What is really meant by the "right" level of pay? The "right" balance of benefits? The "proper" number of employees for a new facility? While industrial engineering has been useful to some extent, employee relations has relatively little hard information about precise manning levels or the employee's actual value to the organization. Instead the specialists have become exceedingly sophisticated at looking to the external commercial environment.

The standards of compensation, benefits, and manpower planning applied in many organizations too often become the standards that are applied for all. While it might be said that a free market system anticipates salary surveys, for example, as a realistic measure of the value of a worker in the marketplace, nowhere do free market economics demand that the comparison always conclude with *continuous escalation*, as one management tries to stay marginally ahead of the next.

94

What is the real "value" of an employee to his or her organization? The concept of an individualized look at a fair day's pay for a fair day's work is extremely attractive in these inflationary times.

Concluding Comments

We have by no means attempted to address ourselves to all functional areas of the broad employee relations field. But we hope the discussion of its place in the hierarchy; the subject matter with which it deals; its relationship with traditional line authority; the absence of adequate career development; its relations with government, labor, and theories of human relations; and the look-alike behavior in compensation, benefits, and manpower planning has been thought-provoking enough to promote meaningful discussion.

Employee relations professionals are anxious to be on the leading edge of change, participating in planning and development—not merely reacting to problems. The Committee believes that employee relations must understand that strategies are necessary to carefully define how a new technique fits into the overall needs and requirements of management, now and for the future. It seems to us that certain issues exist that warrant the attention of those having general management responsibilities.

First, it is important to have a clear understanding of what is required in the employee relations field and to communicate that mission in a positive fashion while interacting with the employee relations staff. To merely pass along information on what is not wanted—law suits, employee unrest, etc.—compounds the already acute problem of a reactive rather than proactive employee relations staff.

Second, a measurable, realistic position must be established for the employee relations function so that it can perform and be held accountable in a real, program-oriented sense.

Third, it should be understood that the nature of the process is such that actions taken today will have impact on the company two, five, even ten years hence. The employee relations staff should be expected to respond firmly and with support to the prolonged character of the process.

Finally, those with executive-level responsibility over the employee relations function should be clear about their mission. They should enlist general management's support for positive, measurable programs and resist the temptation to opt for short-term solutions.

Central to all these remarks lies the shifting concept of the employee relations responsibility. Until that elusive trait can be pinned down and the function becomes a full partner in management—with the attendant accountability—too many employee relations professionals will, for the decade ahead, continue in the role of troubleshooters, unresponsive to the total problems of the employee relations field.

MAJOR EMPLOYEE RELATIONS FORCES
IN THE 1976-85 DECADE

Having started from the premise that employee relations issues have their genesis in the broader society of which each organization is a part, the Committee spent a good deal of time attempting to determine where we are going—as a society and as a nation. In examining the major forces at work, we identified four areas that we believe form the important background for an analysis of employee relations in the decade ahead: (1) the changing social setting of the future, (2) the economic outlook over the coming decade, (3) the role of government as it will affect the management of human resources, and (4) the changing character and interests of organized labor.

The Committee has assumed for the purpose of the report that the free enterprise system will persist and flourish in 1985, although it will continue to be under extreme pressure. It may even be forced to become more bureaucratic itself as it interacts with growing government and union forces. But by and large the nation will continue to accept the principle that primary goods and services of value will be created in the free enterprise system.

Of the major forces identified by the Committee, by far the most significant operating in the United States and throughout the world is social change. But it would be a mistake to assume that social forces operate alone. They are affected by patterns of economic activity and by government and other institutions in their response to social and economic forces. In other words, opinion-makers and leaders can support or diminish the impact of forces in the social and economic setting. The obvious major institutional force affecting employee relations, in addition to government, is organized labor, whose role has been one of instigating change, at least in the past. But for the future, unions will be less the instigators of far-reaching change, at least in their management relations, as they are becoming more institutionalized. Elements of conservatism, aimed at protecting the system that permits them to survive as an institution, are visible.

There are, of course, other institutions—educational, medical, legal—that have affected employee relations in the past and will continue to do so in the future. But we will discuss these only as they interrelate with the other forces in the future environment the Committee envisages.

Social Setting

Workforce

In examining the social setting of the future, one factor that emerges is the changing character of the labor force. The working population will be more diverse than now. Today there are 11 percent nonwhite minorities in the workforce; by 1985 it will be 14 percent, and women will constitute 41 percent. A turning point will be reached in approximately 1985, when white males become a minority of the working population.

There will also be two-worker families and single-head-of-household workers. They will bring to the workforce differences in personal circumstances and needs and a more diverse pattern of expectations regarding employment.

The working population will be older, on an average. In 1968 40 percent of those working were between the ages of 25 and 44; by 1985 they will have increased to 50 percent of the labor force. That 10 percent increase reflects primarily a decline in younger workers.

Finally, the changing labor force will be more highly educated in 1985 than it is today. Retiring older workers, among whom there is a higher proportion of non-high school graduates, will be replaced by younger, more educated employees. Also, the gap between the educational attainment of males and females and of minorities and majorities has been narrowing and is expected to be virtually eliminated by 1985. However, we should not overlook what may well be a growing issue over the decade—the quality of public education, particularly in major cities where it is apparently declining.

In examining the ramifications of a more highly educated workforce, we also need to recognize that the orientation of the educational process is toward questioning, analysis, and understanding. And it can be expected that the workforce will be more skeptical in their approach to their jobs.

Quality of Life

Turning now to less quantifiable social considerations, we find that there appears to be a general recognition among leading futurists that we are gradually evolving from a highly individualistic social philosophy to one that places relatively greater emphasis on humanism—or the welfare of our fellow man—and, parallel to that, greater emphasis on protection of public or community interests. And it is interesting to note that this is not just an academic viewpoint. The *Harvard Business Review* conducted a survey in 1975 to determine the views of management in this area. Of the respondents—76 percent of whom were middle managers or above—73 percent were of the opinion that a humanistic- and community-oriented philosophy would be predominant by 1985. That, of course, does not mean they like it—only 29 percent indicated that they preferred such a philosophy over an individualistic one. This shift in social philosophy brings underlying changes in the values and attitudes of the population—changes in the motivators of life, in what's important—and, in turn, a change in approach to work and the expectations of employees.

We frequently hear the term "quality of life," and while there is no concise definition, there seems to be an underlying notion that affluence alone does not produce the good life. After World War II the nation looked forward to and pursued individual and national wealth. But relative success in attaining wealth has not produced universal satisfaction with life. It was found that other elements of the good life have been neglected—the problems of the cities and the difficulties of their residents, concerns regarding the purity of our waters and our air, and the pressures on our natural resources.

Of course, what constitutes the good life is an individual matter. Designing policies and practices becomes that much more difficult as priorities shift from maximum individual economic attainment to other considerations. But the result of such a shift in priorities is a decline in the relative importance of financial incentives, which will manifest itself in people being less willing to relocate the family, particularly from highly desired geographic locations. It can also be expected to result in less willingness to work overtime and on less desirable shifts for the premiums existing today.

Psychology of Entitlement

The shift in priorities does not mean that money and jobs will not be important in 1985. We are talking primarily about the already employed population, who are earning a reasonable livelihood and have attained a respectable standard of living. In the anticipated 1985 economy, having meaningful work may be even more important to them than it is today.

There likely will be a growing attitude that a job is the "right" of every American—a job that pays well, is interesting, and provides opportunity. This idea is part of an attitude that an affluent society should provide security at a reasonable level for all, which has been called the "psychology of entitlement." It encompasses not only jobs but other vehicles for economic security, adequate health care, and so on.

Generally, equal opportunity is an accepted entitlement today, but employee relations will be struggling with an increasing egalitarianism—equality of result—over the next decade. The trend evolving is toward a no-risk society. As the entitlements, or rights, of the population increase, people will turn more and more to the courts to get what they believe is "rightfully" theirs.

Authority Based on Consent

This psychology of entitlement—a job is a right, not a privilege—erodes individual loyalty and commitment to the organization. When coupled with broader-based priorities than the economic emphasis of the past and with an educational system that places value on questioning, the result is a decline in the acceptance of traditional authority. This, in turn, leads to questioning of organizational decisions and motives: Do they serve personal and community interests, however "community" may be defined in the work setting? To insure that organizational decisions serve the broader interests of people and community, employees will want more participation in the decision-making process. This will lead to demands for openness and disclosure in organizational systems, a prerequisite for employees to participate in reaching sound decisions.

In general, the Committee on 1985 anticipates an evolution in management systems toward authority based on consent. While this may be an alien idea to many, we believe it will create a unique opportunity for employee relations—loyalty and commitment will be earned through adjustment of the management system to quality-of-life demands and the changing concept of authority.

Personal Flexibility

Another value shift related to quality of life is the desire for personal flexibility—the desire to pursue individual interests with a minimum of impeding forces. In a work setting, people will increasingly seek organizational systems that are designed to permit such individual flexibility. Work schedules, vacation schedules, and leave opportunities are examples of areas in which the evolving emphasis on personal flexibility will be manifested. Another manifestation will be the growing demand for personal privacy, in part to prevent the sanction or control of personal activities.

This desire for personal flexibility and for recognition of the individual is an interesting apparent paradox of a less individualistic social philosophy. But on examination it is not inconsistent, for it relates to the *shared* welfare of individuals in the society. And this freedom for individuality will be pursued on a collective basis within the major institutions in our society.

Changing Orientation to Action

The final consideration in the social setting of the future is the changing orientation to action. As the pursuit of individual economic interests declines relative to other values—note that the Committee in no way believes that economic interests will disappear from the American character—and as broader, more socially community-oriented interests expand, the pursuit of those interests also becomes less individual and more collective in nature. The creation of pressure groups and the changing expectations of big government, which have evolved over just the last decade, are examples of this orientation, which the Committee believes will intensify over the next ten years.

Before leaving the discussion of the social forces, which may seem to be truly revolutionary to some, we would like to emphasize that the transition is not new—it is well underway and will continue to evolve gradually.

Economic Factors

The primary ingredient in our ability as a nation and as employers to meet social expectations and employee demands flowing from those expectations is the performance of the national economy. Generally, the Committee is of the opinion that the current economic recovery will not lead to the same kind of growth experienced in the past. Over the long term, we expect slower growth, averaging between 3 and 4 percent, about one-half of the historical increase in GNP. Productivity increases will lag from the traditional 3.5 percent, averaging 2.5 percent over the next decade. Unemployment will continue fluctuating at around 6 percent; persistent inflation will compound, on average, at 6 to 7 percent through 1985. We project significant capital shortages or competition for capital in the 1980s. And we see no reason to believe that it will be more possible to control the business cycle during the next decade than it has been over recent years. In addition, much of the growth that will occur will be in the services rather than the industrial sector, serving to compound the economic concerns of those involved in employee relations.

Government

Of course the shifts in economic values, attitudes, and problems will not go unnoticed by the government. We expect response to take the form of programs or additional citizen entitlements.

There are, however, concerns today regarding the ability of government to deliver the promised results through federal programs, the restraints of the budget, and the impact of government programs on the economy, particularly in the private sector, which can be expected to continue through the decade ahead. These concerns are likely to result in a slowing of the regulatory trend—when compared with the cascading developments of the last ten years—with management and labor taking a larger role in the rule-making processes of the legislative and executive branches.

The new legislation that develops will be significant since it is likely to be concerned with economic security for the population and the expansion of individual rights to privacy (where interest is increasing). It can also be expected that current legislation will be expanded, particularly OSHA and ERISA regulations. It is possible that over the next decade management will capitalize on the opportunity to participate in the making of those rules through the growing partnership of business, government, and labor.

Surveillance by governmental bodies is expected to continue and grow in the future. In the past this was performed primarily by executive agencies. However, Congress is now beginning to operate in its legislative oversight role and will likely exercise its authority in the future.

In addition to playing an expanded role as regulator and overseer, government can be expected to further its partnership with management and labor through growing involvement in dispute settlement. A stronger mediation-arbitration role will inevitably be played in the public sector with the continuing growth of strong unions there. And the techniques and practices employed in that sector will be very attractive to the private sector.

This involvement of government in the private sector will be in keeping with the increasingly accepted view of management as a vehicle for the realization of social expectations. As the federal, state, and local governments attempt to realize social and economic expectations, there will be a continuing battle of conflicting priorities and policies, with management in the middle. It is the opinion of the Committee that the concerns about government's ability to make the necessary strides with limited funds and the pressures of conflicting priorities and objectives will result in increasing interest in some form of national planning. While management recognizes the limitations of planning, it will come to see that some form is desirable to bring order out of the chaos in which it may find itself. In its naiveté regarding the limitations of planning, government will be willing to respond.

Organized Labor

Labor unions and their future are a central concern as we consider the social, governmental, and economic climates of the next decade. As for the unions themselves, the Committee sees dramatic changes.

First, we expect substantial growth in union membership, reversing the trend of declining membership as a percentage of the workforce. Before the Taft-Hartley Act, unions represented somewhat over 30 percent of the workforce—today it is less than 25 percent. Over the next decade we expect an increase to over 30 percent again. It is expected that organization in the public sector will represent perhaps 40 percent of all organized labor, with fully 75 percent of public employees organized by 1985.

We also foresee a significant change in union leadership. The old leadership, steeped in the labor struggles of the past, will no longer play an active role. The new national leadership will be more highly educated and professional, many having risen to power through the staff organization rather than coming from the rank and file. These leaders will be more inclined to seek solutions to membership demands through mechanisms outside traditional collective bargaining.

The trend toward larger unions through merger will continue, the driving forces being dollar savings through consolidation of increasingly professional staffs and the influence on national issues that derives from large membership. More industrywide and national bargaining can also be expected.

The last of the changes we foresee in organized labor is a political orientation even greater than today. This will result from the new leadership and growing influence of public sector unions. Labor also tends to form coalitions with other liberal lobbies to influence legislative issues. As labor's orientation to such political activity grows, unions will increasingly take on the character of representatives of the working class, rather than being simply representatives of their constituencies. Offsetting this growing political orientation, however, is the labor leadership's apparent loss of ability to deliver the vote. That should not be surprising, however; labor is subject to the same social forces as management.

The changing concept of authority will run counter to the centralization of power in organized labor and can be expected to result in greater conflict within labor and the formation of various pressure and splinter groups—for example, the steelhaulers in the recent Teamster negotiations, the skilled trades, and the dissidents among the Steelworkers. These are not unique cases, and we can expect to see more and more of them as the decade progresses.

This climate will create some tough bargaining on emotional local issues. The rank and file will often be dissatisfied with their union's ability to deliver on the expected "entitlements." The problems inherent in this environment will bring the interests of top labor leadership into closer harmony with management as it seeks stability, which can be expected to lead to more cooperation, both in labor relations and in the approach to government. In fact, labor may become more willing to lock arms with management and head to Washington in the quest for common solutions.

Concluding Comments

In concluding this look at the major forces that the Committee believes will affect employee relations in the years ahead, it would be worthwhile to reflect on the changes of the last ten years. They have been substantial, and it is the opinion of the Committee that the next ten years will demonstrate change that will be at least, and almost surely, more significant.

Most people in employee relations would, we think, agree with most of our conclusions regarding the course we are on as a society and as a nation. But most would, given the chance, design a different environment.

CHALLENGES TO EMPLOYEE RELATIONS IN 1985

There are three major challenges that employee relations will have to contend with in the coming decade as it discharges its responsibilities in balancing and integrating the major forces described above. These challenges concern management flexibility, labor costs, and workforce effectiveness.

Maintaining Management Flexibility

It is imperative that management maintain a high degree of flexibility so that it can accommodate the development of products and services to the needs and requirements of the marketplace. That flexibility, however, is hampered by both institutional arrangements, evolved through union contracts or government relationships, and the impact of social requirements. Yet without some degree of management flexibility, it is difficult to effectively marshall the resources necessary for any enterprise to achieve its particular objectives.

There will, however, be several countervailing forces that will constrain employee relations professionals in the exercise of their prerogatives. The likelihood of continued union pressure over the next decade suggests erosion of flexibility in the traditionally safe employee universes. The anticipated rapid gains that labor will achieve in the public sector will undoubtedly have a spillover effect in the private sector. On an even more sensitive note, managers, particularly at the first line, may be increasingly less opposed to unionization and more willing to accommodate the management system to the voice of their employees. Demands for bargaining rights by foremen and supervisors are expected to be more prevalent—adding to the burden of retaining management flexibility. As individuals espouse the right to freely participate and express their opinions, what better way than through a freely elected representative of their choice—the union.

Within the collective bargaining arena itself, two conflicting issues regarding management rights will be paramount during the coming decade. Concern for job security, resulting from slower economic growth, and the expanding psychology of entitlement will bring new union demands for restrictions on layoffs and on subcontracting, guaranteed employment, transfer of work limitations, elimination of overtime, and reduced work weeks. At the same time, management will be increasingly concerned with workforce productivity and will seek the elimination of restrictive work rules and practices. Bargaining on these issues will be tough and settlement difficult to reach.

From another perspective, while there are currently more instances of national bargaining, there will be many issues, such as those of local restrictive work rules, which may be resolved effectively only at the local level. The resolution of such conflicts will be no easy task. Moreover, companies with local bargaining will have an increasingly difficult time maintaining local patterns unless there is careful attention by management to their labor situation.

Finally, the Committee foresees expanded governmental intrusion—by regulation of current legislation such as OSHA and ERISA, plus activity in the areas of economic security, health care, and employee privacy.

Managing Labor Costs

Labor costs are a paramount consideration in a growing, integrated world economy where resource-rich nations can shop the industrial world. Obviously, as the education of the workforce increases, as social requirements further develop, and as economic wants further evolve, workers at all levels seek more for themselves. Inflation, coupled with rising employee expectations, will put pressure on management for wage and benefit increases over the next decade. These will include cost-of-living provisions and retirement securities and guarantees. On the other hand, the projected capital shortfall, rising material costs, and the distressing productivity lag will pressure management to reduce the historical wage and benefit spiral.

It will become more costly to buy response to management requirements—such as shift work, overtime, employee mobility, and relocation. Perhaps even rejection of the opportunity to join the management team will become more frequent.

The Committee also foresees, as a natural consequence of the more heterogeneous workforce, more pressure for benefit flexibility and for new benefits. The new benefits may include such items as prepaid legal services, estate planning, and day-care centers, to mention a few. The flexibility sought could be achieved through cafeteria benefit plans. It is remotely possible that private pension benefits will become stabilized as a percent of the total benefit package because of demands for other benefits.

Other cost pressures are generated by the demands for job and economic security programs, many of which continue to be introduced in contractual agreements. The expansion of supplementary unemployment benefits and other guaranteed-annual-income provisions providing for long-term security clearly contribute to the spiral. Not to be discounted is the further possibility that government may step in and legislate additional security programs.

Another factor which cannot be minimized is the impact of a maturing and stable workforce. The cost escalation associated with this given demographic trend, when linked directly to the seniority-based salary and benefit programs, is substantial.

Thus, labor costs are a serious issue as management seeks to exercise control over product and service costs. There is an obvious trade-off between management flexibility and labor cost levels. One could buy flexibility at a high cost; if too high, labor costs themselves may introduce an inflexibility in management's capability to run its operations. The pressures will be great as organizations attempt to keep labor costs compatible with their bottom-line objectives.

Bargaining will be as difficult as ever, probably more so, with larger units having an even greater and more visible impact on wage rates in nonunion companies.

Maximizing Workforce Effectiveness

It has often been said that it is cheaper to work with highly productive workers at higher costs than with a less productive group since the unit cost per person is less in the first case than in the second. Workforce effectiveness, as management flexibility is tested and as labor costs spiral, will therefore be a key motivating element in management's strategic and tactical planning in the future.

The Committee makes the general observation that the availability of candidates for employment in the future appears to be good, based on our educational and employment data projections. However, the stringent equal opportunity regulations and the scrutiny to which the selection process will be subject in the years ahead must be kept in mind.

There will be conflicting environmental impact on productivity of the workforce. On the one hand, there will be more individuals in the workforce in the 25- to 44-year age bracket, usually considered to be the most productive period. On the other hand, we have cited trends that would suggest a decline in the commitment to work and to the organization. Motivation and commitment will have to be earned, and the degree to which management is successful in earning this commitment will depend on some of the quality-of-life considerations already mentioned. Employees' ability to experience job satisfaction largely through job design, the opportunity for them to participate in decisions (especially where they themselves are involved), and the accommodation or flexibility available to them in meeting their personal needs will have great impact on the effectiveness of the workforce.

The Committee believes that training will become important again in the decade ahead. Aside from the need to increase human productivity, precipitated by capital and energy constraints on technologically induced improvements, it will be necessary to orient a more diverse workforce. Employee relations staffs will have to have greater awareness of the quality of the education the new entrants have received.

There will also be pressure on the grievance and discipline systems within organizations. Employee relations is already familiar with the external channels that OSHA, equal opportunity regulations, and ERISA have provided for complaint hearings. There will be a growing emphasis on, almost encouragement of, due process and the ability of employees to seek redress in diverse forums. This, in itself, will inhibit application of necessary disciplinary action. Compounding the issue is the added factor of forced disclosure by management at the same time that employee privacy and access to corporate records are being facilitated. The consequence may be that employee relations will be compelled to operate in a more legalistic forum with less documented evidence. The pressure on the grievance and discipline system will be further heightened by individual challenge to traditional authority and an increased desire for personal flexibility, which may be manifested in more tardiness and absenteeism in the years ahead.

Concluding Comments

The Committee foresees a complex environment that requires management effectiveness as a vital aspect of overall workforce effectiveness. The competence of those in the employee relations field will be challenged by disclosure requirements. Employee relations staffs will become increasingly accountable for their individual as well as their collective actions. There will be more external interfaces to deal with. There will be a more diverse workforce to contend with. Employee relations will be challenged by more elements of this workforce to allow increased participation in management. Moreover, in light of these increasing developments, there is serious question whether the best people will be willing to make the necessary sacrifices and join the management team.

The challenges of the next decade—maintaining management flexibility, managing labor costs, and maximizing workforce effectiveness—while not new concerns to employee relations, will produce new elements to contend with. The Committee has examined those major forces that will have impact in the years ahead and the challenges that those forces imply for employee relations. We would like to believe that employee relations can do more than just react, that it can anticipate and plan for the challenges ahead. With this in mind, the following discussion will look at where employee relations would like to be in 1985 so that it will be a viable aspect of the management system and make a significant contribution to the success of the organization.

REQUIREMENTS FOR THE FUTURE

The Committee believes there are four significant developments that will deeply affect the employee relations process and management's overall approach toward discharging its responsibilities in the employee relations arena. Before describing the four developments, however, there are two matters not specifically covered by the Committee's report that should be mentioned. The first concerns government as an employer rather than as a regulator; the second, the international aspects of employee relations.

Government as Employer

The government is the nation's largest employer, but thus far it has had relatively little direct impact on the private sector. Though there are many similarities in employee relations between the public and private sectors, in the future there may be significant differences. For example, there has been great concern that the practice of labor relations as carried out in the private sector could be transferred to government. Only recently has it been seen that such a transfer is not likely to be practical, given the character of government management and operations and the executive-legislature structure. Similar differences exist in the areas of compensation, career planning, and so on.

International Aspects of Employee Relations

The international aspects of the employee relations field are many, and there is space here for only a few comments. First, the Committee does not believe that the concepts of codetermination and so-called economic democracy now flourishing in Western Europe will have serious impact in the United States. American institutions and tradition give adequate opportunity for individual expression, and from them patterns will evolve regarding representation of workers. Thus, short of a major change in union attitudes or a collapse of effective management, such concepts are not expected to take hold within the next decade.

Second, while it seems from the union point of view to be sensible to move toward transnational bargaining, we do not expect that development. Union politics within a country, nationalism, and vast differences in objectives by country and industry will frustrate such a move. Further, management can also be expected to vigorously resist this development.

Third, company management patterns will undoubtedly evolve during this decade to find more effective means to interrelate international personnel matters with overall corporate employee relations. Thus the Committee sees the likelihood of a growing sophistication in employee relations within companies as they seek to integrate policy with the diverse employee relations issues confronted round the globe.

Finally, we see the possibility for extensive dialogues developing on corporate responsibilities in the social policy area. These discussions, in addition to efforts in the various countries, will take place in U.N. agencies and the European Community. For managements, the question is whether they will be so organized internally as to be able to respond effectively to such dialogues and to deal with periodic probes by unions seeking to test the resolve to resist transnational bargaining.

Significant Developments for 1985

Nature of the Workforce

Now to return to the four significant developments we see for 1985. The first is that we project a changed workforce. There are changes taking place in the character, orientation, age distribution, and behavior of the workforce that will require fundamental modifications in management's attitudes toward supervision, motivation, maintenance of morale, and organization of work. These changes, while subtle in terms of their step-by-step development and evolution over the past decade, are fairly radical when compared to the situation ten years ago. Given another ten years of evolutionary development, built around the trends mentioned earlier concerning loyalty, motivation, morale, etc., the workforce changes will have so significantly evolved that new techniques and new approaches will be required.

Management as a Vehicle for Social Change

We have already suggested that government will look upon management as a vehicle for social change, and it is our view that management will come to see itself as an instrument of social change and will attempt to balance more thoughtfully its economic requirements with the requirements of society. Management will begin to accept the role of partner in the triad of business, labor, and government in an attempt to maintain stability in the system. It is within a stable system that management has its greatest opportunity to flourish and grow.

Concept of Authority

The Committee does not seek to promote a social objective in terms of our analysis, and we do not assume that a particular social development is either right or wrong. It nevertheless seems clear that there has been a change in attitude toward authority, whether within the private sector, the public sector, the military, or any other institution, that will lead, by 1985, to management systems being less authoritarian. At the same time, however, management will have to deal with the need to exercise leadership, to make decisions, and to have those decisions followed. The problem of balancing the requirement of an organized systematic approach with the desire on the part of individual employees at all levels of the organization to operate in a less authoritarian system will be one of the great challenges of the decade. It will call for new forms of interaction, leadership, and understanding of human relations.

Expectations of Society and of the Individual

The expectations of society and of individual workers, indeed of all of us, with regard to what we would like to accomplish in economic and social terms, and the capacity of the system to fulfill those demands, may be in significant conflict. Unless a way is found to resolve this potential conflict, there is a distinct possibility that the system will become unmanageable. Effective means will have to be found to alert, educate, and expose the public to the realities of the socioeconomic process.

Having looked at the four significant developments that the Committee foresees as affecting the employee relations process, it would seem that there are certain requirements for the future that flow from these developments, which must be addressed by employee relations practitioners.

Priority Areas
Reevaluation of Traditional Approaches

There is need for a reevaluation of the traditional employee relations methods, procedures, and techniques that have been developed in years past. One scholar in the field has described employee relations as the triumph of technique over principle. The decade ahead will require a reversal of that concept, so that principle once again triumphs over technique. In this connection, it would seem that one of the important requirements will be a reexamination of the many technical developments in the employee relations field; they will have to be coordinated, mutually supportive, and intelligently thought through relative to the goals that the system is seeking to achieve. The Committee believes that by 1985 the employee relations function will have to be more geared to a "systems" approach so that programs will be more integrated and more sensitively attuned to managerial requirements.

Reexamination of Employee Relations Role

By 1985 there should be a far clearer role for employee relations in the organization. The field must be more fundamentally related to the employee, his role in the organization, and the forces having impact on that role. With a reexamination and clarification of the function, there should be a more intelligent career-pathing system for its practitioners, a more significant status within the organization, and a more rational way of assessing the merit and worth of the practitioner. Today, one can look upon the field and say that it is not attracting talent as it should, given the scope and dimension of employee relations problems. The Committee agrees. Reexamination would lead to a more effective management function that, because of its contribution, will attract better people both at entry levels and from elsewhere in the organization.

Of paramount importance to the evolution of the employee relations process is that it respond, not by being reactive, but by being proactive, as we have indicated before. Employee relations practitioners must take a more aggressive, imaginative role in helping to manage the organization, in terms of both the business plans of the organization and leadership vis-à-vis the external forces. The process of reaching out to anticipate problems so that they can be dealt with effectively and of positioning the function at the center of the business planning process is what the Committee means as being proactive.

Involving the Individual Employee

Because of the complexities of the modern organization, and because of the importance of maintaining worker support throughout the organization, the individual employee must be given a better understanding of his role within the organization. Achievement of such understanding will require more than the classical idea of economic education. What is required is the involvement of each employee as an individual and as a member of the social system in the realities of the world in which he or she lives. It is an education in depth rather than an education to orient. There are significant experiments in organizations around the country which indicate that there are means of involving individual employees in such a way as to ally them with the goals of those organizations in which they work. The Committee believes that organizations will be going further in this direction in the future as a requirement for success.

111

Involvement with Government

The Committee has said much in its report about the role of government in the future. We have alluded again and again to the involvement of employee relations with government policy and regulation as being perhaps as great as almost any aspect of management. And it is our expectation that this involvement will continue to grow. We have also alluded to the idea that in the classic organizational model there are clear and distinct separations between the responsibilities of employee relations, government relations, legislative liaison, etc. Some organizations have sought, by using committees, to create linkages between these organizational units. Other organizations have coordinated them by having their various functions report to a senior executive. But little has been done that effectively achieves such integration. There is and will be a need to find better ways to integrate the various staff functions so that there can be more aggressive, effective involvement with government at all levels.

Better Planning

Most of the organizations represented on the Committee on 1985, and probably most of the sophisticated management groups in this country and abroad, have long engaged in various forms of planning. In most organizations, strategic business planning is not applied when human resources are concerned. Strategic decisions are made on the basis of financial resources. Human resources plans, if any, are developed to fit other business decisions already made.

This practice apparently assumes an unlimited supply of human skills and complete freedom to hire, fire, transfer, promote, and demote personnel as required. That kind of freedom, in our judgment, is diminishing now, and there will be even less by 1985. Indeed, the really strategic constraints may well include those imposed in the human resources/social arena as well as those in the financial and technological arenas. Thus by 1985 we foresee a requirement for fundamental restructuring of the planning process to better integrate human resources planning and to orient strategic planning more directly to the human resources and social relationship factors. We believe these will be among the driving forces that will have great impact on the management system of the future.

CONCLUDING COMMENTS

Although the Committee's report may have given the impression that we have been overly critical of the employee relations systems, that is far from the case. We believe that the techniques and approaches

112

that have been used have contributed to effective management. However, it is our belief that the characteristics of the employee relations process that have been of value in the past are not necessarily applicable to problems today or to those that will arise in the future. By this we do not mean that all of the skills and techniques of the past must be abandoned. What we do mean is that the future will require a sharply different approach to and by employee relations. Central to the challenge is the need to give sufficient time to a real consideration of the future. The question, What's new? normally means to the employee relations professional, What new technique or program or gimmick might I use? For the future, if we are to reach 1985 in more control of our operations than we have in 1976, What's new? should mean, What are the better ways? How can we be better prepared? How can we affect rather than be affected by the world in which we operate?

CRITIQUE OF THE COMMITTEE'S REPORT

VIEWS FROM SIX PROFESSORS
OF INDUSTRIAL RELATIONS

*As part of its program to "advance the knowledge and practice of human rela-
tions," Industrial Relations Counselors played an active role in the establishment
of industrial relations centers or departments at six universities. The heads of
five of these industrial relations sections—Princeton, University of Michigan,
California Institute of Technology, Massachusetts Institute of Technology, and
Queens College in Canada—attended the conference (Stanford University was
unable to be represented) and formed a panel to review the report presented
by the Committee on 1985. Their informal comments on the report and other
employee relations developments during the 1976-85 period follow. John F.
Simons, the incumbent IRC professor of industrial relations at the Colgate
Darden School, also joined the panel in critiquing the Committee's report.*

J. Douglas Brown, Princeton University: The Committee on 1985
has presented a broad picture of the employee relations field. Rather
than comment directly on what has been discussed, I prefer to act as
observer and look at 1985 in terms of nine problems. I am going to
present each problem as I see it, offer a solution, and highlight the
factors I believe are involved.

The major problem concerns size, bureaucracy, impersonality,
and loss of individual responsibility. The solution I suggest is decen-
tralization: reduce the size of operating units, shorten the vertical
span of control, increase participation, increase delegation of respon-
sibility, reduce detailed controls, and increase overall evaluation of
results. But most of all, more and better leaders are required. A major
factor I see is that we are dealing with a better educated rank and file
and better and more broadly educated executives and supervisors, so
that we can give them greater responsibility. Also, restraint is neces-
sary in the reliance on excessive controls by computers, and greater

emphasis should be placed on judgment; that is, improve leadership rather than take a bookkeeping approach.

The second problem involves improving the plant environment. People are better educated and want a better environment. My solution is that, with decentralization, plants can be moved to suburbs and smaller towns, avoiding decayed central cities unless conditions are improved. Single-dwelling houses should be used, with assistance indirectly by the company but not directly controlled in political, economic, and social terms. "Company housing" carries unpleasant connotations, but the interest of the employer in the community and in housing should not be eliminated. Plant location will become an increasingly critical factor in labor relations and manpower resources, as will inexpensive recreation.

Three, improvement in executive and supervisory quality is necessary. My suggestion is for greater use of midcareer education, not only in specialized areas but also to broaden understanding and judgment. The factor here is that with declining enrollment, universities and colleges will be anxious to develop midcareer education for people in industry.

Problem four is excessive government intervention in employment and employee relations. One answer is to encourage corporation leadership to exercise influence and promote legislation that is related to fundamental goals of sound policy rather than to detailed regulations and methods. The employer must retain the initiative. An important factor here is that public reaction may well swing away from excessive intervention by government bureaucracies, which have proved to be quite inefficient.

Problem five concerns the shifting balance in employee security programs from private to governmental operations. The solution is based on the assumption that government will eventually provide basic protection against old age, disability, survivorship, illness from natural causes, and medical costs. Industry must effectively develop sound supplementary plans, where they are justified and assured. What is important here is to assure maintenance of differential protection related to differential economic contributions beyond the basic needs covered by government. Industry must also assume that the government will require sound and equitable administration of benefits assured by the company as a part of the contract of employment; in other words, the new pension legislation.

Problem six concerns changes in union collective bargaining, more especially for the skilled. It is important to be ready to support differential compensation relative to skill, merit, and contribution, as opposed to following the trend toward egalitarianism. The factor here is that while unions will continue to favor the interests of the majority, unions are political bodies. It can be assumed that union statesmanship will eventually reflect management statesmanship in assuring effective motivation and productivity.

The seventh problem I see is government intervention and interference in hiring and promotion. I suggest that in the next ten years industry maintain a solid front on the principle of individual merit, once the fact and suspicion of discrimination by race, color, sex, and so on, have been eliminated. The important factor here (and I am sticking my neck out) is that I believe that the approach of quotas is not only unconstitutional but also contrary to the common interest of those affected.

Another problem is the shifting age balance in the population. During the next ten years industry will have to be ready to reconsider the normal age of retirement and to raise the retirement age gradually as the proportion of population in the present working ages declines. That's rather radical, but the OASI system is already considering the need to raise the established retirement age from 65 to 68 in small, gradual steps over the next thirty years.

The ninth and last problem I foresee for the next decade concerns the shifting balance of work and leisure. My suggestion is that companies study what the employees really want, and avoid fads. Variations in local conditions should be expected, and it is likely that the five-day workweek will continue as the norm, with leisure time being concentrated in longer vacations.

I feel that whether we get through the next ten years in good shape depends on how much attention is focused on the quality of leadership at all levels in the corporations. That is the essential factor. Stereotypes of leadership must be avoided; they are dangerous. Leadership is a personal art which industry must recognize and develop over the next ten years.

The employer is the active agent. The corporation is the active agent. The government and unions are regulatory. Thus it is industry that must maintain the initiative. It will also be important to balance the forces of governments, unions, and communities in the development of constructive policies and programs and to have faith in response, which does not always come quickly. Finally, we must learn to understand the individual employee and to understand human organizations, which are both lifelong tasks.

Robert D. Gray, California Institute of Technology: The labor force
in the future is going to be better educated, as the Committee on 1985
suggests. But that labor force is also going to be poorly informed. I
base this on my experience with many undergraduates at Cal Tech.
Even though they have been carefully selected and well educated
from a formal point of view, they lack a great deal of information
that we take for granted in the world of business and industry. And
I think it is important to be aware of this.

The Committee appeared quite concerned over the status of the
employee relations function, especially in regard to its role in decision-
making. In the bicentennial year it is well for us to remember what
Mr. Jefferson wrote: that government derives its powers from the
consent of the governed. If that was true two hundred years ago,
it should not be surprising that it is true now.

For example, we often talk about *authority*, but we don't seem
to see its relationship to leadership. Actually, it was one of my stu-
dents who helped me to see that leadership and authority are in a
sense different terms for the same thing. In discussing authority we
usually relate it to position. Obviously, the director of employee rela-
tions in most organizations does not hold a position comparable to
the vice president in charge of manufacturing or of sales. But it is
important to understand that leadership and authority may come
from more than position alone. They are based also on competence,
personality, and genuine interest. Greater competency in the field of
pension planning, for example, would enhance the employee relations
function in any organization.

To further illustrate, let me relate an incident that involved
Clarence Hicks shortly after he became assistant to the president of
Standard of New Jersey (a title he preferred to, say, vice president
of personnel). He was asked by one of his friends then running Stan-
dard of Indiana and an autocrat of the old school what he thought
of the new personnel man at Standard of Indiana. Hicks said, "Well,
I haven't met him, but let me ask you, has he ever come in and
pounded the table and said, 'This is something you have to do' or
'This is something you shouldn't do!'?" The friend answered, "Well,
of course not." To which Mr. Hicks replied, "Well then, I don't think
you have the right man."

That is what is needed in 1976 or in 1985 or at any time in the
future: an employee relations director with initiative who is capable
of pointing out the need for change when and where it is essential.

Although the Committee covered the subject of company per-
sonnel practices and policies broadly, they did not discuss any specific

practices or policies that will be required to meet the needs of the future. Most organizations have policies that need careful review, not just from a semantic point of view but also in terms of how they actually operate in the company. Many policies, for example, assume that there is a difference between wage rates and salary. Years ago there was a difference. But today, despite the differentiations in exempt and nonexempt employees under the wage and hour law, the line is blurring. Such policies must be reviewed and reevaluated in light of current realities to determine if they are really working out in 1976 and if they will work out in the future. Why does a particular policy exist? What problems does it solve? And what problems does the policy create?

The Committee suggested that employee relations anticipate a period of more "openness" but offered no specific suggestions—job bidding, for example. While the terminology too often turns people off because of its association with union contracts, job bidding offers an approach that needs to be examined. Some companies have developed other terminology, such as "opportunities" and "position opportunities." I can think of at least two companies that publicize about a thousand positions in their employee magazine. This produces "openness" because salary schedules and the classification for each position are also publicized. A report is then published about who filled the position. Was it filled, for example, by self-nomination? The records of one company revealed that approximately one third of its vacancies were filled by self-nomination during a one-year period, which indicates that a lot of managers had never reported that they had talented people on their staffs. In the future this is going to change, because supervisors are finding out that they can't hide talent and that they might as well get credit for recommending their bright young stars for promotion rather than losing them and having them say, "I got that job, no thanks to my boss."

Access to records also makes for more openness. California has a state law stipulating that employees have a right to look at the records pertaining to them. Some personnel people began devising ways to limit such access, but they discovered that once employees knew the records were available, they did not flock to see them. This reminds me of an incident in which a supervisor asked one of his subordinates, "What is it you really want to know?" And the fellow answered, "I want to know what you don't want to tell me." If management policy and practice are open, and employees know they can ask for and get the kind of information they want, they are not going to waste their time trying to get it.

There was one brief mention in the Committee's report about a cafeteria approach to benefit plans. Certainly, a few companies are beginning to offer benefit plans that truly meet the needs of employees. Obviously, a standardized benefit package is not going to meet the needs of very many people. Much money is spent on benefits, and it would seem logical to try to provide employees with a package that enables them to pick those benefits that will be of most value to them.

Dallas L. Jones, University of Michigan: I find that the Committee on 1985 brushed over the question of labor legislation and recent labor developments very lightly, but very wisely, by saying, "We expect there will be some legislation." Its report did go on, however, to hint that there will be more surveillance—maybe a partnership of government and labor; maybe national planning; maybe more government security programs. I am going to try to comment upon what the Committee characterized as "some" legislation.

First, my guess is that there will not be much in the way of legislation. I see very little likelihood that our basic labor law will be changed in any substantial fashion. There may be some changes in procedures. The present committee reviewing the operations of the National Labor Relations Board may come up with some suggestions to expedite case load, etc., but these will not be earthshaking. There is little hope, for example, that the emergency dispute provision will be changed. The political balance is just too tight; everyone is afraid to open up any section because this could then lead to other changes. Legalism in industrial relations (and I am speaking particularly of labor relations—grievance handling, etc.) will accelerate, however. I am sure that all of you are aware of this. (I recently heard an arbitration case in which the grievant had filed a charge against the union for failure to represent in good faith. He was grieving a discharge for lack of just cause, and he had charges with the EEOC and the Michigan Civil Rights Commission; he also had outside representation, and an observer from the NAACP. In total, the hearing on this case ran more than six days.)

Perhaps ten years down the line legislation in some states may require just cause for the discharge of any employee—not only unionized employees. There is a growing feeling that this type of protection should be extended, and in a few states legislation to that end has been introduced. Whether it will be passed or not is another question.

We may also have legislation in the public sector—most likely more of the states will regulate public employment conditions. However, unlike the Committee, I do not see any great innovations in public sector legislation. My experience is that the public sector simply adopts private sector solutions, whether they have actually worked or not. If we think in terms of dispute settlement, which is a major issue in the public sector, there is really nothing new—arbitration is not new; fact-finding is not new; mediation is not new. New combinations might be tried, as they have been in Michigan, but nothing different has developed; in fact, in Michigan, we are merely experimenting with gimmicks. Last-offer arbitration, for example, merely adds a few more gimmicks to the whole process rather than, in my opinion, providing equitable solutions. The only feature that I can see as possibly carrying over is unit determination; some states have adopted legislation permitting first-line and high-level supervisors to belong to unions. Now that may have some weight in the future, but I am not certain of it.

Two other questions that the Committee did not discuss but would perhaps like to consider are:

1. What is the higher educational level of the "new workforce" going to mean in the collective bargaining arena? Unions and management have now spent some forty years building up a code of rules (or "web of rules" as John Dunlop would call it), and if a variety of innovative work schemes are adopted, it will mean that those rules will have to be revised, at least within the unionized sector. Are we going to take those big thick books that we have negotiated and paid countless numbers of arbitrators to interpret, throw them out the window, and start all over again? There are some work schemes that cannot be introduced into the unionized sector without substantial revisions in collective bargaining agreements. It may well be that we have held back on innovative approaches in the unionized sector for that very reason, and perhaps the unions have, too. There have been some attempts when new plants are built—International Rockwell and the UAW, for example—to introduce new approaches and then adapt collective bargaining agreements to fit that situation, but in older plants such changes will clearly be a problem.

2. How, in the period leading to 1985, can we deal with the manpower decline in skilled workers? If our economy does begin to recover at a very substantial rate, its resurgence will be blocked by a dearth of highly skilled workers. We have neglected apprenticeship training through the years, particularly in the construction industry, and if construction starts to boom, we are going to be where

we were a few years ago when skilled workers were not available at any price. What the union will do under such circumstances is to send people at the rate who cannot perform the work. My friends in the public utilities industry tell me that if we were, by some miracle, able to start tomorrow on building nuclear power plants, it would be impossible to find the pipefitters and welders to build them. Many corporations, as I am sure you are aware, have started new apprenticeship programs or renewed those dropped a few years ago. It may be, of course, that with the increasing cost of college more people will be interested in apprenticeship programs, but it remains a question we have to consider.

I would also take some exception to the Committee's analysis of what will happen with trade union leadership. I can recall as a young assistant professor back in the 1950s telling my classes that a new union leadership would take over, bringing with it new ideas. In twenty years I have not seen much difference. It seems to me that old leaders are replaced by "old" leaders, and that the world goes on just as before. I am convinced that union staff people will not become the union leaders in this country, not in the coming ten years at any rate. I don't see a Nat Weinburg, for example, of the UAW, or a present Howard Young of the UAW rising to leadership.

Charles A. Myers, Massachusetts Institute of Technology: Judging from the report on 1985 which we have heard, I think the employee relations future is in good hands. Top management should read the Committee's report, for employee relations management, or human relations management, has here an excellent preview of the forces in the broad society that are at work. They are going to necessitate modifications in our traditional segmental approaches, but if we get in an uproar about whether "big brother" is going to be watching us, as George Orwell predicted, or whether some kind of socialism is in the offing, then we may be hampered from being *proactive* rather than *reactive*, and I am using those phrases because I think they ought to be etched in our memories.

I was asked to discuss some of the implications of the Committee's report for national manpower policy. Let me first make five points on future policy; then I want to say a word in conclusion about maximizing workforce effectiveness through a different leadership style.

1. The pressures for equal employment opportunities for minorities and women, particularly at middle and upper levels of management, will continue, with emphasis not solely on recruitment but also

on the movement upward. Many aspects of the personnel policy system will be affected: recruitment, selection, development, promotion, performance, and appraisal, to mention only a few.

2. As the Committee concluded, economic growth may be slower than the current rate, which for 1976 is now estimated at around 7.4 percent—a rate that cannot possibly be sustained. If the Democrats capture the presidency there will be more emphasis on growth and development, including some of the manpower policies that I mentioned earlier, and with a Democratic administration there will be somewhat less concern for inflation. If Arthur Burns carries out his promise to continue as chairman of the Federal Reserve Board he is going to have more problems.

3. Some form of national health insurance or reinsurance is coming, and private plans will probably become supplementary. The pressure arises because private group plans do not cover many low income people, particularly those employed in small enterprises.

4. Possibly there will be a slowing of regulatory trends, as the Committee suggested, but the effort made by John Dunlop to involve organized labor and management in establishing regulations that make sense, as in the emissions standards in coke ovens, is not likely to be pursued as actively under the current secretary (and of course, we don't know who the new secretary will be if the Democrats go into office). An alternative is for the top leaders in management to take the initiative with organized labor in joining hands against public interest groups (self-appointed), whose allies in the present government bureaucracy issue regulations. I'm not condemning government efforts, but there is the risk that those who draw up these regulations draw them up to conform with their personal views of the public interest, and they are not as effective as if they had the total input of top management and top labor people.

5. It seems unlikely that apart from national health insurance there will be much new legislation, especially legislation to curb the powers of the union. Certainly, that will not happen with a Democratic administration, and even with a Republican president I don't think it will occur.

The Committee noted the continuing pressure unions would exert on labor costs and possibly on limiting management flexibility. I think these trends have been persisting for a long time, and some of them, particularly wage pressures, are occurring in many other advanced industrial countries. Recently the Bureau of Labor Statistics put out a study showing relative improvement in the U.S. competitive position. In West Germany, for example, from 1970 to 1975, hourly compensation rose 167 percent; in the same period in the U.S., only 48 percent. The Bureau's conclusion was that there was essentially no difference between German and U.S. labor costs.

A final footnote on national policy: the Committee sees the possibility of unions of first-line supervisors. I think I am correct in saying that the Taft-Hartley Act would have to be amended to give protection to such unions. But if supervisors do try to unionize, the reason will be that, despite all the claims and the statements from management to the contrary, they do not yet see themselves as part of management.

Now, my last point: maximizing workforce efficiency through adoption of a different leadership style that would be less authoritarian, with more interaction and consultation, but with management still making the decisions. I believe the Committee is absolutely right on this because of the social trends that it emphasized, and I suggest that management may not necessarily be as successful in the future in dealing with these as it has been in the past. The external forces at work indicate to me a move in the direction of more consultation and types of participation. This brings to mind the late Douglas McGregor and his two classic books, *The Human Side of Enterprise* and *The Professional Manager*, along with Rensis Likert's book, *The Human Organization*, and Blake and Mouton's, *The Managerial Grid*.

I think McGregor's theory "Y" type of management is consistent with what this young group has talked about, but that it has been misunderstood. In effect, McGregor said that management still has to make decisions; it is not soft management, it is not everybody-be-happy management, but it is based on belief in the integrity of people and their desire to do a good job when the conditions in the organization for which they work encourage self-development and self-motivation. So I find that the ideas about challenging jobs, testing potential, rewarding work, participation, goal-setting, or improved individual performance are ideas already expressed by McGregor, but which are even more important today. Theory "Y" means, not that managers always consult and provide for participation, for when there are time constraints and complex problems, quick decisions have to be made, but that managers build up an atmosphere of trust, within which a tough management style can be accepted for the moment. It is based, as I said, on a deep-seated belief in the integrity of the individual and the importance of self-motivation in an atmosphere where energies are released, and valued.

John F. Simons, Colgate Darden Graduate School of Business, University of Virginia: To the Committee I would like to reiterate that I also think you can be proud of your results and of the acceptance that the whole report has received. All of us do not agree with every detail, but it was a thorough job.

I am going to confine my comments to two aspects of the report. One is the desire for a clearer and bigger role for industrial relations, or as Senator Vandenberg told President Roosevelt once: "We want to be in on the takeoffs as well as the crash landings." I want to consider also the inevitability of trends and the need for industrial relations to affect events more, rather than being affected by them.

As to this first point, there is little doubt of the desire of industrial relations people for a bigger voice, a bigger role, bigger paychecks, and higher status. In some organizations, these exist, but in many they do not. To some extent it may be a state-of-mind problem. In other words, if we think of ourselves as highly competent practitioners, that is probably what we will be. But if we follow the example cited by Bob Gray and are willing to pound on our bosses' desks and maybe risk our skins, perhaps more responsibility, authority, and opportunities for leadership will begin to accrue.

Closely related, of course, is the need, stressed strongly in the Committee's report, to get the best people. This, of course, is much easier to say than to do. For example, take the experience of the Darden School, which has an outstanding group of young people— able, intelligent, articulate, dedicated, and even respectful. Of 134 graduates in this year's class, 130 have already accepted positions. However, only one of these highly competent graduates went into the industrial relations function—and even that is one more than last year, and one more than the year before that. Moreover, I understand there is very little recruiting at the school for industrial relations people. Maybe there is a reason for this: of the 130 students or graduates who have accepted jobs, the average annual salary is $18,000; last year, it was $17,200.

The question I raise is how many industrial relations organizations are prepared to take a student off the campus, even with an M.B.A. degree, and place him or her in their organizations at that salary level? I suspect that there are some who feel they could not do so, and yet marketing functions, financial functions, and operating functions recruit at those salaries to get the good people they think they need. This suggests a subject for introspection on the part of industrial relations executives.

The second aspect of the report which I shall comment on has to do with the desire of industrial relations practitioners to "make things happen" instead of just reacting to events. In a large measure it seems to me we are talking about a matter of leadership, meaning people who *lead*, and not about the kind of person Jack Parker once spoke about, when he said, "There they go, I must hurry and catch up, for I am their leader."

Now, everyone would agree that no one person or one organization is going to devote full time to "making things happen." We are all born into a world we never made, and we must obviously accommodate and "make the best of things" time and again. But there is a fine line between accepting the inevitable on every occasion— often because somebody says it is inevitable—and standing firm now and then for what we sincerely believe in so long as it is not plain foolhardiness. Trends do exist but they are not always inevitable, either in the full impact of their promise, or within the predicted time frame.

The Committee reported, under the "psychology of entitlement" heading, the thought that having a job is a "right," and at "good pay and benefits," and predicted that this would become a reality in our short-range future, that is, ten years.

I don't know whether it will or not. A prominent leader has said: "Society is obliged to provide for the subsistence of its members, either by procuring work for them, or by assuring the means of existence to those who are unable to work."

I'm not quoting Senator Humphrey, speaking in support of his employment bill. That statement was made by Maximilien de Robespierre before the French Convention on April 4, 1793 . . . about 183 years ago. I submit it might have seemed "inevitable" to many listeners at that time. But years have passed, and for one reason or another it is still only a promise, or something less than full reality. Perhaps it is because some leaders felt that however noble in purpose, it was a promise society was not yet in a position to fulfill.

My point is that trends do not always have inevitable results. They are of the times, made and unmade by people who stake out a leadership position because they believe in something enough so that they want to "make something happen," and are willing and courageous and perservering enough to work toward that end. In my judgment, that is what leadership consists of, whether it is in industrial relations or any other function of the business.

Kenneth Clark noted the need for moral monitoring in corporations more than perhaps in any other kind of organization. I ask the question: What function is better prepared than industrial relations to move into this void and to take on a leadership role, considering its experience in dealing with the problems of work and controversy, and in enduring the heat? My thought, in this brief comment, is that to make its full contribution, industrial relations—perhaps one of the nobler professions—must be made up of people who are thoughtful, courageous, who take positions, articulate them, stand by them, and might, as Mr. Jefferson would say, even "be willing to pledge their careers, their fortunes, and their sacred honor" for what they really believe in and stand for.

W. Donald Wood, Queen's University, Kingston, Ontario: I, too, want to congratulate the Committee on 1985 for their excellent report and also for the class and style with which they presented their findings to this conference.

I have been asked to look at the professional, white-collar employee relations field to 1985. Because of time constraints, I am going to be very arbitrary and list ten points, a number of which have been covered in the Committee's report:

1. As the Committee has stated, the white-collar labor force will continue to increase rapidly, and it will continue to be the largest segment of the labor force. According to the U.S. Bureau of Labor Statistics Forecast, 1972-85, the U.S. white-collar group will grow by 37 percent by 1985; the blue-collar by 14 percent. The big engines will be the shift to the service sector and the changing technology within the goods-and-services industry. Within the white-collar group, professional/technical workers will grow the fastest—about 30 percent —and the mixed clerical group about 17 percent. Growth of sales/managerial groups will be fairly flat; in fact, there could be even some slight decline.

2. I agree completely with the Committee's report on the importance of the change in values held by the new workforce. Many of us may have thought these values were disappearing in the last few years, but they were only blunted a bit by the recession; they are still there. In addition, the new, young labor force is very persistent. The new values are not going to be presented with the same militancy and rhetoric as in the late 1960s. But they will be there, and management had better be aware of them and be ready with appropriate responses.

3. With growing numbers in the white-collar field, and its increasing importance, it must receive more employee relations attention. I am afraid we still have quite a bit of a take-it-for-granted attitude. Yet the number of woes expressed by white-collar employees shows that

their dissatisfaction is greater than even that of blue-collar workers. One of the problems is that the employee relations function has been so labor-relations dominated that some of its more positive aspects have been neglected, many of them outlined very clearly in the Committee's report. Thus, we are going to have to pay more attention to the white-collar field, and not just when the union knocks at the door, which may be too late. I am always amazed at the policies and practices companies introduce once white-collar workers become unionized, but not ahead of time. It might be worthwhile, therefore, to review and reassess some of our policies.

4. I am also concerned about the morale problem in the white-collar field in the 1980s, particularly the effect on professionals of slower promotion opportunities. This is related in turn to the unusual age distribution found in the labor force, which is a terribly important statistic for employee relations people to be aware of, both in terms of the total labor force and of their own organizations. Many unique problems are related to age groups. Productive problems occur, I believe, when the age distribution in both the economy and an institution is skewed. It is a critical factor in manpower planning and replacement and in labor costs, particularly on the benefits side.

In the past twenty years there has been a very sparse middle-aged group in the labor force, so it was necessary to move people up very rapidly. This was a good, very healthy situation, but in the 1980s the opposite will occur. According to labor forecasts, the middle-aged group will be in big supply. It will be impossible to move up people as quickly. We will be challenged to balance demands from the administrative hierarchy to maintain morale and efficiency with the rising expectations acquired by our society and the higher educational level of the labor force.

5. A parallel problem with implications for morale is the excess supply of university graduates in a number of areas. Two big demand areas have already slackened—education across the board, and the space program. There are three implications of this change, apart from the serious problem of unemployment among these young people: (a) There will be a tendency, or great temptation, for business to upgrade educational qualifications, leading to underutilization of talent and, in some cases, dissatisfaction of the affected employees. (b) It will limit jobs for no-degree job hunters. (c) It will be much more difficult to satisfy growing demands from women and minority groups for higher level jobs and promotions. In short, the age distribution and excess supply pattern is one that an organization should look at rather carefully in its own environment.

127

6. Against this background, more attention will have to be given to measures for improving job satisfaction and efficiency of white-collar employees. The whole question of organization structure is relevant here. It really should be geared to the kinds of people in the organization, but the tendency has been to transfer systems and structures from the blue-collar field to white-collar areas, thereby creating superfluous layers of supervision. Management needs to look at the occupational mix in organizations. In the goods industries we can get a bit of help from technology, but in the expanding service industries there are no guides from the technology for the kind of occupational mix that is needed.

The Committee has recognized the need for new policies and approaches in the employee relations field. One that needs to be considered, I think, is the whole question of job content. We've tended in the past to treat jobs as sacrosanct. We've had an "X" job and a "Y" job, and although there might be an employee who could fill an X-Y job, and the combination might be more appropriate and more efficient, the X, Y separation has persisted. In this sense, the whole structure of jobs needs some attention.

A number of people have mentioned the importance of more involvement in decision-making. I agree with the Committee that we should not import wholesale the institutions of Western Europe, but university graduates who have been involved in decision-making in their universities for four or more years are going to want to be involved in decision-making in their new organizations. Thus it will be hard to develop mechanisms that keep people "on the reservation" and at the same time get the work done.

7. I am concerned about a top leadership crisis in the decade ahead. In industry, government, institutions—the excessive specialization and departmentalization in our different disciplines is not developing the broad-based people needed for top decision-making. Specialists may move up very quickly during their first five or ten years, but at the high levels it becomes necessary to fit the pieces together in a grand design. Thus we have got to build in more of a liberal arts approach in our various disciplines. I suppose the objective should be to develop more generalized specialists. The most hopeful sign I see is that students are beginning to react to over-specialization and to emphasis on the means and the methodology instead of on the ends.

8. One of the panel members mentioned the middle-management crunch. Certainly, the opinion surveys point up that neither middle managers nor general foremen are overly happy. In the

white-collar field, however, I am not sure how many so-called supervisors and managers really do those jobs. A very important job to be done is to sort out titles from actual functions. Once that is accomplished we need to be sure the supervisors are treated as part of the management team and that they are so rewarded.

I agree also that there is a likelihood of a skilled-trades crunch, which probably reflects the misconception that everybody had to have a "sheepskin." There is still quite a need for apprenticeship training, which we sometimes overlook.

9. In this world of rapid change and knowledge obsolescence, there has to be more emphasis on upgrading and development programs, particularly in the white-collar field, not the band-aid approaches that have often been used in the past, but continuing education and development as a basic-part of the employee relations function.

10. I look for continued strong growth in white-collar union membership. The United States has already experienced explosive growth, and Canada even more, in the public sector in education and health and at state and local levels, and there is still potential, particularly in the States. We have seen less dramatic but more significant growth in the private sector, but in many important industries there is an important base in the white-collar field already, particularly in the clerical/technical areas. The major exceptions would probably be banking, insurance, and finance, which happen to be, and will be, the most rapidly growing sector of industry employment in the 1980s.

In looking at white-collar union growth in the past decade in the United States, I see a 50 percent increase. That is from a low base, but it is a fairly significant increase. And it excludes many employee associations. Often we are misled in examining white-collar unionism by looking for traditional kinds of structures. Much that is happening here is really in the employee association.

Of the ten top unions reviewed by the National Labor Relations Board in 1974, a record white-collar certification year, six were white-collar, and three were industrial unions heavily involved in white-collar organization. I think this growth will continue, and expand more rapidly for three broad reasons: (a) The long-run environmental factors outlined by the Committee will be more favorable, including legislation. (b) There will continue to be short-run frictions and inadequacies in management policies and practice, regarding the white-collar area. (c) Union activity will increase and the approaches will be more sophisticated. The labor force shift to white-collar employment is killing the unions—they have got to tackle that problem.

PART V: THE FUTURE AND ITS CHALLENGE

THE CORPORATE EMPLOYEE RELATIONS ORGANIZATION – CAN IT PRESERVE THE CONCESSION?

RICHARD A. BEAUMONT

RICHARD A. BEAUMONT is director of research of IRC. Since 1964 he has been president of Organization Resources Counselors, Inc., which he joined in 1958. From January 1966 to August 1967 he was on leave, serving as deputy under secretary of the Navy, and from May 1970 to December 1970 he was senior vice president and director of Amerada Hess Corporation. He has long been active in research on management organization and industrial relations, and has served as a consultant to major corporations in this country and abroad, to various branches of the federal government, and to state and local governments. Before joining ORC he was assistant director of research for the Hawaii Employers Council and director of administrative services for the American Management Associations. Mr. Beaumont is a graduate of the University of California and received an M.A. from the University of Hawaii. Among his pub-lications are "Overview of New Dimensions in Organization," in New Dimensions in Organization; *"Investing in Human Resources," in* Manpower and Planning; Management, Automation, and People; Executive Retirement; *and* Productivity and Policy Decisions.

To say something new and different at the conclusion of a meeting like this is extraordinarily difficult. Yet I think there are different ways of looking at the issues of management and employee relations than we have considered over the last three days. So rather than say anything new, I want to examine these issues from a somewhat different perspective. While there may be nothing absolutely new under the sun, I sense, as I travel in this country and around the world, that we are undergoing a unique period of adjustment that affects all of the arrangements that have evolved with respect to the concept of man and his organizations.

IRC was born, as you learned the other day, in the first quarter

133

of this century, after federal troops had to restore order in an industrial workplace. How alien that thought is to us in the United States today, now in the last quarter of the century. In the industrial workplace we have been through much, have made many adjustments, and have adopted many innovations in the course of developing our modern concepts and systems of employee relations. Perhaps it is because we have been through so much in gaining our current sense of balance that there was an initial reaction on the part of some conferees against certain conclusions drawn by the Committee on 1985 about the future of employee relations. Perhaps the desire of some of us to refute the Committee derived simply from the battles which those who are more experienced have already fought to develop and gain positive attitudes and viewpoints among managers and employees, and from the many battles fought with unions and government agencies. Nonetheless, if employee relations is to be a positive force, we must be certain now that we know where we are and where we are going. And that task of examining the future was admirably discharged by the Committee.

As professionals in employee relations, all of us in this room carry the burden of facilitating adjustment to change—in knowing how to accommodate it, and how to use it to spur development. For change is inevitable, whether we are active or passive. As man struggles for a place in the sun, organizations, societies, and people do change. Each permutation introduces new variations, and those variations are what we have to contend with. The language of the IRC charter of "advancing the knowledge and practice" portrays a dynamic concept, recognizing as it does that the interactions of people in their organizations are not only very complex but subject also to a series of changes that are unavoidably and realistically inevitable.

Where are we now? The Committee on 1985 says that the world is at a point where significant changes are occurring in all aspects of man's relationship to work and society. And they are. But more specifically, society is at a historical junction where disruptive, divisive global forces are at work which have the capacity to change the established order. The most dramatic evidence is the recent problems surrounding the world's oil resources and the concerns being manifested over the distribution of wealth among have and have-not nations. Other disruptions in our economies are occurring as a result of the flow of capital from country to country; social and business stability is being threatened by political changes in all parts of the world, particularly in the Middle East and in Africa.

These developments stem from the same type of economic,

political, and social forces that the Committee referred to, and when such forces are seen in a worldwide perspective, their scope is impressive. They are at work in the United States also, and try as we might to ignore them, they have implications for every one of us. They will significantly affect our behavior, our concepts of wealth, property, and the rights of capital, and our views on authority systems and organizations. They will affect our institutions, including unions and their objectives and power, as well as our government and the social and economic order. They will affect our businesses and our colleges.

In fact, the status quo is already being challenged in much of the so-called free world. Before this year is out, elections in Sweden and in Germany may lead to the overthrow or at least the weakening of the entrenched political parties. In Italy a strong communist party already threatens the viability of a centrist government. Even here in the United States we may see a change in focus and direction if a new political party moves into office. In the United Kingdom, in Spain, in Portugal, new definitions of the role of government, business, and unions are taking shape. Even "the Switzerland of North America," Mexico, is going through a period of reexamination in attempting to resolve a new series of internal economic problems.

Perhaps the redefinition process is best exemplified in Japan, the industrial miracle of the modern century. Having struggled through its recent recession to recovery, Japan is still trying to find a new way to operate in the modern world because the past accommodations between business and workers are no longer possible. In the Netherlands, in Belgium, and even Canada there is uncertainty about the future and about the direction that will be taken in the relationship between industry and society. The only Western nation not undergoing the process of redefinition is Brazil—an interesting phenomenon since Brazil is a military dictatorship.

In the center of New York City there is a sign at the top of a building that says, "World Peace Through World Trade." That pious dream, prevalent just five years ago, is already disproved. At this moment we are farther away from "one world" than we were a decade ago. Many in business who believed in the importance of an integrated world economic system as a means of creating social and political order now find that the solution involves much more than that simple concept.

In this country and around the world there is a rising tide of nationalism and ethnocentrism. Germans want industry in Germany; Frenchmen want industry in France. Within nations, groups of citizens are beginning to express an objective first stated by Samuel

Gompers many years ago as simply "We want more." But today the cry is "More for us." This sentiment is being expressed now among the Flemish, among the Galicians; everyone wants more, and on his own terms.

Ethnonationalistic movements are important. Probably one of the great problems in the decade ahead will not be the American problem of dealing with minorities, but the European problem of dealing with the "guest" workers from numerous ethnic groups who represent a massive social force that, if unleashed, has the potential of disrupting the industrial West.

The concept of economic rationalization through the business system remains but a thin veneer which, under the abrasion of even the slightest economic, social, or governmental pressure, is quickly eroded to reveal an intense self-interest on the part of nations, groups, and individuals. In the years ahead this phenomenon will become more and more apparent within the United States and abroad, partly as a result of inflation and partly as a result of a change in social values and social balance. Political parties, governments, and unions will seize upon issues of self-interest to maintain their position, and that will shake our economic and social order.

Such economic, social, and political trends support many of the conclusions of the Committee on 1985 regarding the United States. What they portend for employee relations, particularly in an era of continuing inflation, is extraordinary pressure on tried-and-true practices. It will be most apparent in fields such as compensation and benefits. Merely because of inflation, employee relations practitioners should be examining the question of whether rigid compensation systems built around the scientific management of the late 1920s are necessarily valid today. The extraordinary costs of employee benefits and the impact of the world's financial and capital markets on basic benefits concepts also need reassessment.

Like it or not, the inflationary process at work in the world at large suggests a continuing, persistent flirtation with incomes policies or controls of one sort or another. For one thing is clear, and that is that so far we have not learned how to cope with inflation through the institutions that we have developed. Experimentation with control-type mechanisms is now in order, whether they be called incomes policies, social contracts, or other esoteric names.

The Committee also stated that we will continue to contend with the business cycle. These economic undulations with periods of expansion and contraction suggest the persistence of economic uncertainty for workers. The unprecedented expansion and stability of developed economies during the 1960s have accustomed many to the good life; they have accommodated to it and to the style of living it provides, and they will seek some guarantees to protect themselves. Their desire for security and the need to reduce the range of uncertainty in which they operate will elicit from their political representatives—unions or governments—more promises, and greater pressure on business to provide certainty.

Thus, a widespread movement forcing developed nations to provide guarantees of both income and jobs is in the offing. It is now occurring in Western Europe more than in the United States. The European Commission, for example, is already considering a new directive for establishing the individual's rights in his job. This is quite a shift from the traditional focus in which the social responsibility for alleviating the impact of unemployment was discharged through relocation, unemployment payments, and the like. It marks the emergence of a new questioning of the rights of capital and property.

The concept of job rights is new. It has been a long-standing issue in the United States in the collective arrangements with unions, but in Western Europe we are beginning to see the emergence of quasi-governmental recognition of such rights. And this *is* a different direction.

One of the principles in the wave of new developments and movements now occurring is that political organizations do respond to their constituents. In this process, a promise continues to become a right. Today the promise, explicit or implicit, is a good life in economic terms and the assurance of job protection. Though the guarantee is more explicit in Western Europe than in the United States, experience says that Americans face the same uncertainties as Europeans and that our political parties do respond to constituent demands, whether they are sound economically or not. Thus, in the United States we can look for a spate of bills designed to guarantee income and employment. They may not become law in the near term, but they will lead to an alteration of the old concepts concerning employment, work, and management rights.

As political organizations respond to pressures from the public for satisfaction of its needs, another movement will develop—the further erosion of the rights of capital, the rights of property, and the rights of managers. Participation, the principles of human behavior, the concept of theory "Y" management, and codetermination have been subjects of continuing discussion. But there is little consideration of the real issue underlying each of these concepts—that is, whether or not there is a legitimacy to the right to manage. Can managers rightfully claim legitimacy for the management process itself?

The idea that a manager has authority has precedence, but what does that really mean in the current world, where authority is questioned at the work level by individual workers, by unions, by governments? Moreover, managers themselves even have difficulty demonstrating what management is all about. Perhaps you might have been as startled as I was when I first heard one multinational company report the prevailing philosophy of its international headquarters. It held that two of the few management rights it retained were the right to determine the level of investment, and the appointment of the top manager in each of the countries in which the company operated. Certainly, this is a far more limited view of management rights than most managers generally presume they have. Yet, how much more do we actively retain?

Ultimately, management has to earn the right to manage, and by virtue of a manager's or the organization's effectiveness, demonstrate that the perpetuation of management is in the social good. This will be difficult to do after centuries of believing that management's rights are created by capital and property, protected by government, and perpetuated so long as the operation is a financial success.

At the social level, too, we seem intent on leveling out social and economic differences. Whether this is right or wrong is not the issue. The issue is that the trend exists and that it marks the direction of society. The implications of that phenomenon are of current significance in how we behave in our policies, practices, and actions, both as citizens and as participants on the social, economic, and political stage.

Now, how do some of these broad ideas relate to employee relations? Many of them support one basic thought: *There is a greater and greater need for effective integration of the employee relations process not only within management levels but with the social system and the process of government.* Integration, here, does not mean acceptance of the system; it refers to retention of the capability and capacity to deal conceptually and operationally with behavior patterns reflecting the environmental forces at work in society and impacting upon a given organization. In order to integrate, we must think of tailoring the logic of the organization and our technocracy to the reality of social and political processes, each interacting with and shaping the other. Therefore, I do not envisage a passive role for employee relations; however, its influence will inevitably diminish unless its professionals begin sensitively and intelligently to do the job that has to be done.

In this connection I was somewhat dismayed by the responses to a questionnaire on the employee relations organization sent to a group of companies selected as significant in their industries and important nationally and internationally. In general, they responded:

— We are satisfied with what we've got. Our organizational structure is excellent.

— Our career system is working fine.

— We are sanguine about the way we go about determining our needs.

— We don't need to do very much to formally review our effectiveness; our informal processes—conversation, meetings, reviews with our colleagues in other companies, etc.— do the job reasonably well.

About the only area not described by platitudes was the complicated approval systems operating in many of the companies.

On the positive side, some companies did cite a need for better mechanisms to deal with government and the external environment. A few recognized that the problems of today require more than simplistic reliance on centralized or decentralized modes of management. While they had no answers, they in effect eschewed more centralization or more decentralization as the answer. I was interested in the implications of the General Motors presentation made earlier in our program. What was said was that because of external forces, more centralization within the classical model of decentralization may be the mode for the future, at least in terms of the management of employee relations systems. That is an important consideration. It is the type of issue an intelligent, alert management is debating today, for its response to external forces may determine its survival.

Respondents also expressed great concern over growing "communityism" and the potential implications for unionization. Another intriguing comment favored removal to the line organization of certain activities now in the employee relations function. Specifically mentioned was organization development, which was seen as being more appropriately a line management tool than a staff function.

Early in my career at IRC I was impressed by a report written for a company then operating in the Middle East. The first paragraph said that the primary employee relations objective of the company should be the preservation of its concession. Today, the question of preserving the concession to operate is the material question before us. This is not an abstract issue that relates to whether we can continue to operate in Rhodesia or Tanzania. It is a question of material significance right now, for example, in Sweden, where the idea of capital reformation may take hold in a five-year period; if it does, the management concession will be lost. Germany also, in my judgment, is but five or six years away from dealing with the question of capital reformation, as is the Netherlands. And in fact there might be a similar risk in the United States, though it would come about through far more subtle means. How many of the multinational companies present here, for example, have begun to plan and to prepare for being responsive to the new OECD guidelines which impose drastic new requirements concerning information and personnel policy? The time is growing short for preserving the concession. As we move into the future certain questions and challenges will need to be faced.

First, the structure of organizations. One of the themes heard at this meeting, and at many meetings I have attended, is that top management has got to direct more of its attention to employee relations problems and to become more involved in these issues. The difficulty, of course, is the little time that top managers have to spread over many areas of responsibility. The issue was never clearer to me than a little over a year ago when Helmut Schmidt sought to convene a meeting of the chief executives of multinational companies to discuss German codetermination. I wondered what would have happened if, on the same day, the shah of Iran had summoned a similar group. While an oil company executive would probably have gone to Iran, what would he have done about Helmut Schmidt?

It is possible that the typical classical organizational structure focusing on one top leader may no longer be able to serve the total management system in handling the issues that will have to be faced. In employee relations alone, the problems of interaction and confrontation are growing ever greater and straining the classical model.

Second, during this meeting we have flirted with the perpetual problem of defining the staff role of employee relations vis-à-vis the line. Personally, I have long viewed the "line and staff" terminology as reflective of an archaic, simplistic concept. When, for example, today's tax expert tells the management of his company what it can do, he is not advising but is in effect making the decision. In employee relations the differentiation is more complex because there are no hard facts or exclusive terminology. Thus it appears that anyone can analyze employee relations situations and draw conclusions, when, actually, more expertise is required because of the scope of employee relations decisions. At this stage more objectivity is needed in delegating authority to make decisions, as well as greater sensitivity to the need of an organization to utilize its best talent to decide what is actually best. The idea of sharing and pooling resources to reach a better decision is spreading, and as it does, the distinctions between line and staff will blur further. Slowly newly merged roles will have to be accommodated in organizational dogma and practice.

Third, where does personnel and employee relations really fit in? I urge that you carefully reread Douglas Brown's definition of a "learned profession," which he appended to his remarks at the outset of our conference. The elements he cited, of action, of philosophy, and of being willing and able to pick and choose from the various fields of knowledge, are essential ingredients for the future. But is that all our employee relations function, structure, and system is about? How should it fit into the organization, how must it be positioned to draw on the talent and to develop the initiatives needed by management systems today, if it is to cope with the broader demands of modern society? That is the underlying issue.

Fourth, if my thesis about nationalism and ethnocentrism is correct, and if we add a dimension to the matrix by taking account of the many differences in our employee populations—race, sex, religion, locality of orientation, age, and education—are the basic tenets that have governed fundamental employee relations philosophy in the past valid for the current era and valid for the future? The system has been based on a concept of homogeneity and equality of treatment. I believe that heterogeneity will be a characteristic of employee populations in the future. But we are not philosophically oriented or structured to deal with it; we are structured to deal with homogeneous population groups, and this applies to management as well as to unions. Perhaps we lose sight of the fact that true equality of treatment identifies specific needs and seeks to satisfy those needs at the same relative level.

Fifth, in the private sector, private enterprise system, have we actively considered whether we are prepared to adequately distribute the profits of the system in terms of wages, dividends, or social need? Or do we in fact simply follow past practice as modified by day-to-day events? The greater burden being imposed on the enterprise system to satisfy the needs of the society generally requires that we actively respond, and responsible managements and boards of directors cannot avoid facing questions of balancing competitive demands. Kenneth Clark suggested that an ombudsman on the board with moral and ethical responsibility in this area might be useful.

Some of you have been concerned about the idea now flourishing in Western Europe of codetermination and of having outsiders present on your boards when critical questions of management arise. Nonetheless, in a somewhat chaotic, ad hoc way, we in the United States are developing a representational system on our boards of directors that involves not only women and blacks, but other representatives of the community. As this trend develops further, and it will, I urge you to consider the likelihood that these new representative bodies will behave more like legislatures than like the traditional business. Slowly but persistently they will move us to the point where the distribution of the gains of the system will focus on social needs to a greater and greater extent. Are we prepared for that?

Sixth, as I observe managements, I am troubled by the persisting issue of whether an organization should be more, or less, centralized or decentralized. So much energy is spent in determining the internal balance that too little time is devoted to employee needs and external pressures. All organizational arrangements lead to some conflict which requires attention to control mechanisms and methods of coordination. The reality is that all organizations are a system of "treaties" between the center and the group, and the group and the division, and the division and the plant. But these treaties should recognize that each level has certain rights. Thus, rather than decentralization, what we really should have in mind is centralization and devolution. Devolution is a slightly different concept than decentralization, for the latter suggests vested rights in the operating unit that the central organization simply cannot have. New rational approaches to such devolution must be arrived at for each new situation.

Seventh, where are we in the process of planning? The Committee's concern that planning is typically seen in the framework of financial constraints is valid. But for the future the real constraints (now operating elsewhere in the world more dramatically than in the United States perhaps) will be social in nature. What I would suggest is that we have been on a philosophical and psychological plateau. Now a gargantuan effort is required to move ahead. A true revolution is not in the offing, but the consequences of needing to make a commitment to change in a new social and political environment should be reckoned with. This is going to be hard to plan for because, on the one hand, change will occur ever so slowly and, on the other, the prospect of entrapment will confront us continually because of having to deal with fundamental problems in a public relations mode.

We must continue to focus on the individual and his needs, regardless of his level in the organization, balanced against the organization's needs. We will need to know and understand our organizational goals and to seek better interaction methods and communications. We must understand if the rewards will truly reward, and I refer not only to financial ones. We must look for systems that are capable of integration and management in a way that gives operating units their proper role, and this is what I meant in my remarks above by forms of rational devolution.

Most important, we must orient ourselves to the future, the concept, the vision, the dream. I think that one of the roles of leadership is to constantly point out to our organizations that they should be expanding their reach, that they should be preserving the concession. We must recognize that there are new social dimensions and be prepared to deal with them.

Kenneth Clark said that he had faith in the ethical practices represented by the individual's actions. Perhaps, because we are pragmatists, we bridled a little at some of the points emphasized by the Committee because we know we will cope—I am convinced of that. However, my fear is that our professionalism in the essential though abstract art of management—in engineering, in finance, or in the employee relations areas of labor relations and compensation—can lull us into the false sense that we are coping with the total world when, in fact, we are not. What the future will require is a degree of boldness to look beyond our organizational boundaries, a degree of willingness to take the initiative based not on facts but on vision. This means commitment to our ideals and accepting jeopardy and risks. In the long run, if we are dedicated to the principle of advancing the knowledge and practice of human relationships in our own organizations, we may find that commitment to be the best way of preserving the concession for the next decade and beyond.

SURVEY OF CORPORATE EMPLOYEE RELATIONS ORGANIZATIONS

A Summary of Responses from Leading Companies

As a part of the activities surrounding its Fiftieth Anniversary, Industrial Relations Counselors initiated a number of studies in an attempt to assess the present and future prospects of the field of employee relations. One of the studies undertaken was designed to generate basic data on the organization, conceptualization, and discharge of the employee relations function in industry.

A standardized questionnaire, consisting of 13 individual items on corporate employee relations organization—an area in which there has characteristically been a dearth of significant comparative information—was developed and forwarded to 90 well known companies (see Appendix B). Care was taken to reach a good cross section of the business community in terms of size, industry, philosophy, and corporate structure. Forty companies responded, outlining their general patterns and approaches to employee relations. They varied considerably with respect to both industry and size, ranging from finance to extractive industries and consumer goods, and employing from just under 3,000 to over 600,000 people. Statistically 12 of the responding firms employed fewer than 30,000 people, an additional 12 employed between 30,000 to 100,000, and the remaining 16 had in excess of 100,000 employees. All of the firms play a significant role in their own industries, and many are of considerable importance nationally and internationally as well. Of the 38 American industrials responding, 27 may be found on the Fortune 100 listing for 1976.

STRUCTURE OF THE EMPLOYEE RELATIONS FUNCTION

Despite the variations in corporate size and industry and in employee relations structures, the responses exhibited a significant degree of homogeneity in outlook, although exceptions did exist, notably in the two international European firms. The responding companies are generally quite satisfied with the way employee relations structure has developed up to this time. Most of them feel that their individual employee relations organizations embrace all of the relevant functional specialities required for smooth and comprehensive operations, an attitude reflected in the following typical comment: "We have just reviewed our employee relations function and believe the organization is all inclusive and can relate to all levels of management both corporate and divisional."

Only six of the companies, all of which have less than 30,000 employees, identified responsibilities or individual functions that they believe should probably be excluded from what is presently included in their corporate employee relations area. In three of the companies, functions that were seen to be more normally handled by the comptroller's department (payroll and liability and property insurance) had been included among the tasks of employee relations. In the other three companies routine administrative functions relating to clerical employees, the management of the headquarters building, and security were seen to be more properly the function of the auditing department.

About one-third of the responding companies identified some functions that they felt should be included in the employee relations area, although some of the exclusions were results of the historical development of the individual firms. Perhaps the most frequently mentioned were formal management and organizational development programs (which in some cases had not even been identified as specific corporate functions) and a number of specialized legal areas, such as labor law and equal opportunity law, that are presently handled by law departments. Two of the smaller firms presently exclude the safety function from the employee relations organization. In one case the employee relations function was the responsibility of the public affairs manager.

Of all the responding firms, only the two European companies felt that a comprehensive social planning function should be included in employee relations activities. Although such a function is now being carried out in a piecemeal fashion with no direct assigned responsibility, both companies recognize the importance of the social research and planning area for the future and believe that some centralization of these activities on a formal basis will soon be required. Although the corporate or employee relations philosophies of several of the larger U.S. firms recognize the concept of social responsibility, none of these firms indicated a desire to establish a formal area of responsibility within the company.

The high degree of uniformity and sense of satisfaction with the employee relations function which the responses as a whole reveal would indicate either the maturity of employee relations as a function or rather widespread complacency about what has often been an amorphous management area in the past.

CENTRALIZATION VERSUS DECENTRALIZATION

Generally, most companies, as shown below, reported themselves as being strongly committed to either centralization or decentralization, and only a few indicated any present reassessment of either concept.

Company Size	Centralized	Decentralized
Under 30,000 employees	7	5
Between 30,000 and 100,000 employees	7	5
Over 100,000 employees	10	6
Total	24	16

The companies reporting a decentralized decision-making structure tended to respond as though there were something inherently good in decentralization and seemed to take pride in using this approach without really justifying it. Most of those companies organizationally emphasized the divisional or profit-center approach, and they seemed less concerned about corporate consistency and more with flexibility of policy interpretation to meet the needs of their operating units.

The companies reporting a centralized decision-making structure tended to include more justifications for their form of corporate organization than did those describing themselves as being decentralized. The centralized corporations maintained that among the primary advantages of their system is the ability to insure consistency of policy and its application throughout the firm. This tends to decrease the response time on issues for which policy has been determined but simultaneously increases the response time for issues for which no policy exists. Other reported advantages included increased control by corporate headquarters, the enhancement of the employee relations function that results from this, and greater follow-up potential. It was noted that in highly centralized corporations, the employee relations function may almost be described as a line function rather than a staff service.

One of the medium-sized companies indicated that it had undergone a consolidation of subsidiary company employee relations staffs into a centralized function at the corporate level. After two and a half years of experience with this format, the company believed it had made the right decision. According to its analysis, "Consolidation has several advantages, among which are that it (1) brings to bear a greater concentration of functional expertise; (2) generates a long-term cost savings by eliminating subsidiary company central employee relations staffs; (3) greatly improves ability to move employee relations people into various field assignments, regardless of subsidiary company; (4) improves caliber of staffing at the general office because of the 'one company' concept; and (5) provides for more consistent application of policies and plans among the various subsidiaries."

Some disadvantages of the centralized system identified by the respondents are fewer opportunities for the development of middle management, occasional communications problems, need for more reports, and more nonproductive time in terms of administrative requirements. None of the respondents chose to make any comments dealing specifically with the impact of decentralization on the line organization.

Twenty-four of the responding firms either characterized themselves as being highly centralized with regard to decision-making or, based on overall examination of their questionnaire responses, had what amounted to a de facto system of centralization, despite official pronouncements to the contrary to the one particular question utilizing these terms. A typical pattern focused on policy-making and decision-making as a top-level corporate function, with responsibility for implementation generally delegated to lower levels in the organization. The latitude of action available to lower echelon corporate units varied considerably but tended to be highly issue-oriented and dependent on the existence of articulated corporate policies. The lack of any formal corporate policy on a particular area tended to lead to that function, e.g., salaries, being characterized as decentralized.

Of the 16 companies that considered themselves to be decentralized in their decision-making, most reported that the corporate staff functions, including employee relations, fulfill advisory and consulting roles. In one case it was noted that in the determination of corporate policy, input from line units always takes precedence over input from corporate staff. A small number of the companies did, however, indicate that it was becoming increasingly difficult to retain the decentralized decision-making style because of increased government regulatory pressures. Such pressures are forcing an ever greater degree of centralization and are presently generating the requirement for stricter controls and increased monitoring activity at the corporate level. As one respondent put it, "Under [our] philosophy, the *overall* objectives and the decisions are determined at the corporate level. Practices and procedures implementing these policies are the responsibility of the divisional employee relations organization. Decision-making, within the overall corporate guidelines, is a decentralized function.

"Forces stemming from today's social and legislative climate—for example, increased government regulations and the tendency toward litigation—signal the need for decision-making to move more in the direction of centralization."

CHANGES IN THE EMPLOYEE RELATIONS FUNCTION

Government pressures, in the form of regulations in such areas as equal employment opportunity, safety, and pensions, were identified by the majority of respondents as being responsible for the significant differences in the employee relations function of today as compared with that of ten years ago. The major difference cited was the increase in scope and responsibility which has resulted in increased specialization of the individual employee relations function and in increased professionalism among those in the field. It was also reported that government pressures have significantly increased top management's acceptance and recognition of the employee relations function.

According to the respondents, the major change occurring in employee relations departments over the last decade—one not related to increased government involvement—is the trend toward comprehensive reorganization, particularly during the last five years. Corporate movements toward centralized or decentralized decision-making systems, depending on the original system, have resulted in changes in reporting relationships, power, and, in some cases, areas of responsibility for the employee relations departments. Several of the companies responding appeared to regard these essentially administrative changes as the most significant developments to have taken place in employee relations over the past years. Four responding companies indicated that they believe that there had been no significant changes, in either function or organization, in employee relations during the past decade.

In addition to internal organizational changes and a growing functional sophistication, the respondents mentioned such changes as the increased importance being placed on training and management development; greater concern for, and more formalization of, programs dealing with executive and professional employees, such as compensation and benefits; and concern over possible unionization. The importance of functions related to overseas operations has also increased greatly. And, particularly among the larger firms, respondents indicated growing recognition of the importance, within the employee relations sector, of planning and research in this area.

Several respondents reported that as the result of the various changes that have taken place, the entire process of corporate employee relations has developed from the generally reactive function of ten years ago into the more initiating and active function of today.

CURRENT PROBLEMS FACING EMPLOYEE RELATIONS

The increased government involvement in business, characterized as perhaps the single greatest element of change in the conduct of employee relations, was also cited by the great majority of the responding companies as the major problem area in employee relations today. The situation was described by one respondent as the "cancerous encroachment of the federal government into the affairs of business, as well as [into] other elements of the private sector." Another referred to the "regulation, pressure, interference, and plain meddling on the part of various government agencies."

Although many government programs, such as OSHA and ERISA, were mentioned, the most consistently cited was equal employment opportunity. Government regulations and involvement in this area have, in the view of one respondent, created the problem of "protected classes" (minorities, women, etc.). Many of the responding companies have found it necessary to delegate responsibility for dealing with government regulations and initiatives to specific employee relations practitioners within their organizations—the level of expertise and specialization required being considered beyond most personnel generalists. One company noted that the proliferation of federal regulations had made necessary the establishment of a corporate employment practices unit. Another firm felt that the time pressures associated with the changes being fostered by government intervention were creating a "bureaucratic mentality" rather than an "enterprise mentality" among employee relations practitioners.

The second most-cited problem facing employee relations was management selection, development, and training. The need for good managers and skilled employee relations practitioners was repeatedly stressed in the completed questionnaires, with the inadequacy of present training procedures, especially in the area of employee communications, being frequently cited.

Along with general economic concerns involving maintenance of competitive compensation policies and coping with increased costs, the third major concern of the respondents was the general area of employee attitudes. Many companies have recognized that problems in attendance, productivity, turnover, and loss of "loyalty" may stem from broad social concern with the quality of life. Other manifestations of this change in employee attitudes cited by respondents were challenges to management authority, white-collar and professional unionization, and the tendency of employees to refer complaints to third parties, such as government agencies. Several of the responding companies reacted with near indignation to this shift in employee attitudes, with one observer commenting on employees' "apparent lack of appreciation of the contribution of corporate enterprise based on profits." One large company, however, expressed the hope that "changes in employee attitudes may result in employees' becoming more active in controlling their environment and resolving their own individual disputes. This increased participation could serve to reduce the tendency to resolve problems through litigation."

Most companies saw solutions to these problems in the development of increased motivational techniques and greater flexibility of employee relations policies. Only the two European respondents and one U.S. company saw as a possible solution the development of effective means of gaining employee involvement in the decision-making process and management of the firm. They suggested that employee relations work toward increasing management-employee communication and cooperation, making better and more use of employees' capabilities, and achieving meaningful employee participation in management and decision-making, while still maintaining final management control. It should be noted that the U.S. firm indicated a somewhat different rationale for those employee relations objectives than did the Europeans. After dealing with its efforts at increased communication, participation, and integration of minority employees into all levels of the organization, the respondent effectively qualified the corporate policy by stating that "the principal objective of all of the foregoing is to increase productivity."

PROBLEMS PROJECTED FOR THE NEXT FIVE YEARS

Looking ahead five years, the single largest concern of the responding companies is the problem of equal employment opportunity—questions about promotions, maintaining merit policies, the potential male or white "backlash," and the relationship between retirement plans and age discrimination were all mentioned. It is interesting that although government regulation of business was cited frequently as a continuing problem, equal opportunity was consistently singled out for specific mention. The variety of other government programs, such as OSHA, were usually included together in a single grouping. Benefits were the only other area of government intervention specifically noted by respondents. Expectations of a national health insurance plan, requirements for Health Maintenance Organizations, dental plans, and a portable pension retirement system seem to be widespread among the responding corporations.

There was also significant concern about various social issues, including the possibility of social audits of corporations by outside agencies. Also cited were problems likely to arise because of increased employee expectations in terms of the quality of life—job enrichment, longer vacations, shorter working hours, and a general desire among the workforce to be included in the decision-making process of the firm. Both of the European firms, and a number of the U.S. respondents, also noted a trend toward income equalization, or salary compression, between managers and the workforce and between blue- and white-collar workers in general.

It was noted that specific problems generated by increased employee expectations would be the maintenance of discipline and the need to balance those expectations with the corporate desire for productivity and efficiency. There was some recognition that these divergent needs are not necessarily mutually exclusive, and finding a method to bring about a reasonable balance was mentioned as an important challenge for employee relations for the future.

The respondents, in considering the next five years, were also concerned about the development of a more globally oriented management style and a reduction of American parochialism; restrictions on corporate privacy of information, particularly with regard to employee records; job security for professional and other salaried employees; white-collar and professional unionization; and a number of internal corporate problems such as succession, cost effectiveness of training, and promotions. The unavoidable impact of the unstable world economic situation, inflation, and increased competition from non-American multinationals were also cited as being areas of increasing significance.

Given the various forces seen as impacting on employee relations over the next five years, it would seem logical to expect certain changes in the function to be called for, either organizationally or functionally, during that period. This, however, is not the case. The majority of the responding companies believed their present employee relations structure was perfectly adequate to meet the challenges of the coming years. As one company noted, it does not "anticipate that any further changes will be required in the employee relations function or process to be fully responsive to increased governmental intervention or other external forces. The flexibility of our present organizational structure and personnel should enable us to handle effectively any unforeseen development with minimal adjustments."

Of those companies that did foresee a need for some changes, many were concerned with avoiding duplication among staff and with a general streamlining of the employee relations function. Two companies thought that the employee relations function should report directly to the chief executive officer and not to a vice president. Some new functions were suggested. The two European companies thought there is need for a social affairs section with a specific budget, and some U.S. companies believed that a specific organizational development function should be created. One company, however, reacted adversely to this point, and suggested that it would be appropriate to "get organizational development into operating departments and normal training activities."

Generally, most of the suggested changes were internal and bureaucratic in nature and are not significant for cross-company comparisons. Most comments regarding the future indicated satisfaction with the present system and an assumption of built-in flexibility that would enable the employee relations function to handle any new problems that might arise. In light of the reported current and projected needs, the overall complacency and confidence in current employee relations methods and structure is somewhat surprising.

CAREER PATHS

Given the reported concern over the selection, training, and development of managers that was expressed, it might be expected that there would be some concern over the career development aspects of staffing the function. Surprisingly, most of the respondents, when specifically questioned about career paths in employee relations, indicated that they are satisfied with the manner in which things are being handled. This was the case regardless of whether the corporation had mapped out a formal path or career development strategy for their employee relations personnel. Less than 20 percent of the responding companies indicated any dissatisfaction with their present method of operations.

Overall, the total number of respondents was almost evenly divided between those who had a clear career path and those who did not. As shown below, none of the 12 companies employing under 30,000 people indicated that any such clear path existed, while a majority of the remaining firms had initiated a clear career development program. Several of the smaller firms indicated a dissatisfaction with the present, somewhat ad hoc method of career development and noted that efforts to review the situation were underway. Levels of dissatisfaction among the remaining firms in the survey were relatively low, with most being pleased with their career development systems, or lack thereof, and with the quality of the managers produced. Perhaps the most succinct statement was made by a medium-sized company, which simply replied, "No clear [career] path, and we are satisfied."

Company Size	Clear Career Path Exists		Clear Career Path Does Not Exist	
	Satisfied with the Results	Unsatisfied with the Results	Satisfied with the Results	Unsatisfied with the Results
Under 30,000 employees	—	—	8	4
Between 30,000 and 100,000 employees	6	2	3	1
Over 100,000 employees	9	—	4	3
Total	15	2	15	8

In general, the key areas of commonality among the clear career paths described are the desire for line experience and job rotation. These two elements were also highly valued by firms that used a more informal method of development. For example, a respondent who reported the existence of clear career paths for the development of employee relations executives in the firm made the statement that "it is my opinion that the best employee relations representatives are those who come from line operations." Similarly, a respondent who noted the lack of any clear career path in his company stressed the need for a variety of assignments both inside and outside of employee relations: "Somewhere along the line one has to have assignments to learn management problems firsthand, to learn the corporation's business, and to develop the credibility needed to be effective with other corporation executives."

A formal career path in employee relations, allowing for some individual variations, would seem to begin with a low-level plant position, movement to either a higher level within the same plant or an almost lateral position in a larger plant or in corporate headquarters. The next move would be to a higher level of corporate or division staff and then a reassignment back to the field in a senior position. The final move was generally a return to corporate staff at the vice presidential or senior employee relations level. It should be recognized, however, that most employee relations specialists were not a part of this process and that their career paths were often shorter and much more rigid. The compensation, training, and equal employment specialist was often characterized as moving along a short track within his speciality at the corporate or division level, with the track terminating with a position analogous to that of director of training, director of compensation, or the like. With one exception, none of the responding companies indicated any access to the vice presidential level by anyone pursuing the employee relations specialist path of development.

It is apparent that despite their indicated concern with the need for increased specialization and professionalism, the majority of respondents still adhere to the procedure of training generalists for top company positions. The importance of line experience and job rotation to eventual success within an overall employee relations career path was pointed out repeatedly. The exceptions were usually regarded as being the specialists, who would be highly developed within their functional area as a continuing resource for the traditional generalist managers. There were variations on this theme, although one company expressed the desire for more behavioral science among the employee relations staff in order to augment the line experience already normally a part of employee relations career development. And another company pointed out the possibility of a problem arising from the line personnel generalist/personnel staff professional dichotomy: "The view is generally taken that a personnel manager must be first a manager and then a personnel expert. This has led, over the last few years, to a number of positions in personnel being filled from the line, and there is a belief among personnel staff that it is difficult for them to reach the top positions in personnel and in general management. Although this is coincidental, action should be taken to correct the situation."

CONCLUDING COMMENTS

It is apparent that the degree of initiation, diversification, and general willingness to gamble on new ideas within the employee relations function is relatively low among the companies surveyed. There appears to be a general desire to maintain the status quo, both in corporate policies and in relations with the corporate workforce. Reorganizations and changes are represented and regarded as almost overwhelmingly difficult and complex tasks, not to be repeated too often. Any intrusions on the internally defined smoothness of operation within personnel—whether by government, consumers, workers, or innovators within the corporate structure itself—that diverge from familiar and almost predictable patterns are regarded with discomfort. The paramount position of "line" experience, usually defined in terms of plant rather than decision-making experience, is maintained in the selection and development of top-level employee relations managers, despite a simultaneous recognition of the ever-growing requirements of functional specificity and professional sophistication. And, despite encouraging signs among some of the respondents, the entire concept of employee relations still seems to be largely reactive in the majority of cases.

Employee relations seems to be viewed predominantly as a closed system within a corporation subjected to untimely and highly resented intrusions from beyond the confines of the organization. Other than a few highly perceptive firms, most respondents did not take into account the possibility of further changes in social norms and values and of increasing demands for the corporation actually to justify its role in society. The responses to the questionnaire tended to focus inward, with only a very few indications that efforts were being made to assume any role greater than the traditional profit-loss accountability and the relation of all corporate functions to those ends. There was, in other words, evidence of a distinct resistance to change and caution regarding innovation in the character of the employee relations function. The function tends, as characterized by many respondents, to be supportive and a pacifier, but rarely is it an agent of change, a leader, or a philosopher.

QUESTIONNAIRE (SURVEY OF EMPLOYEE RELATIONS ORGANIZATIONS – January 1976)

To Participating Company

A. *Corporate employee relations functions vary considerably in organizational structure and focus because of the differences among companies' orientation, products and markets and the way they manage their affairs.*

B. *This questionnaire (a duplicate is enclosed for your files) on corporate employee relations organization is designed to elicit information on how different companies organize in this area and to provide a guide on how management discharges its employee relations responsibilities. It is part of a study of employee relations that will be reported to those attending the IRC Fiftieth Anniversary meeting in June 1976. Each participating company will also receive a copy of study findings.*

C. *All information reported will be confidential; no company will be identified in the report on the study.*

D. *Please attach additional sheets keyed to each question as required and return your responses to:*

> *Richard A. Beaumont*
> *Director of Research*
> *Industrial Relations Counselors, Inc.*
> *P.O. Box 228*
> *New York, New York 10036*

---

1. Please describe your company's top corporate and divisional (or profit center) employee relations organization in terms of:
    a. Functions included (e.g., compensation, labor relations, management development, training, safety, etc.).
    b. Functions excluded which you believe should be in corporate employee relations, and their current reporting relationship within the company.
    c. Functions included which you feel should be excluded.

d. How the employee relations organization relates to line management at the corporate level and to major divisional or profit center organizational levels. (Please include international operations.)

e. The responsibilities of corporate employee relations staffs as contrasted to those of major divisional or profit center employee relations staffs.

If available, attach an organization chart.

2. Summarize the main features of your company's employee relations philosophy. If you have a written statement of such philosophy, please attach a copy.

3. What are the major characteristics of the employee relations process in your company in terms of how new policies and programs are developed, approved, implemented and monitored?

4. Describe how and to what extent the employee relations responsibilities and major activities vary within your company for different groups of employees —e.g., salesmen, managers, professional employees, unionized workers, etc.

5. Characterize the degree of centralized decision-making in your company, and then indicate how that pattern of organization/management affects the employee relations function.

6. What major differences in functions and organizational relationships exist today in the present employee relations structure versus that of ten years ago?

7. What methods are used to evaluate the employee relations program and its effectiveness —

a. At the corporate level, and by whom?

b. At the divisional or profit center levels, and by whom?

c. At field or plant locations, and by whom?

8. What is the basis for allocating employee relations costs, if an allocation system is used?

9. What are the most significant problems in employee relations that you believe the company faces at this time?

10. What major organizational changes would you like to see in the employee relations function in the next five years?

11. What major organizational or policy issues do you believe will have to be dealt with in the next five years?

12. If there is a clear career path in the development of employee relations executives, please describe it. If there is not such a path, are you satisfied with the developmental process for employee relations practitioners?

13. If you anticipate further changes in the employee relations function or process based on increased regulatory scope or pressure from government or forces external to the company, please describe them.

SOURCE DATA USED BY THE COMMITTEE ON 1985

This appendix contains the interview guidelines and bibliography used by the Committee on 1985. Conclusions on demographic, economic, and relevant forces are drawn from citations contained in the bibliography. A list of economic/demographic data used by the Committee and a list of those interviewed are available on request from IRC, Inc.

INTERVIEW GUIDELINES

GOVERNMENT AS A REGULATOR

Purpose

To determine the legislative, executive, and judicial trends affecting employee relations in 1985.

1. Characterize the relationship you anticipate between government and business in 1985. Will the interaction typically be that of partner, adversary, other?
2. Will government's role be exercised in traditional or new ways? Consider:
   a. Changes in balance of power among the levels and branches of government.
   b. Changes in federal, state, and local government relationships of significance to employers.
   c. Changes in the relative authority of the judicial, regulatory, and legislative functions.
   d. What will be the role of the bureaucracy, independent commissions, advisory committees, etc.

3. What will be the special character and role of the judiciary, particularly as the judiciary tends to create "new" law by its extensions to general laws? Is there any possibility of reaffirmation of legislative authority in such areas?

4. Will the influence on government of management, labor, public interest and civil rights groups or others change in nature or shift in power?

5. What do you see as the legislative/regulatory trends in the following areas, and what will the role be of government and the employer in each of these areas?

   Health care
   Retirement income protection
   Employment security
   Health and safety
   Labor-management relations
   Civil rights
   Economic stabilization
   Social responsibility

6. What is the probability of the passage of comprehensive legislation reordering government's approach to employment and social welfare, such as is currently proposed by Congressmen Hawkins and Reuss and Senator Humphrey?

7. Will government take a major role in seeking to redistribute income, and what will the effect be on employee relations?

MANAGEMENT (PUBLIC AND PRIVATE)

Purpose

To determine the trends in management which will influence how employees will be utilized (required) in 1985.

1. What significant changes do you foresee in the overall mission and/ or direction of government (federal, state, local) by 1985, particularly in terms of service orientation, social responsibility, funding? (Note: This question applies only to management in the public sector.)

2. What changes in direction over the next ten years would you project in the character of your corporation's service/product orientation, profitability goals, social responsiveness, etc.?

3. What type of trends do you anticipate there will be in organizational structure approaches by 1985? Consider current forces affecting your company—facility location, employment mix, government impact—and their influence on centralized/decentralized management process, etc.

4. With regard to your management process,
   a. Will the locus of decision-making change? If so, how?
   b. Will management prerogatives be broadened or narrowed?
   c. Will the balance of your staff-line relationship be altered?
   d. Will a culturally diverse employee and community population lead to any change in management values?
   e. What are the trends in employee participation, job restructuring, etc.?
   f. Will there be a trend toward bureaucratization of management?
   g. Will more emphasis be placed on proceduralistic approaches rather than on creativity?

5. What changes by 1985 do you anticipate in the relationship between the public and private sectors in the following areas: nationalization, antitrust, and contracting-out? How will personnel practices be influenced?

6. What trends or changes do you expect in the relationship between management and the following: individual employees, unions, interest groups?

SOCIAL TRENDS

Purpose
To project prevalent attitudes and mores which will have a significant impact on management and its employee relations activities in 1985.

1. What will be the attitudes regarding the importance of financial incentives, materialism and economic equity? Discuss in terms of the following specifics:
   Compensation and benefits package
   Standard of living
   Equality of opportunity vs. equality of result

2. From the employee's point of view, what will be the attitudes toward work and toward leisure? From the corporate and social point of view, what is the tradeoff between pay and other rewards? Consider such matters as:

Quality of work
Work time
Work ethic
Job content
Job satisfaction
Corporate recreational programs
Vacation, leave of absence, sabbatical leave, hours of work

3. In seeking personal satisfaction and fulfillment, what priority will people place on:

Job
Neighborhood
Family
Religion
Education
Avocations

4. What will be the attitudes regarding authority and individuality? What effect will these attitudes or trends have on the corporation with respect to traditional management systems, participative management, "industrial peace," employee theft, sabotage? What will be the tendency toward more extensive alliance of individuals with groups? How will privacy be regarded and what will be the balance between uniformity and pluralism?

5. What expectations will people have of government, business, unions, etc., in terms of personal goals and security, identification and involvement, and social responsibility?

OTHER INSTITUTIONS

Purpose

To identify significant trends in the areas of health, education, and legal services, and in individual rights and perceptions which will impact on management and employee relations in 1985.

Health

1. What role will management as the employer play in health care in 1985?

2. Will health institutions serve employer needs, and, if so, in what way?

3. What impact would the enactment of a National Health Program have on management and employee relations?

4. Will there be any change in the extent of employer liability for occupational health and safety by 1985?

Education

1. What impact will the rising cost of education have on management and employee relations?
2. Will the educational system be able to provide the mix of human resources needed by business? If so, how?
3. What role will management play in educational curriculum development in 1985?

Individual Rights and Legal Services

1. Will there be any change in the degree to which individual rights are protected by 1985? What effect would such change have on a corporation's employee relations?
2. Will there be a need for management to move toward the provision of legal services as a fringe benefit?

Media

1. What impact will increased public awareness have on corporate social responsibility?
2. How will the shrinking world concept affect employee attitudes?

NATIONAL RESOURCES/TECHNOLOGY

Purpose

To determine the nature and availability of technology and natural resources in 1985 and the impact on employee relations.

1. What will be the changes in technology capital investment over the next ten years and how will these changes affect:
   Total employment
   Skill requirements
   Productivity
2. If the changes are material, will the nation be able to support its growth or will there be significant limits based on physical, economic, or political forces?
3. If natural resources are available only on a limited basis, does this portend an export of talent from the U. S.? What are the implications?
4. What significant technological developments do you foresee that will have a major impact on the economy? What will be the impact on productivity?

a. Will available manpower skills be a constraint on application of emerging technology in 1985?

b. Will such technology require extensive retraining or a shift in educational programs or systems?

c. What level of capital investment will be required to utilize these technological developments?

5. How will the service industries change over the next ten years in terms of application of new technology?

LABOR

Purpose

To consider the nature of the labor union movement in 1985, and the relationships among labor, management, and other institutions.

1. What will be the direction and composition of organized labor?

2. What internal and external pressures will there be on organized labor, and how will these pressures manifest themselves in union political, legislative, and social activities?

3. What organization forms or structures may be dictated by internal union finances or other factors, and how will these affect union relations with management and other institutions?

4. What will be the nature of the collective bargaining process and union/management relationships in 1985? What will be the major collective bargaining issues?

BIBLIOGRAPHY

"America in the Seventies: A More Integrated Society," *ISR Newsletter*, Institute for Social Research, The University of Michigan, Autumn 1975.

Bach, George L., "Inflation and the Redistribution of Wealth," *Reprint Series No. 136*, Graduate School of Business, Stanford University, Palo Alto, California, February 1974.

Baier, K., and N. Rescher, editors, *Values and the Future*, New York: The Free Press, 1969.

Bell, Daniel, *The Coming of Post-Industrial Society*, New York: Basic Books, 1973.

Bell, Daniel, "The Post-Industrial Society—Expectations for the 1970s and 1980s," in *The Future of the Corporation*, New York: Mason and Lipscomb, 1974.

Bradford, William D., "Inflation and the Value of the Firm: Monetary and Depreciation Effects," *Reprint Series No. 135*, Graduate School of Business, Stanford University, Palo Alto, California, January 1974.

Brown, George H., "1984 . . . Plus One," *The Conference Board Record*, December 1970.

Browne, N. Neil, and Paul F. Haas, "Social Responsibility: The Uncertain Hypothesis," *MSU Business Topics*, Summer 1974.

Cassell, Frank H., "The Social Cost of Doing Business," *MSU Business Topics*, Autumn 1974.

Chamber of Commerce of the U.S. (Washington, D.C.), *Employee Benefits, 1973*, 1974.

The Conference Board (New York, N.Y.), *Challenge to Leadership, Managing in a Changing World*, 1973.

___, *The States in the 70s*, October 1974.

___, "U.S. Labor Force: Projection to 1985," *Road Maps of Industry*, No. 1660, February 15, 1971.

Cyert, Richard M., "The Behavioral Theory of the Firm and Social Responsibility," Public Lecture Sponsored by The Japan Economic Journal (Tokyo, Japan), March 14, 1975. (An Administration Paper, Carnegie-Mellon University, Pittsburgh, Pennsylvania).

___, "Energy, Environment and the Price System," Talk before the Pennsylvania Forum, Hershey, Pennsylvania, May 1, 1975. (An Administration Paper, Carnegie-Mellon University, Pittsburgh, Pennsylvania).

Data Resources, Inc. (Boston and Cambridge, Massachusetts), *Data Resources Long-Term Review*, May 1975.

Decker, Robert L., "Future Economic Developments: A Delphic Survey," *Futures*, April 1974, p. 148.

Drucker, Peter F., "Management's New Role—The Price of Success," in *The Future of the Corporation*, New York: Mason and Lipscomb, 1974.

Drucker, Peter F., "Six Durable Economic Myths," *Wall Street Journal*, September 16, 1975.

"Explosive Pension Costs," *Labor Trends*, April 27, 1974.

Feldstein, Martin S., "Unemployment Insurance: Time for Reform," *Harvard Business Review*, March-April 1975.

Foulkes, Fred K., "The Expanding Role of the Personnel Function," *Harvard Business Review*, March-April 1975, pp. 71-84.

The Futurist, August 1974, pp. 192-94.

Gibson, J. Douglas, "Inflation and Private Pension Funds: Impact on Corporate Costs," *The Canadian Business Review*, Winter 1975.

General Electric Company (Fairfield, Connecticut), *Annual Mapcast Forecast*, March 1975.

Gordon, T. J. and R. E. Le Blue, "Employee Benefits, 1970-1985," *Harvard Business Review*, January-February 1970.

Greenwood, William T., "Business in Reaction to Social Pressures," *The Conference Board Record*, May 1975.

Gross, Leonard, "Is Less More?" *Newsweek*, July 14, 1975.

Hyer, Douglas K., "Employee Benefits: No Longer on the Fringe," *Pension World*, September 1975, p. 46.

"Into a New Era—How Your Life Will Change," *U.S. News and World Report*, March 1975.

"In What Direction Can Private Pension Programs Now Be Expected to Develop?" *Employee Benefit Plan Review*, October 1975.

Jones, R. H., "Our Future: The Challenge of Capital Formation," Address, December 1974 (General Electric Company, Fairfield, Connecticut).

Kahn, Herman, editor, *The Future of the Corporation*, New York: Mason and Lipscomb, 1974. Especially "Forces for Change," and "The Future of the Corporation."

Kahn, Herman, and B. Bruce-Biggs, *Things to Come: Thinking About the Seventies and Eighties*, New York: Macmillan, 1972.

Kahn, Herman, and A. J. Wiener, *The Year 2000*, New York: Macmillan, 1967.

Kinard, Jerry L., "About This Business of Social Responsibility," *Personnel Journal*, November 1974.

Kostelanetz, Richard, editor, *Social Speculations*, New York: William Morrow & Co., 1971.

"Labor Force and World Population Growth," *Bulletin of Labor Statistics*, Special Edition, 1974, 86 pp.

Lien, Arthur P., Paul Anton and Joseph W. Duncan, *Technological Forecasting: Tools, Techniques, Applications*, American Management Association, Research and Development Division, 1968.

Lodge, George Cabot, *The New American Ideology*, New York: Alfred A., Knopf, 1975.

Mansfield, Roger W., "The Advent of Public Sector Multiemployer Bargaining," *Personnel Journal*, May 1975.

Mesarovic, Mihaslo, and Eduard Pestel, *Mankind at the Turning Point—The Second Report to the Club of Rome*, New York: E. P. Dutton & Co., 1974.

Michell, James M., and Rolfe E. Schroeder, "Future Shock for Personnel Administration," *Public Personnel Management*, July-August 1974.

Mills, Ted, "Human Resources—Why the New Concern," *Harvard Business Review*, March-April 1975.

Names, Bert, "The Future-Oriented Corporation," *Business Horizons*, February 1975.

Napier, Herman S., "The Futurist: Vice-President of Tomorrow," *Personnel Journal*, April 1975.

"National Health Insurance, Which Way To Go?" *CU Viewpoint, Consumer Reports*, February 1975.

"1975—Looking Ahead," *Training and Development Journal*, January 1975.

Organization Resources Counselors, Inc. (New York), *Maintaining Balance in 1974*, February 1973.

Paul, Robert D., "Can Private Pension Plans Deliver?" *Harvard Business Review*, September-October 1974.

Perloff, Harvey S., editor, *The Future of United States Government*, New York: George Braziller, 1971.

Predicasts, Inc. (Cleveland, Ohio), *Occupational Outlook Quarterly*.

___, *Predicasts*, April 29, 1975.

Rockefeller, John D., III, *The Second American Revolution: Some Personal Observations*, New York: Harper and Row, 1973.

Rosenthal, Neal, "Occupational Outlook for the Mid-1980s," *Occupational Outlook Quarterly*, Winter 1974, pp. 3-11.

Sullivan, John F., "Planning Compensation Programs for the Future," *Personnel Administrator*, July-August 1974.

"A Think Tank That Helps Companies Plan," *Business Week*, August 25, 1973.

"The Traditional Relationship between the Business Community and the Employees," *Personnel Journal*, July 1975.

Turner, Robert C., *Economic Growth: The Outlook for Ten and Twenty-Five Years*, Committee for Future Studies, Indiana University, Bloomington, Indiana.

U.S. Department of Commerce (Washington, D.C.), *U.S. Industrial Outlook, 1975*.

___, Bureau of the Census, *Population Estimates and Projections*, February 1975.

___, Bureau of the Census, *Statistical Abstract of the U.S.*, (95th edition), 1974.

___, Bureau of the Census, *U.S. Trends and Prospects: 1950-1990*, p. 187.

___, National Petroleum Council/Federal Energy Administration/Commerce Technical Advisory Board, *Recommendation for a National Energy Program*.

Weinstein, Ted, "Work in the 1980s," *The Labor Gazette*, July 1974, pp. 490-493.

Whyte, William F., *Organizations for the 1980s*, Ithaca, New York: Cornell University Press, 1974.

Wolfbein, Seymour L., "Seven Signs for the Seventies," *Journal of College Placement*, Fall 1974.

"Xerox Implements a Social Service Program Worldwide," *Business International*, June 14, 1974.